OXFORD HISTORICAL MONOGRAPHS

Music in the Holocaust

Confronting Life in the Nazi Ghettos and Camps

SHIRLI GILBERT

CLARENDON PRESS · OXFORD

OXFORD

UNIVERSITY PRESS

Great Clarendon Street, Oxford OX2 6DP

Oxford University Press is a department of the University of Oxford.
It furthers the University's objective of excellence in research, scholarship,
and education by publishing worldwide in

Oxford New York

Auckland Cape Town Dar es Salaam Hong Kong Karachi
Kuala Lumpur Madrid Melbourne Mexico City Nairobi
New Delhi Shanghai Taipei Toronto

With offices in

Argentina Austria Brazil Chile Czech Republic France Greece
Guatemala Hungary Italy Japan South Korea Poland Portugal
Singapore Switzerland Thailand Turkey Ukraine Vietnam

Published in the United States
by Oxford University Press Inc., New York

British Library Cataloguing in Publication Data

Data available

Library of Congress Cataloging in Publication Data

Data available

ISBN 0-19-927797-4 940.5318

1 3 5 7 9 10 8 6 4 2

Typeset by Kolam Information Services Pvt. Ltd, Pondicherry, India
Printed in Great Britain on acid-free paper by
Biddles Ltd.
King's Lynn, Norfolk

In memory of Sara and Moshe Steinberg

PREFACE

This book began its life simply as a history of musical life amongst inmates in the Nazi ghettos and camps. On one level, it still is that: a documentation of a wide scope of activities, ranging from orchestras and chamber groups to choirs, theatres, communal sing-songs, and cabarets in some of the most important internment centres in Nazi-occupied Europe. But it is also more ambitious in its scope. At its core it is a social history, taking as its focus the lives of individuals and communities imprisoned under Nazism. Music opens a unique window onto the internal world of those communities, offering insight into how they understood, interpreted, and responded to their experiences at the time.

The book focuses primarily on the music created, circulated, and performed on an informal basis by prisoners in various internment centres, and on the musical activity initiated there by the SS. While I discuss numerous songs and compositions, I am interested as much in how music functioned as a participatory activity involving larger prisoner communities as in individual musical works that survived. I have chosen not to include issues associated with professional musical life, such as the fates of professional musicians and composers deported to the camps and ghettos, or the continuation of their activities in these places, except where they have direct bearing on everyday musical life. Also outside the book's scope are Nazi music policy and its effects in the public and professional spheres—the Nazification of music from 1933 onwards in schools, universities, concert halls, and religious establishments in Germany; the banning of certain categories of 'degenerate' music; the political use of music at party congresses and in organizations such as the *Hitlerjugend* (Hitler youth). The distinction between the latter aspects of musical activity under Nazism and my subject is a fundamental one, particularly in the context of later discussions about 'spiritual resistance' and the social and political factors within inmate communities that affected music-making in the camps and ghettos.

I have also made a deliberate decision not to include Theresienstadt in my study, since it has been the focus of a number of studies. Theresienstadt, a fortress town located on the outskirts of Prague, assumed an exceptional position in the Nazi camp system as a 'model' or 'show' camp, one of whose functions was to convince the outside world of the humane treatment that

Jewish prisoners were enjoying. In order to serve these propagandistic aims, the Nazi authorities tolerated, and later encouraged, an unparalleled range of cultural activities: operas, instrumental and orchestral concerts, vocal recitals, a coffee house with regular jazz performances, choirs, cabarets, and more. The prominence that Theresienstadt has assumed in the popular imagination has meant that it has come almost exclusively to represent musical activity in the ghettos and camps. The uniqueness of its situation makes this problematic, however, and it is this—aside from the fact that it has attracted so much academic attention—that motivated my decision to focus on other areas.

I have drawn on a broad range of testimonial literature in this study, from archives in Israel, Europe, and the United States. Although I expected to find little original musical material to supplement this literature, my initial archival searches were fruitful—so much so that I was forced to limit the scope of the book significantly. My four case studies are based on seventeen original songbooks and around seventy newly written songs in German, Yiddish, and Polish. One of my most important sources was the Aleksander Kulisiewicz Collection at the United States Holocaust Memorial Museum, named after a Polish musician and activist imprisoned in Sachsenhausen from 1940 to 1945. While still an inmate, Kulisiewicz began what became a massive post-war project to collect songs from the camps; he also composed at least forty songs of his own. He was not able to publish his work during his lifetime, and his enormously valuable collection only became publicly available in the early 1990s when it was purchased by the Museum.

My work has benefited from a number of studies that preceded it: in particular, Gila Flam's *Singing for Survival*, on songs in the Łódź ghetto; Gabriele Knapp's *Das Frauenorchester in Auschwitz* (The Women's Orchestra in Auschwitz); and wider-ranging accounts by Milan Kuna, Guido Fackler, and Moshe Hoch. These studies have made important contributions to the ongoing process of gathering primary musical and testimonial material; moreover, in an area of study where scholarly rigour and sophistication are regrettably often lacking, they have established the groundwork for a more complex and nuanced understanding of musical life in the ghettos and camps. Beyond my immediate subject area, my thinking has been stimulated by the work of several prominent scholars on the subject of writing and remembering the Holocaust, in particular Lawrence Langer, Omer Bartov, Saul Friedländer, and James Young.

Some brief notes on terminology and translation: I have generally used the names employed by the Nazis themselves to differentiate between types of internment centres—ghettos, concentration camps, labour camps, and so on—although I use the term 'death camps' rather than 'extermination camps' (*Vernichtungslager*) in referring to the places where organized mass killings took place (Auschwitz, Majdanek, Sobibór, Treblinka, Chełmno, and Bełżec). I use 'camps' to refer generally to all camps in the Nazi system. Where places under Nazi occupation had their original names replaced by German alternatives (Theresienstadt for Terezín, Auschwitz for Oświęcim), I have for purposes of consistency used the German names. I have made an exception only in the case of Łódź, which although renamed Litzmannstadt is still usually referred to by its Polish name.

All translations from Hebrew, Yiddish, German, and French are my own unless otherwise indicated. Transliteration from Hebrew follows the guidelines of the American National Standards Institute; transliterations from Yiddish follow the guidelines of the YIVO institute.

At various stages in the writing of this book, I received advice and support from numerous individuals and institutions that I would like to take this opportunity to acknowledge. Thanks are due first of all to the supervisors of my doctoral research, on which this book is largely based: to Nick Stargardt, for his genuine interest in and enthusiasm for my work, and his continued moral and intellectual support; and to Roger Parker, for giving so generously and warmly of his time even after his official obligations had ended. I would also like to thank Mark Roseman and Ruth Harris for their confidence in my work and their helpful advice. An enormous debt of love and gratitude goes to Pauline Nossel, who has been an untiring source of wisdom and generosity.

I have been fortunate to receive financial assistance for this project from the Skye Charitable Trust in South Africa and the Commonwealth Scholarship Commission (British Council) in the United Kingdom. I was also privileged to hold the Bryce Research Studentship in Modern History at Oxford University (2001–2). Grants from Magdalen College, the Oxford University Music Faculty, the Batya Lyons Trust, the Oxford University Oriental Institute (Segal Fund), and the Skye Charitable Trust allowed me to spend time in archives in Israel, Poland, the United States, and Germany. A Postdoctoral Research Fellowship at the University of Cape Town and an Honorary Research Fellowship at the University of the Witwatersrand, Johannesburg supported me through the final stages of preparing the manuscript for publication.

Archivists and librarians too numerous to mention made the task of tackling the archives a more fruitful and enjoyable one. I am grateful to staff at Yad Vashem, the United States Holocaust Memorial Museum, the

Akademie der Künste, Berlin, the archives and depository of the Gedenk-stätte und Museum Sachsenhausen, the Fortunoff Video Archive for Holo-caust Testimonies at Yale, the Imperial War Museum Sound Archives in London, and the Auschwitz-Birkenau State Museum Archive for their valu-able assistance and advice. I am particularly grateful to the staff at the Wiener Library, London, for their consistently helpful advice, friendly conversation, and generous supplies of tea. For opening their homes to me so hospitably during my travels, I would like to thank Mickey Blumberg in Jerusalem, Mark and Jill Wexler Greenstein in Washington, DC, Erica Drath in Washington, DC, Gundula Kreuzer in Berlin, and Richard Mansell in New York.

Thanks also go out to Ritika Prasad, Richard Mansell, Chaya Herman, Martin Kerem, Paul Rabiner, Tim Elfenbein, and Sandra Swart, who read and made helpful comments on various parts of the manuscript. Gundula Kreuzer, Helen Beer, Miriam Trinh, Zosia Sochańska, and Michal George gave generously of their time on matters of translation.

The last and most important thanks are reserved for family. To Jesse, Tal, Leah, and Dave—infinite thanks for your good humour, patience, careful readings and re-readings, and constant love, support, and encouragement. This book is dedicated to the memory of my maternal grandparents, Sara and Moshe Steinberg, who endured the war in Poland and later the Soviet Union, and lived to pass on their stories. The memory of their strength has sustained me through many of the challenges that accompanied the writing of this book.

S.G.

ACKNOWLEDGEMENTS

Chapter 3 is adapted from Shirli Gilbert, 'Songs Confront the Past: Music in KZ Sachsenhausen 1936–1945', *Contemporary European History*, 13/3 (2004), © Cambridge University Press, reproduced with permission.

I would like to thank the following for permission to cite from unpublished archival material:

Gedenkstätte und Museum Sachsenhausen (citations of song lyrics and extracts from letters)
Wiener Library, London (citations from eyewitness testimonies)
Yad Vashem Archives (citations from eyewitness testimonies)
United States Holocaust Memorial Museum Record Group 55 (Aleksander Kulisiewicz Collection), Selected Records:

    RG-55.004.18 ('Koncentrak' text and musical example)
    RG-55.004.18 ('Egzekucja' text and musical example)
    RG-55.004.18 ('Chorał z Piekła Dna' text and musical example)
    RG-55.004.18 ('Maminsynek w Koncentraku' text only: brief quotes)
    RG-55.004.18 ('Hej, pod Berlinem!' text and musical example)
    RG-55.004.23 ('Jüdischer Todessang' text and musical example)
    RG-55.003.07 ('Gazownia' text and musical example)
    RG-55.019.09 ('Frauenlager' text only)
    RG-55.004.14 ('Pieśń Oświęcimska' text and musical example)
    RG-55.003.15 and RG-55.003.16 ('Birkenau' text and musical example)
    RG-55.004.02 ('Wiązanka z Effektenkammer' text and musical examples)

Permission to reprint published materials from S. Kaczerginski and H. Leivick (eds.), *Lider fun di getos un lagern* (New York: Altveltlekher Yidisher Kultur-Kongres: Tsiko, 1948) was granted by CYCO, Central Yiddish Cultural Organization, Inc., 25 East 21st St., 3rd floor, New York, NY 10010, Phone: 212-505-8305, Fax: 212-505-8044, Email: cycobooks@aol.com. CYCO Publishing House and Yiddish Book Distribution Center is a 501 (c)(3) non-profit organization established in 1937.

I have made every effort to obtain permissions for all materials cited or reproduced in this monograph. However, numerous attempts to secure permission for citations from I. Lammel and G. Hofmeyer (eds.), *Lieder aus den faschistischen Konzentrationslagern* (Leipzig: Friedrich Hofmeister, 1962) were unsuccessful. Should the copyright holders come forward, I will be pleased to make full acknowledgement, in subsequent editions of this monograph, of this and any other relevant sources not acknowledged here.

CONTENTS

LIST OF ILLUSTRATIONS

The plates appear between pp. 132 and 133

LIST OF MUSIC EXAMPLES

A NOTE ON THE MUSIC EXAMPLES

Sources for the music examples sometimes contain inconsistencies between two or more versions of the text and the music for the same song. It has thus been dii;cult in some cases to reproduce exact citations. I have attempted to represent musical texts as accurately as possible, preserving what I perceive to be the most important and characteristic musical features where there are variations. Where sources offer differing versions of lyrics, particularly between stanza form and music examples, I have generally chosen to cite the former. Many sources do not indicate clearly how lyrics should be set in relation to the music; here I have exercised my own judgement, taking into account extant recordings, language, and other relevant information.

ABBREVIATIONS

AdK	Akademie der Künste, Berlin, Arbeitlerliedarchiv
CENTOS	Centralne Towarzystwo Opieki nad Sierotami (Headquarters of the Society for the Care of Orphans)
FLK	Faraynikung fun Literarn un Kinstler (Association of Writers and Artists)
FPO	Fareynigte Partizaner Organizatsye (United Partisans Organization)
GMSA	Gedenkstätte und Museum Sachsenhausen, Archiv
GMSD	Gedenkstätte und Museum Sachsenhausen, Depot
Kaczerginski and Leivick	Shmerke Kaczerginski and H. Leivick (eds.), *Lider fun di getos un lagern* (New York: Altveltlekher Yidisher Kultur-Kongres: Tsiko, 1948)
KPD	Kommunistische Partei Deutschlands (German Communist Party)
USHMM	United States Holocaust Memorial Museum
WL	Wiener Library, London
YIKOR	Yidishe Kultur Organizatsye (Jewish Cultural Organization)
YIVO	Yidisher Visnshaftlekher Institut (Jewish Scientific Institute)
YV	Yad Vashem Archive
ŻTOS	Żydowskie Towarzystwo Opieki Społecznej (Jewish Society for Social Welfare)

Introduction: Redeeming Music—'Spiritual Resistance' and Beyond

> For the purpose of defence, reality can be distorted not only in memory but in the very act of its taking place.
>
> Primo Levi, *The Drowned and the Saved*

With this sentence, Primo Levi introduced the story of Alberto D., a fellow Auschwitz inmate with whom he developed a close friendship during his year-long imprisonment. Levi described this man as courageous, robust, and unusually clear-sighted. His most defining quality, however, was his critical attitude towards the 'consolatory illusions' regularly fabricated and spread by prisoners: 'the war will be over in two weeks', 'there will be no more selections', 'the Polish partisans are about to liberate the camp', and so on. These rumours were always eventually belied by reality, and Alberto refused to seek refuge in them.

Alberto had been brought to Auschwitz together with his 45-year-old father. During a selection in October 1944, his father was chosen for the gas chambers. According to Levi, Alberto's attitude changed within the space of a few hours. Suddenly the rumours he had heard seemed worthy of belief: the Russians were approaching; the impending selection was not for the gas but for weakened, salvageable prisoners; those chosen would be taken to a nearby camp, Jaworzno, for light labour. Of course, his father was never seen again. For Levi, however, Alberto's abrupt and unexpected transformation signalled the immense power of consoling stories to those who faced an unbearable reality.[1]

I

'Consoling stories' of various kinds continue to shape our understanding of the Holocaust today.[2] As Levi's account suggests, however, the 'distortion' of

---

[1] Primo Levi, *The Drowned and the Saved* (London, 1988), 19–20. The quotation in the epigraph comes from p. 19.

[2] 'Holocaust' has become a value-laden term, subject to much political wrangling. In both the academic and public arenas, there is general indecision as to whether it refers only to the Jewish

reality is an activity in which human beings engage not necessarily for dishonest purposes, but as a way of making certain situations more assimilable and easier to bear. This relates not only to the victims of the Nazi genocide, who recreated their reality in various narrative forms—diaries, chronicles, artworks, songs, testimonies—both after the war and 'in the very act of its taking place', but also to us, the post-war generations, who have constructed understandings of the genocide 'in memory'.

Narrative reconstructions of the past are of course the stock of the historian's trade: we must inevitably rearrange and 'distort' what happened in order to identify themes, highlight important points, and draw wider conclusions. In the case of the Nazi genocide, however, there has been a peculiar tendency, in certain areas, towards unsophisticated narratives of redemption and consolation. My book grew out of a profound concern with one of these narratives, best represented by the term 'spiritual resistance' and often closely related to the subject of music. Spiritual resistance is by now a common concept in secondary writing on this subject, defining music not only as a channel through which Nazism's victims derived emotional comfort and support, but also as a life-affirming survival mechanism through which they asserted solidarity in the face of persecution, the will to live, and the power of the human spirit.

When I began working on this subject, I was impressed by the enormous scope of musical activities that existed. Most of the larger ghettos in Nazi-occupied eastern Europe established choirs, orchestras, theatres, and chamber groups that existed for periods of months or even years. Official orchestras established on the initiative of the SS were also a feature of many camps. Aside from these institutionalized activities, a wide range of informal and spontaneous music-making took place. The music that inmates performed ranged from popular pre-war songs to opera and operetta, folk music, standard classical repertoire, choral music, and dance melodies. In addition, a large number of new songs and pieces were created, not only in the ghettos but in the camps as well.

Initially, it seemed logical to construe these enthusiastic and largely voluntary activities as an incongruity in the violent world of Nazi internment.

victims, or whether it is taken to include other victims of the Nazi genocide such as homosexuals, the Roma and Sinti, Jehovah's Witnesses, and countless others. As far as public memorials are concerned, major museums such as Yad Vashem in Jerusalem and the United States Holocaust Memorial Museum have clearly faced pressure to include sections on non-Jewish victims of the genocide, although 'Holocaust' is still taken to refer primarily to the Jewish victims. I have chosen deliberately to include in this book not only Jewish inmates but also non-Jewish German, Polish, Czech, and other prisoners in the camps, as I explain further in this chapter. My use of the word 'Holocaust' should be understood in this context.

People who asked me about my work would indeed often make comments about its macabre nature, or the incongruity of music in such a setting. It took some time to realize, however, that this understanding was based on tacit assumptions about the nature of music and the kinds of roles it should play: the idea that music comforts and uplifts people, or acts as a vehicle for asserting humanity and dignity. Deeper involvement with my subject led me radically to reassess these assumptions. In particular, why was it assumed that music was inviolable by social forces, or that it was immune to the processes of politicization and corruption that infiltrated so many aspects of life at that time? Especially in the ghettos and camps, where the perverted moral codes and deeds of the regime had their most concentrated expression, nothing could escape contamination.

My initial concern with how musical life had been represented in retrospect led to a renewed interest in the ways in which Nazism's victims understood and represented their experiences at the time. For this, it soon became apparent, the music itself is a particularly valuable source. While most sources relating to Holocaust historiography originate from the post-war period, the songs are a significant body of texts originating from the time itself. In this they stand alongside the few diaries and chronicles that were preserved. They are also distinctive among these contemporary sources as oral texts, disseminated—and, ultimately, preserved—within large-scale group frameworks. They convey to us not the retrospective understanding of individuals that survived (as do post-war testimonies), but the uncertain and constantly shifting perspectives of prisoner communities facing new daily realities over an extended time period. They are, in other words, a unique legacy of the time: fragments of shared ideas and interpretation, orally conveyed and preserved, from communities that otherwise left few traces.

Taking this distinctive body of sources as its basis, my study contributes in several ways to our understanding of the experience of Nazi internment. It challenges the widespread and simplistic conception of music as spiritual resistance, a conception based on unrealistic assumptions about inmate solidarity and the possibility of resisting Nazism's calculated policy of dehumanization. In its place, it presents a more complex, multi-layered portrait of what Primo Levi called the 'Grey Zone' that constituted captive life.[3] It explores hierarchies and other patterns of power within inmate communities, and illustrates how a variety of social and political factors affected the ways in which different groups could make use of music. Detailed consideration of

---

[3] This concept is explained and discussed further on in this chapter.

Jewish, Polish, Czech, and German prisoners in various settings reveals the diversity of experiences that could exist within the same ghetto or camp, and the markedly different ways in which people viewed their experiences.

The ghettos and camps in the Nazi system housed a wide array of prisoners, representing national, political, and religious affiliations from across the European continent. Acknowledging this diversity is important for several reasons, the first being a simple one of historical accuracy. For the most part, portrayals of musical activity have relied on assumptions about the uniformity of prisoners' experiences. In the process, the experiences of certain groups have been marginalized or ignored. Considering the preoccupation in Western society with the memory of Nazism, the question of why certain aspects of experience have not been given equal attention is an important one. An emphasis on diversity helps to redress some of the simplifications of memory, laying the path for more complex historical representations.

As we shall see, music operated not in homogeneous communities, but in communities divided on the basis of power, wealth, class, language, and other factors. It was not only a medium for the discussion and documentation of social disparity, but also a place where disparity was played out. Individual initiative was significant only until a certain point where inmates' participation in musical activity was concerned: beyond this, they relied for their opportunities on externally imposed factors, such as social standing and connections, support of prisoners higher up in the camp hierarchies, or the permission of the SS. Music was also mobilized for explicitly political ends. Inmate groups with active agendas—particularly those involved in resistance activity, like partisans in the ghettos and political prisoners in the camps— used songs to promote narratives of optimism and solidarity, and to encourage people to join in the opposition struggle. Ghetto authorities, especially in Vilna and Łódź, used cultural life for their own, somewhat different purposes: in order to calm and reassure their populations, as a forum for promoting policies such as the importance of work, and subtly to discourage involvement with resistance movements.

The focus on diversity also allows us to recognize the multi-faceted nature of human behaviour rather than reducing it to assimilable stereotypes. Under extreme conditions, where the struggle for individual survival was paramount, people responded in different ways. Some withdrew into themselves; some provided support to those around them; some bribed, stole, or informed in order to improve their situation. As well as encountering pockets of solidarity and protection, inmates experienced widespread antagonism, deception, and hostility. Ghetto and camp societies were stratified in much the same way as our own societies are, and exploring this complexity helps to dispel simplistic assumptions about what life within them was like.

Music opens a window onto the internal world of these societies when they were not yet distant past but raw present, when feelings were volatile, and understanding fragmentary and shifting. Because of the insight it can provide, it has important implications for the ways in which we understand the experiences of Nazism's victims. Most significantly, it challenges conceptions of the Holocaust that rely on quasi-mythicized rhetoric of sacred martyrs and inhuman beasts—worryingly pervasive in both academic and popular writing on the subject—revealing instead a profoundly *human* world within which people tried to interpret and understand what was happening to them in complicated, contradictory, and changing ways.

II

Let us begin with Levi's idea of the construction of reality 'in memory'. The motivation underlying the spiritual resistance argument here is not difficult to recognize: put simply, music presents a seemingly natural opportunity for hope-tinged discussion about the Holocaust. Secondary writing on the subject has been dominated by redemptive narratives, with 'redemptive' defined in a dual sense: music not only redeems victims from total dehumanization, but is also framed in such a way as to impart affirmative meaning to representations of life during the Holocaust. In other words, music not only affords the victims a certain retrospective moral victory, but also restores *for us* a certain measure of closure and meaning to the events. My objection in this book is not directed at affirmative explanations per se: as will become clear, musical activity fulfilled many constructive functions within inmate communities. I am troubled, however, by discourse that is concerned more with abstract concepts of heroism and resistance than with a contextualized understanding of how music functioned in different situations.

From the late 1940s, Holocaust discourse—particularly in Israel—has placed clear emphasis on active heroism and resistance. This is most obvious in the choice of Yom ha'shoah v'ha'gvura (Day of Holocaust and Heroism) as the name for Israel's official memorial day, and the decision to commemorate it on the anniversary of the Warsaw ghetto uprising. Although direct condemnation of the victims' behaviour was generally avoided, the glorification of armed resistance revealed a tacitly critical approach to the great majority of the victims' submissiveness and inaction.[4]

Armed resistance during the Holocaust, in fact, was infrequent and largely unsuccessful, for several reasons. Primarily in western Europe, but in eastern Europe as well, Jews tended to participate in resistance activity as citizens of the countries in which they were living, or in support of political movements. Distinct Jewish resistance movements usually appeared only in areas of mass concentration—ghettos or camps. Even in these places, resistance was seldom the most reasonable or obvious course of action. In the first place, most people were unable to believe what was happening to them, even when information had begun to emerge from the death camps. Taking advantage of this denial mechanism, the Nazis employed tactics of deception in order to heighten the uncertainty and confusion, and consequently to discourage organized activity. Those who engaged in resistance endangered not only themselves but the entire community, thanks to a calculated policy of collective responsibility. In addition, resistance organizations were cut off from the free world, faced the hostility of local populations, and encountered great difficulty in obtaining arms. Thus, even in those cases where a decision was taken to resist, organizations—where they existed—were ultimately unprepared. Despite the many obstacles, there were some cases of armed resistance: ghetto uprisings in Warsaw (April 1943) and Białystok (August 1943); revolts in the death camps Treblinka (August 1943), Sobibór (October 1943), and Auschwitz-Birkenau (October 1944); partisan activity chiefly in occupied eastern Europe; and isolated acts of resistance in other ghettos and small towns.[5] These revolts were almost invariably acts of desperation, carried out when no foreseeable hope of survival remained.

The revolts in the death camps were aimed primarily at opening up opportunities for escape. In the ghettos, however, particularly during the first few years of war, underground movements did not confine themselves to the struggle for physical survival. They were involved with publishing underground newspapers, organizing illegal education, establishing contact with isolated Jewish communities, and arranging various other social and political activities.[6] It is to these activities that Holocaust historiography has gradually extended its focus. In an attempt to mitigate the critique of passivity that emerged (whether explicitly or implicitly) from the emphasis on armed

---

[4] Yael Zerubavel, *Recovered Roots: Collective Memory and the Making of Israeli National Tradition* (Chicago and London, 1995), 75.

[5] Leni Yahil, *The Holocaust: The Fate of European Jewry* (Oxford, 1990), 462–6.

[6] Ibid. 458–78.

resistance, there developed a trend to honour what became known as spiritual resistance. Yehuda Bauer explained that while community leaders in many cases advised people not to take up arms, they proposed that instead 'the struggle should be carried on ... by other, life-affirming means'.[7] These means have ranged, in post-war interpretations, from the organization of clandestine education, religious activities, and social welfare, to musical and artistic life, rescuing religious artefacts, sharing rations, and writing diaries and chronicles. As the historiography of the period developed, many of these activities came to be couched in what is now the familiar redemptive rhetoric of defiance and determination, the struggle to survive against all odds, and the assertion of spiritual autonomy in the face of physical persecution.

Lawrence Langer, perhaps the most outspoken critic of redemptive discourse, has focused on the 'verbal fences' that we—the post-war generations— construct between atrocity and what we are psychologically prepared to confront.[8] Understood in this sense, the motivations for attributing redemptive meaning are straightforward. When confronted with an event that radically shocks our sense of order and sanity, we want to reduce indeterminacy into a knowable, coherent representation. We rebel against the idea that suffering can have signified nothing, that it has left nothing but 'a gaping, black, empty hole'.[9] Instead, we look for justifications and interpretations of what has happened in order to make the events easier to assimilate.

The rhetoric of spiritual resistance arguably has good intentions—above all, to counteract depictions of victims as passive, attribute some retrospective dignity to their actions, and impute meaning to their suffering. However, it also has a tendency to descend into sentimentality and mythicization. For one writer, for example, music was proof that 'the human spirit cannot be repressed even if the human body is tortured and finally destroyed'; another wrote that

> Music in the Holocaust served a dual purpose. On the one hand, the songs expressed the anguish of the situation—agony for which words alone were an inadequate vehicle. On the other hand, music was the means by which the dehumanised could maintain their humanity, the link that allowed the condemned to cling to life. This is music that is optimistic and life-affirming. As Terezín survivor Greta Hofmeister stated so powerfully, 'Music! Music was life!'[10]

---

[7] Yehuda Bauer, *They Chose Life: Jewish Resistance in the Holocaust* (Jerusalem, 1973), 33.

[8] Lawrence L. Langer, *Admitting the Holocaust: Collected Essays* (Oxford, 1995), 6.

[9] Omer Bartov, *Murder in our Midst: The Holocaust, Industrial Killing, and Representation* (Oxford, 1996), 107.

[10] Joseph Rudavsky, *To Live with Hope, to Die with Dignity: Spiritual Resistance in the Ghettos and Camps* (Lanham, Md., and London, 1997), 68; Joshua R. Jacobson, 'Music in the Holocaust', *Choral Journal*, 36/5 (1995), 9–21 at 18.

In most cases, rhetoric of this kind shifts our understanding further away from the events described rather than illuminating them. Scholarly writings since the 1980s have usually relied on the implicit assumption that music, by its very nature, provides pleasure and spiritual comfort. Far from being an inherent and universally acknowledged truth about music, however, this idea is firmly rooted in the German Romantic philosophical tradition, which conceived of music as the paradigm of artistic expression, and the ultimate language of the emotions.[11]

The seeming appropriateness of redemptive discourse also arises out of what Michael André Bernstein has described as the impulse to foreshadow history. By this he refers to a teleological model in which the event in question is seen as a terrible inevitability. For Bernstein, by knowing which events were 'significant' in terms of the final outcome, those writing in retrospect are in danger of denying the ongoing struggle of victims to create an unknown future, and of ignoring the unpredictable contingencies and potential paths of action that informed their experiences at the time.[12]

As we have already seen, musical activity has been construed by some writers as a conscious communal attempt to impede demoralization, or as a deliberate means through which victims asserted their spiritual tenacity in the face of their imminent physical destruction. These explanations assume that music was fashioned as the deliberate response of a community that knew what fate had in store for it. They are thus problematic on many levels.

First, the concept of spiritual resistance has often relied on a tacit assumption of solidarity between Nazism's victims. Correspondingly, it has avoided discussion of less agreeable dynamics within inmate communities. Perhaps the most important reason for its inadequacy, however, is the enormous range of social differentiation that existed in the camps and ghettos. Primo Levi's concept of the 'Grey Zone' is a useful starting point in this regard. While Levi identified in Holocaust historiography 'the tendency, indeed the need, to separate evil from good, to be able to take sides', he stressed that

the network of human relationships inside the Lagers was not simple: it could not be reduced to the two blocs of victims and persecutors . . . it did not conform to any model, the enemy was all around but also inside, the 'we' lost its limits, the contenders were not two, one could not discern a single frontier but rather many confused, perhaps innumerable frontiers, which stretched between each of us . . . It is

---

[11] Philip Alperson (ed.), *What is Music?* (University Park, Pa., 1994), 7–8.

[12] Michael André Bernstein, *Foregone Conclusions: Against Apocalyptic History* (London, 1994), 9, 30.

naïve, absurd, and historically false to believe that an infernal system such as National Socialism was, sanctifies its victims: on the contrary, it degrades them, it makes them similar to itself.[13]

Although it relates to the camps, Levi's observation has some relevance for the ghettos as well. Far from there being consistent solidarity between the victims, corruption, class antagonisms, and general hostility were rife. While communities were often an important source of identity and support, inmates were nonetheless first and foremost engaged in a struggle for individual survival. This meant that pre-war notions of civil engagement changed radically: stealing, bribing, and smuggling became commonplace, and even became some of the most constructive ways of surviving. In the ghettos, some communal structures were more or less retained, or new ones created, but social conflicts did not disappear. In fact, new power structures brought with them new antagonisms. In the larger ghettos, elite members of society— prominent among them employees of the Judenräte (Jewish Councils) and the Jewish Police—ate, worked, and lived better than the majority of the population. In the camps, functionaries wielded enormous power over their fellow prisoners. While these dynamics affected more essential areas of camp and ghetto life, they also affected the nature of musical activity.

As I have mentioned, resistance was often not organized and deliberate in the way that some have suggested. For most of the time, the victims did not have a clear understanding of what was happening to them. Even when they received information that was precise—jumbled in amongst the countless rumours and reports with which they were regularly confronted—they would not or could not believe it; and when full realization came, if it came at all, it was almost invariably too late to react. This was not a result of their failure to anticipate danger, but of a carefully planned strategy of deception on which the Nazis relied. In the face of this uncertainty, communities did what they could to keep themselves going: kept up some form of religious life, organized clandestine get-togethers, smuggled food and shared rations, established social welfare groups, and tried to preserve some of their pre-war cultural practices. These impulses were manifestations of a human instinct to stay alive, regardless of whether or not hope was realistic—a powerful instinct that cannot simply be construed heroically. Instinctive coping strategies such as these might also ironically have made it even more difficult for victims later to assimilate their reality. Relating to these issues, Langer has rightly pointed out that the term 'staying alive' is more appropriate than the consoling and

---

[13] Levi, *The Drowned and the Saved*, 23, 25.

value-laden 'survival'.[14] People feared death, however inconceivable the imminence of their own, and searched for markers to re-establish order in the chaotic ghetto or camp environment.

Where the props of pre-war existence had been taken away, musical activity was only one of a number of ways in which communities attempted to restore a sense of security, familiarity, and continuity. It provided a place where the illusion of normality could be perpetuated, and where people could escape temporarily from the ghetto or camp world. It also provided a framework within which victims could laugh at, express despair at, or try to make sense of what was happening to them. While the word resistance suggests active intent, it seems more likely that music was only a small part of the coping framework, and a less essential one than smuggling or soup kitchens. At a certain point in the world of atrocity, when people were exhausted, diseased, freezing, and dying of starvation, music could simply no longer flourish.

Continuing along Bernstein's line, we might thus more usefully understand musical activity through a process of 'sideshadowing'. By this Bernstein suggests that we consider the alternatives the victims might have imagined for themselves at the time, and acknowledge that their inability to predict their own victimhood must inflect our understanding of their actions. In short, we must come to the subject with an awareness that events now in the past were once in the future.[15]

This process requires tireless imaginative work. When we talk about symphony concerts, or communal sing-songs, or café shows, we need to imagine the streets through which the victims walked in order to get there, the living spaces they left and returned to, and the things they might have witnessed along the way. When we think about theatre revues, we need to imagine the oppressive atmosphere that must have redescended on the audience once the performance had finished. We need to consider who would have attended what events, how often, and what extent of their mental space they would have occupied. The significance that music held for the victims cannot be understood independent of this context: just as it informed every activity, it should qualify and complicate every observation. These seemingly obvious points need emphasis, as it is in their absence that redemptive descriptions have been able to flourish.

---

[14] Lawrence L. Langer, *Holocaust Testimonies: The Ruins of Memory* (New Haven and London, 1991), 175.
[15] Bernstein, *Foregone Conclusions*, 24.

III

Because its aim, whether overt or implicit, is to defend the victims and the way in which they are remembered, the rhetoric of spiritual resistance has enormous power. In reverent tones, it tells us: this is how determined and courageous the victims were; despite tragic circumstances, they did not give up, and their spirits could not be broken. It is precisely *because* it honours the victims in this way that it tacitly silences opposition: if one asserts that victims should not be construed heroically, one risks being accused of violating their memory. Within the safety of this framework, the language of heroic resistance does what is arguably more dangerous work as far as the truthfulness of the historical record is concerned: it does not honour the complexity of human life in the camps and ghettos, and in my case hinders a richer understanding of the work music did there.

From the construction of reality in historical retrospect, let us move to the realm of Alberto and the victims themselves. Langer has argued that the concept of spiritual resistance 'may have been exaggerated by us, the heirs and descendants of the Holocaust experience, instead of its having been recruited as an accurate description of their activities by the victims and survivors of the event'.[16] While the point about post-war exaggeration is indisputable, the question of how the victims chose to describe their activities is more problematic. As far as music is concerned, victims writing both during and after the war often used the terminology of spiritual resistance. It must be stressed that although this exposes a state of affairs far less straightforward than the one Langer depicts, it in no way justifies the prominence that terminology has assumed in scholarly writing. It does, however, reveal that the motivations for attributing redemptive meaning do not stem solely from present-day concerns, but almost certainly acquired their initial impetus from the victims themselves.

Writing in 1948, surviving victim H. Leivick declared:

In the bitterest days of our nation's Holocaust—yes, even then—none of us doubted the spiritual powers, the spiritual heroism of our brothers who died in God's holy name...In mines, in bunkers, in sewerage pipes, on the threshold of the gas chambers Jews sought strength in prayer, in poetry, in song...We are pierced by a singular feeling of admiration: The nation is always singing. Yes, always.[17]

---

[16] Langer, *Admitting the Holocaust*, 53.
[17] Kaczerginski and Leivick, pp. xxviii–xxx.

Many survivors used similar rhetoric to describe the musical events they remembered. Recalling the premiere performance of Verdi's *Requiem* in Theresienstadt, the inmate Josef Bor imagined that what motivated the conductor, Raphael Schächter, was a sense of communicating to the audience that 'we endured, we never gave way, we never succumbed'. For his fellow Theresienstadt prisoner Ruth Elias, music was viewed as 'a revolt against the regime' and '[weapon] against the Nazi terror'. For the Vilna inmate Sima Skurkovitz, the songs were 'an expression of what was in our hearts . . . They gave us hope to survive.'[18]

There were also occasions on which contemporary writers—those writing at the time of the events—tended towards redemptive rhetoric. Unlike in post-war testimonies, however, the difficult context within which they were writing almost always intruded into their descriptions. The entry in the Łódź *Chronicle* for 24 November 1943, approximately nine months before the liquidation of the ghetto, read as follows:

Though life weighs heavily upon people in the ghetto, they refuse to do without cultural life altogether. The closing of the House of Culture has deprived the ghetto of the last vestiges of public cultural life. But with his tenacity and vitality, the ghetto dweller, hardened by countless misfortunes, always seeks new ways to sate his hunger for something of cultural value. The need for music is especially intense, and small centres for the cultivation of music have sprung up over time; to be sure, only for a certain upper stratum. Sometimes it is professional musicians, sometimes amateurs who perform for an intimate group of invited guests. Chamber music is played and there is singing. Likewise, small, family-like circles form in order to provide spiritual nourishment on a modest level. Poets and prose writers read from their own works. The classics and more recent works of world literature are recited. Thus does the ghetto salvage something of its former spiritual life.[19]

While emphasizing the 'tenacity and vitality' of the ghetto inhabitants and their urge for 'spiritual nourishment', the *Chronicle* also acknowledged that these 'modest' activities were enjoyed only by a small elite. Similar trends were evident in the Warsaw diary of Chaim Kaplan. According to his translator, Abraham Katsh, Kaplan was acutely aware of his own contradictory responses to his experiences. He feared that the Jews would not survive Nazism, and was all too conscious of the ways in which the Nazis deluded their victims as to their ultimate fates. However, like many ghetto inmates he also frequently

---

[18] Josef Bor, *Terezin Requiem* (London, 1963), 58–9; Ruth Elias, *Triumph of Hope: From Theresienstadt and Auschwitz to Israel* (New York, 1998), 84; Sima Skurkovitz, *Sima's Songs: Light in Nazi Darkness* (Jerusalem, 1993), 26.

[19] Lucjan Dobroszycki (ed.), *The Chronicle of the Łódź Ghetto, 1941–1944* (New Haven, 1984), 412.

succumbed to 'wishful thinking'. As Kaplan's narrative proceeded, there were recurrent adjustments in his conception of the events. His early entries in particular were marked by relentless pessimism: he described how depression and fear had gripped the ghetto, how people had begun to act like animals preoccupied only with their individual survival, and how the Jewish leadership had abandoned the community. On 7 March 1940, he wrote:

Our desolate and miserable lives go on without the spark of hope to which our people have always been accustomed. The days when the oppressed Jewish masses would console themselves with nonsensical political rumours are past. Reality shows us that our redemption is still far from us. Those who understand the military and political situation well are going about like mourners. There is no ground for hope that the decisive action will come this spring, and lack of a decision means that our terrible distress will last a long time.

However, elsewhere there were frequent shifts into language of hope and defiance. On 10 March 1940, Kaplan described the Jewish community's will to live as 'the outward manifestation of a certain hidden power whose quality has not yet been examined . . . as long as this secret power is still within us we do not give up hope'. His entry for 1 August 1940 asserted that although Jews had always lived in material and spiritual straits, 'Jewish creativity never ceased throughout all the days of our exile'. In February 1941 he wrote: 'It is almost a *mitzvah*[20] to dance. The more one dances, the more it is a sign of his belief in the "eternity of Israel". Every dance is a protest against our oppressors.'[21]

In a letter smuggled to the New York YIVO Institute from Warsaw in May 1944, A. Berman and Emmanuel Ringelblum detailed the wide-ranging cultural life that had existed in the ghetto. They described how, taking up the exhortation to 'live with honour and die with honour', the inmates had established the Yidishe Kultur Organizatsye (Jewish Cultural Organization), clandestine schools, an underground archive and press, youth organizations, and numerous theatrical and musical activities. Laying emphasis on the community's dedication to cultural activity, they wrote:

The source of social and cultural work flowed as long as life still pulsed in the Jewish communities. It should be known that the last living activists remained devoted to the ideals of our culture until the last moment. They carried the flag of culture and struggle against barbarism in their hands until their deaths.[22]

---

[20] Hebrew word meaning both commandment and good deed.

[21] Chaim A. Kaplan, *Scroll of Agony: The Warsaw Diary of Chaim A. Kaplan*, trans. and ed. Abraham I. Katsh (London, 1965), 10, 129, 131, 174, 244–5.

[22] Ringelblum and Berman cited in Meilekh Neustadt, *Khurbn un oyfshtand fun di yidn in Varshe: eydes-bletter un azkores* (Tel Aviv, 1948), 313.

Writing several years earlier from within the ghetto, however, the same Emmanuel Ringelblum presented a rather different picture. In his *Notitsen fun Varshever geto* (Notes from the Warsaw Ghetto), he recorded a wide spectrum of cultural activities. However, his descriptions were always grounded in the ghetto context, and his evaluations were often critical. According to his translator Jacob Sloan, his most frequently used term to describe the psychological state of the ghetto in the *Notitsen* was 'demoralization'.[23] In addition, the social inequality in the ghetto, which was one of his recurring concerns in the *Notitsen*, was not expressed in the May 1944 letter.

The conflicting emphases in these examples shed light on the distinctive purposes contemporary and post-war writings were intended to serve. In the case of contemporary writings, the uncertainty of lived events saw frequent and often radical shifts in the victims' perceptions, depending on the latest happenings, prevailing moods, and other contingencies of daily existence. Moments of abrupt change—moving into the ghettos, or deportations, for example—could quickly shatter inmates' fragile emotional stability. The discourse of spiritual resistance in this context often signalled a desire on the part of the victims to attribute meaning *for themselves* to their otherwise suffering-filled lives, as well as a need to rebuild hope.

Post-war accounts necessarily adopted a different approach. While Ringelblum's *Notitsen*, for example, were part of a documentary project carried out during the existence of the ghetto, his letter was already a gesture of memorialization written more than a year after its destruction, and addressed directly to a community removed from the events. It seems, as David Roskies has pointed out, that while some of the writings from within the ghetto were focused on internal corruption and hostilities, post-ghetto reports tended to suppress these in the attempt to impart a greater sense of community cohesion. This was based on the premiss that 'bringing the external enemy to justice was far more important than settling old internal accounts'.[24] It also stemmed from the fear that audiences removed from the events—even those sympathetic to the Jewish plight—would fail to grasp the magnitude of what had been perpetrated and suffered. The impulse to frame wartime experiences in unambiguous moral terms derived logically from this position: in the wake of raw suffering, conveying to an external audience the enormity of the

---

[23] Emmanuel Ringelblum, *Notes from the Warsaw Ghetto: The Journal of Emmanuel Ringelblum*, trans. and ed. Jacob Sloan (New York, 1974), 101.

[24] David Roskies (ed.), *The Literature of Destruction* (New York, 1989), 382.

atrocity and bloodshed unquestionably outweighed all other aspects of the story.

The issue of how to approach testimonial material of this kind is obviously a sensitive and complex one, and has in recent years been the subject of an important and dynamic debate. In their retrospective testimonies, victims could do little more than describe their own individual experiences; in doing this, they necessarily emphasized some events while consciously or unconsciously misrepresenting or omitting others. Their attempts to talk about traumatic events long after they occurred also often meant that problems generally associated with conveying memory were magnified. In addition, the complex process of readaptation to society in the post-war period inevitably affected their constructions of events: potential factors that informed their narratives included guilt about survival; shame for acts committed that may have been essential to survival but which in hindsight violated the ethics of 'civilized' existence; or a trauma so severe that crucial aspects of experience could not be recalled. Further exploration of this issue lies beyond the scope of this book, but the crucial point here is an awareness that testimony cannot be taken at face value, but should be approached—as any other historical source—with care and discretion.[25]

The preceding discussion should make it clear that redemptive narratives in the context of the victims' accounts have a markedly different relevance than those that characterize some secondary writings. As Bernstein rightly points out, 'there is nothing self-evidently deluded in the fact that it was the *wrong* prediction, the fatally *incorrect* interpretation of public events that won the intellectual and emotional allegiance of the vast majority of European Jews'.[26] Theirs was a powerful instinct to hope for survival even when prospects were grim, and to make some sense of what was happening to them even when the structure of their lives seemed to be disintegrating. This does not mean, however, that we can straightforwardly appropriate the meaning that they ascribed to things. Rather, we need to acknowledge that the interpretations they made, both during and after the war, were part of an

---

[25] The debate regarding testimony as a historical source is an important one in the context of my subject, particularly since it is uncritical approaches to testimony that have hindered deeper, more searching studies of music during this period. For more detailed discussion, see Shirli Gilbert, 'Music in the Nazi Ghettos and Camps (1939–1945)' (D.Phil. diss., University of Oxford, 2002), 21–30. See also Langer, *Holocaust Testimonies*; James Young, 'Between History and Memory: The Uncanny Voices of Historian and Survivor', *History and Memory*, 9/1 (1997), 47–58; Annette Wieviorka, 'On Testimony', in Geoffrey H. Hartman (ed.), *Holocaust Remembrance*, 23–32; Bernstein, *Foregone Conclusions*, 47; Shoshana Felman and Dori Laub, *Testimony: Crises of Witnessing in Literature, Psychoanalysis and History* (London, 1992).

[26] Bernstein, *Foregone Conclusions*, 24.

ongoing struggle in their own conception of the events, and part of their inability to predict what was going to happen to them, or to evaluate things 'correctly'.

IV

The spiritual resistance theme is complicated by one further, crucial group of contemporary writings: the musical texts. As we shall see, a substantial number of the songs produced during this time contained uplifting, encouraging messages. Most of those associated with resistance organizations in particular—amongst German political prisoners in Sachsenhausen, for example, and partisans in the Vilna ghetto—were bold, defiant, and optimistic. Nonetheless, the vast majority of the songs told more complicated stories. They often engaged directly with the actualities of camp or ghetto life—hunger, hard labour, death, disease—and expressed emotions ranging from nostalgia for the past to anger, pain, despair, loss of faith, guilt at having survived family members, frustration, uncertainty, and the desire for revenge. While they were sometimes used for voicing thoughts about the Nazi authorities, they also provided a forum for criticism directed within the prisoner communities themselves—towards the Jewish Councils and welfare organizations in the ghettos, for example, or functionaries in the camps. Some detailed specific events and responses to them, while others dealt with new social problems that had arisen. They offer us hundreds of portraits, from the time, of different perceptions of and responses to camp and ghetto life. Even the triumphant and optimistic songs resist simplistic evaluation, not least because descriptions of hardship often account for the bulk of the song texts.

Songs were, above all, a medium through which narratives of understanding and response to the events were constructed. Communities used music to process and make sense of what was happening to them, but in different contexts they framed and interpreted the events in particular ways. While some construed internment as part of a larger, ongoing political struggle against the Nazi regime, others tried to situate their experiences within pre-existing national or religious frameworks. Their narratives took many forms, and involved multiple layers of identity: pre-existing religious, cultural, social, and political identities, and identities that were developed or imposed in these radically new social environments. The process of construction was ongoing, and subject to frequent shifts and changes depending on the circumstances.

Considered in this light, hopeful messages frequently suggest a struggle to *encourage* resolve and perseverance, rather than merely to reflect their existence. Particularly in the ghettos, optimistic songs grew in number as conditions deteriorated. The less cause there was for hope, the more people needed to hope; they hoped instinctively because they could not assimilate the possibility that they would not survive. To take the songs at face value is to overlook what was surely a more complicated interaction between them and the reality they not only described, but also participated in.

In short, we should not attribute to music a singular power it did not and could not possess in the circumstances. The diction of heroic resistance mythicizes and decontextualizes the phenomenon, choosing instead to espouse clichés and comforting stories. The rejection of redemptive narratives need not presuppose a refusal of all affirmative meaning, however. Musical activities in many camps and ghettos were prolific and diverse, and afforded the victims temporary diversion, entertainment, and opportunities to process what was happening to them. The key word here is temporary. Whatever its power, music could ultimately be only a small component of the ghetto or camp structure. And while it gives us insight into some of the most compelling aspects of captive life—the ideas with which victims were preoccupied, and the ways in which they framed their experiences for themselves—it is most usefully and honestly viewed from a wide-angle perspective. That is to say, even while we focus in on the isolated times and places where it existed, we should have as a constant mental backdrop the atmosphere of fear, uncertainty, violence, illness, hunger, and death that characterized the camps and ghettos, and permeated their every aspect. For Levi's Alberto and countless other victims, whatever little consolation could be mustered was almost always punctured and undermined by reality. In the case of retrospective narratives, however, particularly secondary accounts by those who did not experience the events, reality no longer arrives of its own accord to belie its reconstructions.

V

In the light of the preceding pages, one point must be made clear. The scope of musical life under Nazi internment was a remarkable demonstration of the integral role culture can play in constructing communal meaning and identity, particularly in times of crisis. My book is an attempt not to negate that role, but rather to widen the frame of reference within which it can be understood, and to explore it in its myriad dimensions through detailed examination of musical life as embedded in particular social contexts.

I chose to adopt a case-study approach with this underlying motivation. Rather than using disparate, decontextualized examples to support generalized conclusions about the 'triumph of the spirit', I have sought to understand the distinctiveness that characterized people's interactions with music in particular places and times. While 'resistance' was undoubtedly part of what sometimes motivated inmates to participate in musical activity, it is not the whole story. The book will consider under what circumstances and for whom resistance was a possibility, and explore the manifold functions that music could play for those who did not enjoy sustained or approved access to it.

The four case studies that make up the book take as their focus the Warsaw and Vilna ghettos, and the Sachsenhausen and Auschwitz camps. I wanted to include examples from different types of internment centres—ghettos, concentration camps, and death camps—as well as to include places that were, if not representative of other institutions of their kind, at least among the more prominent in general awareness. This decision was based on the consideration that findings and conclusions could later be applied to studies of a wider range of places, including labour camps, and transit camps such as Westerbork.

I have also deliberately chosen to consider the activities of Jewish inmates alongside those of German, Polish, Czech, and other prisoners in the camps. The existing literature has kept these areas of enquiry largely separate. As will become clear, the experiences of these groups were indeed widely differing; nonetheless, drawing connections between their experiences shifts emphasis away from wranglings about 'uniqueness' and allows for a richer understanding of the human experience of internment. This is perhaps most significantly what the book seeks to explore and understand: the diverse and changing ways in which human beings imprisoned under Nazism responded to and interpreted what was happening to them.

In the first chapter, I show how music as a social activity reflected the stratification of Warsaw ghetto society, and the considerably varied lifestyles that Jews of different classes were able to lead. I also look at people's perceptions of ghetto life as expressed in the songs newly created there. The songs draw us into a world of uncertainty and collapsing moral frameworks, where begging, smuggling, and stealing were becoming pressing social issues, and overt hostility was being directed at the Jewish Council and welfare institutions.

The second chapter, 'Vilna: Politicians and Partisans', considers musical activity both as a continuation of the community's rich pre-war cultural life, and as a vehicle for promoting agendas within new political structures in the ghetto. The structures in question were the Jewish Council, particularly under the leadership of Jacob Gens from mid-1942, and the underground Fareynigte Partizaner Organizatsye (United Partisans Organization, FPO), established in the early part of that year. In this chapter we see how the partisans used musical activity to encourage active resistance and defiance, while the Jewish Council promoted passive acceptance and continued productivity as the best way of ensuring the survival of at least a portion of the community.

In the second half of the book I explore the forms that musical activity took within the 'Grey Zone' of the camps. In both Sachsenhausen and Auschwitz, the experiences of different groups demonstrated how profoundly access and opportunity differed on the basis of social placement. Music was a potent symbol of difference, marking the division between those who had free access to it, and those who did not, and reflecting the diverging treatment of national, political, or religious groups within the prisoner hierarchies. As a voluntary activity it tended to be the preserve of the 'privileged', and although it sometimes functioned as a means for inter-group communication and solidarity, it was equally often the sign of one group's advantages over another.

In Sachsenhausen we encounter 'privileged' German Communist inmates, who were able to integrate musical activities into their ongoing underground struggle against fascism. We then shift our focus to Polish prisoners, whose music reflected the radically different tenor of their lives in the camp—disempowered, angry, and cynical. Jews were severely restricted in their opportunities, but compelling evidence survives to show how the largely assimilated German-Jewish prisoners in the camp used Yiddish folksong to forge links with their past, and situate their experiences within a Jewish historical trajectory.

The final chapter, 'Fragments of Humanity: Music in Auschwitz', examines how forced music-making in the camp—particularly the prisoner orchestras, daily marches, and forced singing sessions—might have served positive personal functions for the SS authorities themselves. Beyond its functions of punishment and torture, music is seen to provide a framework within which the SS could maintain a self-image of refined German culture and personal 'decency', not apart from but precisely in the context of the murderous activities in which they were involved. The chapter also explores the limited voluntary activities that could take place amongst 'ordinary' prisoners, and the wider range of opportunities open to 'prominents', including discussion of a full-length cabaret created and performed in Auschwitz-Birkenau.

As a final point, it is worth emphasizing that as these are case studies, their observations and conclusions are intended to shed light not only on the histories of individual internment centres, but also on the ways in which daily life in other camps and ghettos might come to be viewed.

I

'Have compassion, Jewish hearts': Music in the Warsaw Ghetto

Shortly after the war, three surviving inmates of the Warsaw ghetto related to the collector Shmerke Kaczerginski the song 'Moes, moes' (Money, money), which they recalled being popularly sung (see Ex. 1.1).[1] The song provides a glimpse into the complicated social landscape that the move into the ghetto engendered:

> Moes, moes, moes iz di ershte zakh.
> Hostu nit keyn moes, iz tsu dir a klog,
> Gib avek di bone un zog a gutn tog.
> Moes, moes, moes iz di beste zakh.
>
> Moes, moes, moes iz di beste zakh,
> Di yidishe gemine nemt fun undz danine
> Un git dokh undz tsu esn broyt mit sakharine.—
> Moes, moes, moes iz di beste zakh.

Mo - es,　　mo - es,　　mo-es iz di er - shte zakh.

Ho - stu nit keyn mo - es,　iz tsu dir a klog,　Gib a - vek di bo - ne un

zog a gu-tn tog. Mo - es,　　mo - es,　　mo-es iz di be - ste zakh.

Ex. 1.1. 'Moes, moes'. Kaczerginski and Leivick, 401

[1] Kaczerginski's collection, edited by H. Leivick, entitled *Lider fun di getos un lagern* (Songs from the ghettos and camps), constitutes the most comprehensive source of Yiddish songs from this period. The word 'moes' comes from the Hebrew 'ma'ot', which literally means coins or small change.

Moes, moes, moes iz di beste zakh,
Ale fakhn lign haynt in dr'erd,
Nor di bekers raytn oyfn ferd.—
Moes, moes, moes iz di beste zakh.

Moes, moes, moes iz di beste zakh,
In der heym hob ikh gegesn pomerantsn,
Haynt esn mikh oyf di layz mit di vantsn.
Moes, moes, moes iz di beste zakh.

Moes, moes, moes iz di beste zakh,
Der yidisher politsyant er iz dokh a lobuz,
Zetst aykh oyf der mashine un shikt avek in 'obuz'.
Moes, moes, moes iz di beste zakh.

Moes, moes, moes iz a gute zakh.
Hostu nit keyn moes, hob yakh far dir a plan:
Gib avek di bone, un rik zikh in Pinkerts kestele aran . . .
Moes, moes, moes iz an eydele zakh.[2]

Money, money, money is the first thing.
If you have no money, woe to you,
Give away your ration card and say good day.
Money, money, money is the best thing.

Money, money, money is the best thing,
The Jewish Council takes taxes from us
Yet it feeds us bread with saccharin.—
Money, money, money is the best thing.

Money, money, money is the best thing,
All trades have had it these days,
Only bakers ride on horses.—
Money, money, money is the best thing.

Money, money, money is the best thing,
Back home I ate oranges,
Today I am eaten by lice and bedbugs.
Money, money, money is the best thing.

Money, money, money is the best thing,
The Jewish policeman is just a scoundrel,
Puts you on the train and sends you away to a camp.
Money, money, money is the best thing.

Money, money, money is a good thing.
If you have no money, I have a plan for you:
Give away your ration card, and crawl into Pinkert's little box . . .
Money, money, money is a fine thing.

[2] Kaczerginski and Leivick, 177–8.

Another version of the song collected by Ruta Pups and Bernard Mark suggests that numerous additional verses were in circulation.[3] Set to a pre-war American jazz hit, 'Moes, moes' was a biting satire of corruption and moral decline. It exposed the ghetto as a place of economic and social inequality, and in particular criticized the ill treatment of the ghetto masses at the hands of the powerful and wealthy elite. The Judenrat could impose taxes and provide nothing in return; the Jewish Police protected their positions by deporting members of their own community to the camps. Those who were left could hope for little more than to 'crawl into Pinkert's little box'—Motl Pinkert being the head of the ghetto's Khevre Kadishe (Burial Society).[4] The singer's advice for coping with the situation was resignedly good-humoured; beyond the theatres where the song was performed, however, it is doubtful whether people accepted the situation with such equanimity. In fact, the disparities that characterized Warsaw ghetto society were for many a source of anger and despair. The effects of stratification were most strongly felt in critical areas such as food and housing, but they also trickled through to most corners of ghetto life, among them the dynamic range of musical activities that continued for most of the ghetto's existence.

The Landscape of Jewish Warsaw

On the eve of the Second World War, Warsaw's Jewish population was the largest and most socially diverse in Europe. The city had already established itself as one of the most important Jewish centres a century earlier: welfare, educational, and religious institutions had their headquarters there, as did political parties, youth movements, and sports organizations, and it was the hub for the Polish-Jewish press. Particularly after 1881, it had attracted thousands of Jewish migrants not only from within the borders of Congress Poland, but from the Russian Pale of Settlement as well.[5] In 1939 its 380,000 inhabitants made up almost a third of the city total, and by the time the

---

[3] Ruta Pups and Bernard Mark, *Dos lid fun geto: zomlung* (Warsaw, 1962), 46–8.

[4] Ibid. 48.

[5] The assassination of Czar Alexander II in 1881 was followed by anti-Jewish violence and pogroms in Congress Poland as well as in Russia, which led to mass migrations. See Celia S. Heller, *On the Edge of Destruction: Jews of Poland between the Two World Wars* (New York, 1977), 38; Chone Shmeruk, 'Aspects of the History of Warsaw as a Yiddish Literary Centre', in Wladyslaw T. Bartoszewski and Antony Polonsky (eds), *The Jews in Warsaw: A History* (Oxford, 1991), 232–45 at 232; Yisrael Gutman (ed.), *Encyclopedia of the Holocaust* (London, 1990), 1601–3.

ghetto was established in November 1940, they numbered well over 400,000.[6]

Jewish Warsaw was characterized by a diversity of cultural trends. On the one hand, it housed the largest numbers of Yiddish-speakers in Europe, and was the leading centre for Yiddish literature. Despite the rising influence of Polish and Russian among early twentieth-century Jewish communities in Poland, Yiddish had continued to gain strength as a language of cultural and political activity, and Hebrew was also advocated by a substantial contingent as the language of the Jewish future.[7] At the same time, Warsaw was by far the largest centre of Polish-speaking Jews. The process of Jewish acculturation had been more rapid here than anywhere else in Congress Poland, and although it affected only a small minority of the population, by the nineteenth century the city had already become famed for its plutocracy of assimilated and converted Jews. Those who had chosen to convert before the war did so in order to gain access to employment otherwise forbidden to Jews, but also to some extent because they wanted to dissociate themselves from the poor, uneducated Jewish masses. There were also those who retained their Jewish religion but insisted on speaking Polish rather than Yiddish, and advocated education for their children in Polish schools.[8]

The diversity of this sizeable population was manifest to an even greater extent when it was concentrated within the ghetto walls. The establishment of the ghetto also saw the growth of new inequalities. The priorities and values that had driven the pre-war community were quickly modified or abandoned in the new environment, where the struggle for survival took precedence. In their absence, a new elite gained control. Apart from those in top-ranking occupations—members of the Judenrat and the Jewish Police, or skilled workers employed outside the ghetto—some of the most prosperous and comfortable of the ghetto's inhabitants became those involved in illegal or criminal activities: smugglers, blackmailers, black marketeers, and other underworld figures. The powerful positions held by these characters afforded them adequate food and shelter, higher wages than the majority of the ghetto inhabitants, more security from forced labour, and sometimes temporary exemption from deportation.

[6] Although the outbreak of war led to a substantial emigration from the city, over 75,000 refugees were taken in from Łódź, Kalisz, and about 700 other settlements during 1940. Lucy S. Dawidowicz, *The War against the Jews, 1933–1945* (London, 1975), 250.

[7] Stephen D. Corrsin, 'Aspects of Population Change and of Acculturation in Jewish Warsaw at the End of the Nineteenth Century: The Censuses of 1882 and 1897', in Bartoszewski and Polonsky (eds.), *The Jews in Warsaw*, 212–31 at 222.

[8] Shmeruk, 'Aspects', 233; Charles G. Roland, *Courage under Siege: Starvation, Disease and Death in the Warsaw Ghetto* (Oxford, 1992), 30.

To be sure, and as we shall see, a number of welfare institutions attempted to lessen the enormous burdens faced by the community's weaker members in particular; nonetheless, those of limited financial means in the ghetto were invariably the first to suffer the effects of victimization.[9]

Cultural life was deeply rooted in this diversity. The musical landscape of the Warsaw ghetto was one of impressive scope: it offered more performances, of more varied range and subject matter, and in a greater number of locations than any of its counterparts. It boasted a symphony orchestra, several Polish and Yiddish theatres, choral groups, and cafés, and hosted countless concerts and informal events. Even in the months before its closure, a wide range of musical entertainments had sprung up to suit the needs of the community. But the parts of musical life with which different people were likely to engage depended almost entirely on their social standing. For many, the only musical sounds in the ghetto were those of beggars singing for money on the streets, or the occasional free concerts in the soup kitchens. Others could partake of the bourgeois pleasures of symphony orchestra and chamber concerts, or attend performances at one of the ghetto theatres. Only a small upper stratum had access to the cafés, and to the private house concerts given by some of the ghetto's leading artists.

This chapter considers the ways in which music as a social activity reflected the stratification of the society, and the considerably varied lifestyles that people of different classes were able to lead. In addition, it explores the diversity of people's perceptions of and responses to ghetto life as expressed in the newly created songs. These engaged with some of the ghetto's most pressing social issues, including begging, smuggling, and the allocation of welfare benefits, and directed sharp criticism at the Judenrat and welfare institutions. In this they mirrored the preoccupations of other ghetto communities.[10] Some also took up the exhortation to document for posterity the experiences that had befallen the community, while others were an outlet for the expression of pain, desperation, religious belief, and survival guilt.

Most musical activity in Warsaw, including the newly created songs, drew on pre-war repertoire. This was not surprising, and was also the case in most other internment centres; communities evidently found value in music that drew on their national or religious origins. In addition, the use of pre-existing melodies as a basis for new songs, which was a widespread practice in most of the ghettos, was a long-standing tradition in Yiddish folksong. Of course, the

---

[9] Dawidowicz, *The War against the Jews*, 265–6.

[10] See, for example, Gila Flam's discussion of Łódź in *Singing for Survival: Songs of the Lodz Ghetto* (Urbana, 1992), 102.

process by which old songs were modified to the new conditions took manifold forms. Songs of hunger and oppression (an integral part of the Jewish experience prior to the Second World War) were particularly adaptable,[11] but even songs from 'normal' life—lullabies, love songs, and songs about children—acquired radically altered associations and provided revealing commentary about the new events. Many new songs were also composed in direct response to what was happening; at least seventeen of those written in Warsaw were preserved.[12]

The Extremes of Ghetto Life

The ghettos were a transitional phase in the 'Final Solution', intended primarily as places where Jews could be concentrated prior to mass emigration and killing. A directive issued by Reinhard Heydrich on 21 September 1939 regarding policy towards Jews in the occupied territories stated that the first prerequisite for the fulfilment of the 'final aim' was concentrating Jews from the countryside in the larger cities. As few concentration centres as possible were to be set up, and only at locations with rail junctions.[13]

Plans for the establishment of a ghetto in Warsaw were considered as early as November 1939. It was only on 12 October 1940, however, that the official decree ordering the establishment of the ghetto was issued. A map indicating the boundaries of the area was published, and on 16 November the district was sealed. Situated in the Jewish quarter in the northern section of the city, the walled-in ghetto occupied only 2.4 per cent of the city's area, and included no parks or open spaces. According to a document issued on 20 January 1941 by the district Resettlement Department, the 403 hectares of the ghetto housed 410,000 Jews. The situation worsened steadily as refugees poured in from outlying areas throughout 1941. By January 1942 the ghetto's size had been reduced to only 300 hectares, and was inhabited by about 400,000 Jews.[14]

[11] Flam, *Singing for Survival*, 131.

[12] A listing of these songs is given in the Appendix, §I.

[13] Yitzhak Arad, Yisrael Gutman, and Abraham Margaliot, *Documents on the Holocaust: Selected Sources on the Destruction of the Jews of Germany and Austria, Poland, and the Soviet Union* (Jerusalem, 1981), 173–4.

[14] The periodic influxes of refugees meant that although the mortality rate in the ghetto was high, the population figure remained relatively stable. The population reached a peak of over 450,000 in Apr. 1941. Numbers began to decrease in the latter half of 1941, but dropped dramatically only after the great deportations during the summer of 1942. See Roland, *Courage under Siege*, 29; Gutman (ed.), *Encyclopedia*, 1607–8; Wladyslaw Bartoszewski, 'The Martyrdom and Struggle of the Jews in Warsaw under German Occupation 1939–43', in Bartoszewski and Polonsky (eds.), *The Jews in Warsaw*, 312–48 at 313–14.

Although mass killings were seldom carried out in the ghettos, they served as powerful instruments of indirect destruction. They were generally located in the poorest and most dilapidated parts of cities, in areas that lacked basic sewerage and sanitary facilities, or where apartment buildings had suffered from bombing and shelling. Living conditions in Warsaw were some of the worst in any of the ghettos of eastern Europe. The population density meant severe overcrowding; on average, six or seven people shared a room. During the winter months, the scarcity of fuel made it difficult to keep warm. Starvation was rife, and the illegal smuggling of food became a thriving industry. The squalid conditions also bred rampant disease: the most prevalent was typhus, but thousands died of heart disease, dysentery, tuberculosis, diseases of the digestive tract, or simply of starvation and exhaustion. Added to the inhospitable physical conditions was the constant possibility of seizure for forced labour for those aged between 14 and 60; between 1940 and 1942, a total of 15,000–20,000 people were taken.[15] In its lead article on 23 May 1941, *Biuletyn Informacyjny* (Information Bulletin), the underground organ of the Union for Armed Resistance, reported of the ghetto:

Further crowding has resulted in conditions of ill-health, hunger and monstrous poverty that defy description. Groups of pale and emaciated people wander aimlessly through the overcrowded streets. Beggars sit and lie along the walls and the sight of people collapsing from starvation is common. The refuge for abandoned children takes in a dozen infants every day; every day a few more people die on the street. Contagious diseases are spreading, particularly tuberculosis. Meanwhile, the Germans continue to plunder the wealthy Jews. Their treatment of the Jews is always exceptionally inhuman. They torment them and subject them constantly to their wild and bestial amusements.[16]

Only a small proportion of the ghetto population had access to basic food supplies. According to a calculation made by the Żydowskie Towarzystwo Opieki Społecznej (Jewish Society for Social Welfare, ŻTOS), almost half the inhabitants—over 200,000 people—had no means of support.[17]

However, there were also those who continued to live well in the ghetto. An entry in the Łódź ghetto *Chronicle* in May 1941 recorded a speech by Judenrat chairman Rumkowski in which he shared his impressions from a recent trip to Warsaw:

---

[15] Gutman (ed.), *Encyclopedia*, 1609; Bartoszewski, 'Martyrdom and Struggle', 313.
[16] Cited in Bartoszewski, 'Martyrdom and Struggle', 314.
[17] Gutman (ed.), *Encyclopedia*, 1610.

There is a striking contrast in the Warsaw ghetto between the tragic poverty of the enormous majority of the people and the prosperity of the small handful who still remain wealthy and have access to every sort of restaurant, pastry shop, and store, where the prices are, of course, dizzyingly high. Aside from that 'frippery' and the small number of fortunate people who are dressed in the latest fashion and perfectly well fed, one sees immense crowds of unemployed people whose appearance is simply frightening.[18]

The 'prosperity' enjoyed by this elite 'handful' was manifest in many areas of ghetto life, particularly in the early months of the ghetto's existence. Those with money and connections had access not just to basic food supplies, but to a wide variety of delicacies, meats, and alcohol that had been smuggled in. They continued to live in comfortable houses, in hygienic conditions, with adequate bedding and clothing. As Ringelblum noted, they were also able to buy their way out of forced labour, ensuring an enviable degree of safety and comfort for themselves and their families.[19]

 Among the items to which these people had access was entertainment, particularly music. Even before the sealing of the ghetto, numerous cafés and clubs offering plentiful food, drink, and live musical entertainment were opened. Leszno Street was jokingly referred to as 'the Broadway of the Warsaw ghetto'.[20] In April 1941 Ringelblum recorded that sixty-one café-type establishments were in existence, and a report in *Gazeta Żydowska* on 17 June 1941 revealed that stiff competition had arisen between them: 'The demand for artists is big . . . Each coffee house, each bar and restaurant . . . advertises its own rich program of sensational attractions'.[21]

Many of the cafés opened with the help of Gestapo or Judenrat members, and could continue to operate only through high-ranking connections.[22] They made little attempt to hide their activities from the rest of the population: the 11 April 1941 issue of *Gazeta Żydowska*, for example, advertised a café offering 'a concert every day' and 'tasty luncheons'.[23] The former inmate

---

[18] Dobroszycki (ed.), *The Chronicle of the Łódź Ghetto*, 58.

[19] Ringelblum, *Notes*, 37, 47, 159.

[20] Jonas Turkow, *Azoy iz es geven* (Buenos Aires, 1948), 130.

[21] *Gazeta Żydowska* was the official newspaper of ghettos in the Generalgouvernement. Emmanuel Ringelblum, *Ksovim fun geto* (Warsaw, 1961–3), 241; Isaiah Trunk, *Judenrat: The Jewish Councils in Eastern Europe under Nazi Occupation* (New York, 1972), 222.

[22] On 19 Feb. 1941 Ringelblum wrote about a carnival held at one of these venues: 'The Law and Order Service tried to break up the good time, but it turned out that one of the owners of the Melody Palace was one of Them, and she couldn't be touched. The same goes for most Jewish entertainment places.' See *Notes*, 125.

[23] Cited in Yisrael Gutman, *The Jews of Warsaw, 1939–1943: Ghetto, Underground, Revolt* (Brighton, 1982), 108.

Ya'akov Tselemensky drew the following picture of the Sztuka café, where high-ranking musical performances, risqué comedy shows, and fine cuisine were the order of the day:

In the ghetto, light was permitted until a certain hour. After that we had to sit around the house by the light of candles or kerosene lamps. When we reached the nightclub the street was dark. My escort suddenly said to me: 'Be careful not to step on a corpse.' When I opened the door the light blinded me. Gas lamps were burning in every corner of the crowded cabaret. Every table was covered by a white tablecloth. Fat characters sat at them eating chicken, duck, or fowl. All of these foods would be drowned in wine and liquor. The orchestra, in the middle of the nightclub, sat on a small platform. Next to it a singer performed. These were people who once played before Polish crowds. Now they were reminded of their Jewish heritage. When I came in, M.Z., the renowned Polish actor, played the role of a comic character, eliciting lots of laughter. Afterwards a singer, U.G., sang old Polish hits and romantic songs. The audience crowding the tables was made up of the aristocracy of the ghetto—big-time smugglers, high Polish officers and all sorts of big shots. Germans who had business dealings with the Jews also came here, dressed in civilian clothes. Within the walls of the cabaret one could not sense the tragedy taking place a few yards away. The audience ate, drank and laughed as if it had no worries.[24]

Other witnesses gave similar descriptions of the decadent cafés, remarking angrily on people's astonishing lack of concern for the tens of thousands outside exposed to starvation and disease. Chaim Kaplan complained that there were 'dozens of pigs who live and enjoy every comfort even in these evil times, people with money and large incomes . . . who find it difficult to give the smallest amount from their clenched hands'.[25] The pianist Władysław Szpilman, who performed at several cafés, described how the wealthy clientele looked down on poorer Jews, and rarely gave alms. Beggars were even expressly prohibited from standing outside:

The café was frequented by the rich, who went there hung about with gold jewellery and dripping with diamonds. To the sound of popping champagne corks, tarts with gaudy make-up offered their services to war profiteers seated at laden tables. I lost two illusions here: my beliefs in our general solidarity and in the musicality of the Jews.[26]

Although accounts suggest that the café entertainments were often cheap and vulgar, on the whole it seems that their performance quality was superior to that found in other entertainment establishments in the ghetto. Many of the

---

[24] Cited in Moshe Fass, 'Theatrical Activities in the Polish Ghettos during the Years 1939–1942', *Jewish Social Studies*, 38 (1976), 54–72 at 57–8.
[25] Kaplan, *Scroll of Agony*, 184.
[26] Władysław Szpilman, *The Pianist: The Extraordinary Story of One man's Survival in Warsaw, 1939–45* (London, 1999), 13.

best musicians, struggling to earn a livelihood, sought employment in these places in order to supplement their meagre incomes. Szpilman, for example, claimed that through his work as a café pianist he could support his family of six.[27] The most popular artists and ensembles performing at these venues were Marysia Eisenstadt, Diana Blumenfeld, Yosef Hirschfeld, the Rosner brothers, the orchestra of Leopold Rubinstein, the 'Jolly Boys' orchestra, and the ensemble of Artur Gold (later to become conductor of an inmate orchestra in Treblinka).[28]

On a slightly lower end of the class scale, there were families such as Janina Bauman's, who led a relatively comfortable existence thanks to the help of a relative living on the other side of the ghetto wall. Bauman visited cabarets and restaurants with live musical entertainment, regularly attended the concerts of the ghetto orchestra, and even acquired a gramophone. Aware that it was only her 'privileged' status that afforded her these opportunities, she expressed feelings of guilt and hypocrisy. Marcel Reich-Ranicki's family led a similarly secure existence: his brother's income as a dentist was a good support, and he himself worked in the Judenrat. As a music critic, he was able to attend the symphony concerts regularly, and, like Bauman, recalled getting together with other young people to listen to classical records.[29]

Music on the Streets

At the other end of the ghetto spectrum, music was a radically different affair. In the first place, there were occasions when it ceased to function as entertainment at all. In Warsaw, as elsewhere, the SS used forced music-making as a means of humiliation. In May 1942 Ringelblum described a new amusement devised by the Gestapo: dragging musicians from all over the ghetto to the Pawia Street prison, where they would be forced to provide entertainment for hours on end.[30] Szpilman similarly recalled the sadistic games played by Nazi guards at the gates:

As the crowd grew so did its agitation, nervousness and restlessness, for the German guards were bored at their posts here, and tried to amuse themselves as best they

---

[27] Szpilman, *The Pianist*, 16.

[28] The orchestra in Treblinka is discussed further in Ch. 4.

[29] Janina Bauman, *Winter in the Morning: A Young Girl's Life in the Warsaw Ghetto and Beyond, 1939–1945* (Bath, 1986), 94, 97–9; Marcel Reich-Ranicki, *Mein Leben: Autobiographie* (Stuttgart, 1999), 215, 230.

[30] Ringelblum, *Notes*, 278.

could. One of their favourite entertainments was dancing. Musicians were fetched from the nearby side streets—the number of street bands grew with the general misery. The soldiers chose people out of the waiting crowd whose appearance they thought particularly comic and ordered them to dance waltzes. The musicians took up a position by the wall of a building, space was cleared in the road, and one of the policemen acted as conductor by hitting the musicians if they played too slowly. Others supervised the conscientious performance of the dancers. Couples of cripples, old people, the very fat or the very thin had to whirl about in circles before the eyes of the horrified crowd. Short people or children were made to partner the strikingly tall. The Germans stood around this 'dance floor', roaring with laughter and shouting, 'Faster! Go on, faster! Everybody dance!'[31]

These punishments, however, were not a common phenomenon in the ghetto. Another element of street life with which music became more extensively associated was begging. From early on in the ghetto's existence, Ringelblum noted the chronic increase in this activity. On 11 July 1941 he observed:

Lately, whole families have been out begging, sometimes even well-dressed people. Musicians and singers take their children along with them to 'work'. The father plays an instrument, while his child or children put out their caps for a coin. There's one singer who stands outside with his young wife, who is dressed with real elegance. As he sings his wife collects alms. Nearby stands a cradle with a small child in it—the parents have no one to leave the child with. The child is being trained to be a beggar, literally in the cradle. Generally speaking, family begging has become the mode. Some parents do it because children attract attention, others because they can't leave the children alone at home...Some of the beggars have taken to singing in the courtyards.[32]

In most Polish cities before the war, street entertainment was a common phenomenon. However, as Ringelblum suggested, even the community's previously more prosperous members now had to resort to playing in the streets. While some found occasional employment at cafés, theatres, or giving private concerts for the wealthy, most were forced to transport their trade to wherever it was likely to earn them money. A contemporary document noted that

musicians have organized small groups wandering from backyard to backyard as long as the weather is warm. Sometimes they make some money, but often they make nothing. During the winter they could not work at all. Some could be seen with their fiddles in the streets, freezing and begging.[33]

---

[31] Szpilman, *The Pianist*, 66–7.
[32] Ringelblum, *Notes*, 205.
[33] Cited in Trunk, *Judenrat*, 223.

Kaplan similarly described street performances by instrumental bands and soloists, and even a cantor and his choir singing prayers and hymns outside, all in a desperate attempt to earn a few pennies.[34]

Ringelblum noted that despite the institutions maintained by the Centralne Towarzystwo Opieki nad Sierotami (Headquarters of the Society for the Care of Orphans, CENTOS), children constituted the majority of the beggars. Kaplan also described the singing of groups of young children, 'the emissaries of mothers and fathers who supervise them from the sidelines'. Numerous photographs testify to this phenomenon: young boys, usually undernourished and dressed in rags, playing the violin or the harmonica, sometimes holding open empty caps for donations from passers-by. Occasionally entire children's choirs sang for money in the streets.[35]

Particular songs began to circulate among these beggars. The former inmate Irke Yanovski recalled a short refrain sung by a man who begged on the ghetto's main streets at night with his wife and six children (during the day he hid for fear of being taken away for forced labour). The song, which opened with the words 'Hot's mitlayd, hot's rakhmones' (Have pity, have compassion), was a simple plea for bread, set to a short, typically Jewish tune (emphasizing the augmented second of the minor scale).[36] In a song entitled 'Hot's rakhmones, yidishe hertser' (Have compassion, Jewish hearts), the Polish writer and inmate Paulina Braun depicts the plight of the omnipresent beggars, invoking the same refrain that Yanovski remembered as a resounding and inescapable part of the ghetto's aural landscape:

> Arumgetsamt mit moyern, mit drotn,
> Ranglt zikh dos geto kegn toyt,
> M'zet nit mer fun mentshn vi dem shotn,—
> Oysgedreyte beyner, trukn hoyt.
>
> Du zest: m'loyft, m'tumlt in di gasn,
> Mitamol—zestu a toytn guf.
> S'glantsn oygn fun dem ponim blasn,
> Un du herst a shvakhn, shtiln ruf:
>
> 'Hot's rakhmones, yidishe hertser,
> Git mir esn, oder epes gelt;
> Hot's rakhmones, yidishe hertser,
> Kh'vil nokh lebn, kh'vil nokh zen di velt!

---

[34] Kaplan, *Scroll of Agony*, 221.
[35] Ringelblum, *Notes*, 283; Kaplan, *Scroll of Agony*, 221.
[36] Kaczerginski and Leivick, 141.

To hot's rakhmones, yidishe hertser,
Varft arop a shtikl trukn broyt!
Hot's rakhmones, yidishe hertser,
Helft aroys a yidish harts fun noyt.'

Fun likhtikn frimorgn biz di shtern
Shteyt a kind mit oysgeshtrekter hant.
Un afile ven du vilst nit hern,—
Yogt dikh 'hot's rakhmones' nokhanand.

Der toyt in geto mitamol gekumen,
Groys iz der gedrang geven tsu im,
Un in a shtot mit mentshn tsugenumen,
Farblibn iz in geto nor di shtim:

'Hot's rakhmones, yidishe hertser,
S'vartn meyler hungerike fir.
Hot's rakhmones, yidishe hertser,
A khay-vekayem bin ikh dokh vi ir!

Hot's rakhmones, yidishe hertser,
A groyse Varshe iz geven a mol,
Hot's rakhmones, yidishe hertser'—
Klingen vet eybik der kol.[37]

Fenced in by walls, by wires,
The ghetto wrestles with death,
People are little more than shadows,
Twisted bones, dry flesh.

You see people running, making a racket in the streets,
Suddenly—you see a dead body.
Eyes shine out of a pale face,
And you hear a weak, quiet cry:

'Have compassion, Jewish hearts,
Give me something to eat, or some money;
Have compassion, Jewish hearts,
I still want to live, I still want to see the world!

So have compassion, Jewish hearts,
Throw down a piece of dry bread!
Have compassion, Jewish hearts,
Help a Jewish heart in need.'

From the bright morning until the stars at night
Stands a child with outstretched hand.
And even when you do not want to hear,—
'Have compassion' keeps chasing you.

---

[37] Ibid. 156–7.

Death came suddenly in the ghetto,
There was a great rush towards it,
And in a city with people taken away,
There remains in the ghetto only the voice:

'Have compassion, Jewish hearts,
Four hungry mouths are waiting.
Have compassion, Jewish hearts,
I am a common man just like you!

Have compassion, Jewish hearts,
Warsaw was once great,
Have compassion, Jewish hearts'—
The voice will resound for ever.

The song presents a vivid picture of the tortured beggars: 'pale' creatures made of 'little more than shadows' and 'dry flesh', caught in a constant struggle to avoid death, and appealing in desperation to the common humanity of their fellow Jews. Ironically, their 'weak, quiet cries' generally went unheard below the lively café entertainments. Nonetheless, Braun implied that for many the presence of the beggars was haunting and distressing, something that would 'keep chasing you' and 'resound for ever', even once death had laid claim to the ghetto.

The Theatres

These were the extremes of ghetto society. Between them, making up the bulk of Warsaw's musical landscape, were a host of activities intended primarily for the entertainment of the ghetto masses. These included a symphony orchestra, five theatres, chamber groups, choirs, and the numerous events organized by social welfare organizations in the soup kitchens.

Given the size of the population, it is perhaps unsurprising that music existed on such a wide scale. Different types of activities catered for different sectors of the community, although performers were often involved in several of these simultaneously (some singers, for example, performed in the cafés and the theatres as well as the soup kitchens). Many of these activities were essentially a continuation of the community's active pre-war cultural life. Satirical theatre revues, for example, had by the inter-war period become one of the most popular entertainments amongst east European Jewish communities; during the war, many of the ghettos, including those in Warsaw, Vilna, and Łódź, modelled new revues on their basis. The ghetto orchestra and other musical groups drew the bulk of their members from their pre-war counterparts. Singers were regrouped to form choirs and folk choruses such as Shir and the Choir of the Great Synagogue.[38] Emphasizing continuity with pre-existing cultural trends is important, as Flam has observed, because it focuses attention on the rich cultural tradition of east European Jewry rather than exclusively on its destruction.[39]

The extent to which musical life was able to re-emerge under ghetto conditions is nonetheless worthy of note. With the Nazi occupation in 1939, Jewish schools and businesses had been closed, and pre-war institutions and organizations banned. Within weeks of these closures, however, underground activity had already begun. House concerts were organized, and amateur groups sprang up all over the city, giving performances in clandestine, makeshift venues. Jonas Turkow described one such venue located in an attic on Wałowa street: benches were placed in rows, a stage and curtain set up, and the room lit with kerosene lamps; audience members were directed through ruined buildings and courtyards by sentries who also kept watch for unwanted German visitors.[40] These activities were intended to substitute, albeit on a limited scale, for the rich cultural life that had now been suppressed. Although their quality was not always first-rate, they were a means through which the embattled community could restore some sense of familiarity and 'normal' functioning.

In place of the banned pre-war institutions, only two frameworks were allowed to function in the ghetto: the Judenrat and welfare organizations. Made up of people who had held important posts in Jewish public life, as leaders of Jewish political parties and their representatives in the Polish parliament, the Warsaw Judenrat was largely regarded as a continuation of the pre-war *kehilla* (Jewish Community Council), and had its offices in the same building. Adam Czerniakow, who had been appointed by the Polish mayor Stefan Starzyński as *kehilla* chairman in September 1939, become the Judenrat chairman when the body was set up the following month. The role of the *kehillot* in the pre-war years was confined to religious tasks, but since the Judenräte were the only executive bodies authorized by the Nazis, a broader range of social functions had to be conducted under their auspices. However, cultural life in Warsaw came under the Judenrat's jurisdiction only to a limited extent. In most instances it was run by independent organizations, some of them clandestine.[41]

---

[38] Trunk, *Judenrat*, 223.
[39] Flam, *Singing for Survival*, 17.
[40] Turkow, *Azoy iz es geven*, 202.
[41] Gutman (ed.), *Encyclopedia*, 1603–4, 1614; Trunk, *Judenrat*, 186.

The first of these clandestine organizations came into being in September 1940, when growing concern about the variable quality and haphazard organization of amateur activity led to the establishment of a special committee for the supervision of cultural life, under the auspices of ŻTOS. The committee's central aims were to regulate all performances, raise their artistic level, use them as a means of social education, and to protect the interests of those professionally employed in the field. Special care was also devoted to the fostering of young talent. In the first year of its existence, the committee organized close to 2,000 performances, and registered approximately 270 professional artists and 150 musicians.[42]

It was only after the ghetto was sealed that extensive programmes of organized cultural activity could begin. The revival of established institutions and practices, which began almost immediately, helped to bring back something of the familiar environment of pre-war life. It also strengthened the sense that the community was still intact, and that its most important values and objectives could still be pursued. The way in which social and cultural life was organized suggests that, for community leaders at least, the aim was to keep the society functioning in a sustainable way, and in particular to provide guidance and education for children. The emphasis was on continuity: working through the challenges that presented themselves in anticipation that the occupation would eventually come to an end and things would return to normal.

It must be emphasized, at this point, that music was not a pressing concern for the Nazi authorities. Although all performances in the ghettos were by law to be approved by the German censorship board—an order was published in *Gazeta Żydowska* on 20 September 1940—no uniform law applied. While in some places works by Aryan composers were outlawed, for example, in others they were permitted and even encouraged. Policy was generally left in the hands of local authorities, and thus saw many variations.[43]

Musical activities helped to perpetuate the illusion that Jewish life in the ghettos was reasonably stable and autonomous. In truth, Jews did feel more protected in the newly sealed ghettos than they had previously: the severe restrictions on movement and activity they had faced initially were relaxed, and they had little contact either with the SS or with the surrounding population. They thus had more scope to organize their communities' cultural and social life without interference. However, this semblance of

---

[42] Turkow, *Azoy iz es geven*, 210.
[43] Fass, 'Theatrical Activities', 67.

self-sufficiency also sometimes functioned as a powerful means of control. In an ironic inversion of the spiritual resistance argument, it seems that music was one of many activities tolerated by the SS precisely because by diverting their attention from what was really happening to them, it helped in deflecting any urge on the part of the victims to resist. It has been argued elsewhere that similar motivations underlay the Propagandaamt's support for cheap forms of amusement in the occupied countries.[44]

Jewish self-sufficiency was also most likely tolerated to the extent that it was because the Nazis perceived it as having little political potency. A memorandum from the Rassenpolitischesamt on 25 November 1939 read:

Jewish political groups should be forbidden along with Polish ones. But Jewish cultural societies might be more tolerated than Polish ones. Jews may certainly be allowed more freedom in this respect than Poles, for the Jews have no such real political power as have the Poles.[45]

Ultimately, as this memo suggests, cultural activities were permitted because they were unlikely to change in any significant way the fate of the ghetto populations.

Perhaps the most representative and popular of the musical events aimed at the Warsaw ghetto masses were found in the theatres. Within weeks of the sealing of the ghetto, *Gazeta Żydowska* reported that official permission had been granted for the establishment of a theatre. Like other leisure activities, this was almost certainly viewed by the authorities as a way of keeping the ghetto population docile. Nonetheless, it was an important development for musical life. Serious dramas were sometimes presented, but the most common entertainments were revues consisting of comic sketches and musical pieces.[46]

Five professional theatres operated in the ghetto. The first, a Yiddish theatre called the Eldorado, was opened on 6 December 1940. The actor Simcha Pustel and the Zeyderman family (David, his wife Chana Lerner, and their son Harry) performed at this venue, and a resident orchestra played under the baton of A. Walstein. A favourable review in *Gazeta Żydowska* on 20 December 1940 described the opening presentation: a variety show including men's choir, Chassidic dancing, musical comedy, and other skits. At least eight additional programmes were staged between January and August 1941; they included the shows *Rivkele dem rebns tokhter* (Rivke the Rabbi's

---

[44] Trunk, *Judenrat*, 216.

[45] Cited ibid.

[46] Moshe Hoch, 'Ha'tarbut ha'muziqalit b'kerev ha'y'hudim tachat ha'shilton ha'natsi b'polin 1939–1945' (Ph.D. diss., Bar-Ilan University, 1992), 88; Turkow, *Azoy iz es geven*, 126.

daughter), *Tsipke fun Novolipye* (Tsipke from Novolipye), *A heym far a mame* (A home for a mother), and *Undzer rebenyu* (Our dear Rabbi).[47]

The next theatre to open was the Polish *Na Pieterku* in April 1941. This small venue staged at least three performances between April and July 1941, when it ceased activity. Joining the Eldorado in May 1941 as the only other Yiddish theatre in the ghetto was the Nowy Azazel. Classic Yiddish plays by Sholem Aleichem, Sholem Asch, and S. Ansky were staged, as were the comedy-musicals *Hertser tsu farkoyfn* (Hearts for sale) in July 1941, and *Dovid's fidele* (David's fiddle) in March 1942. The last two theatres, both of which performed in Polish, were the Femina and the Teatr Kameralny.[48]

The Warsaw theatres relied heavily on pre-existing repertoire: film music, American ragtime, cabaret, tangos, operettas, and musicals. This was in contrast to ghettos such as Vilna, where revue programmes consisted almost entirely of original material. The emphasis on well-known repertoire suggests that the theatres were intended primarily to help restore a sense of familiarity, rather than as places where new experiences could be confronted in the public realm. People went to the theatres to distract themselves from their difficult daily lives, and to see lively performances of the kind they had enjoyed before the war.

Nonetheless, post-war song collections from the ghettos included at least seventeen new compositions that emerged from Warsaw.[49] It was primarily in the theatres that these songs, often on topical ghetto themes, were popularized. Although little information exists regarding where and when particular songs were sung, as a group they cast an interesting angle on our perceptions of singing in the ghetto. Several of the songs, especially the religious ones, were clearly written in order to provide encouragement. None, however, approached the spirit of heroic defiance to be found among other inmate communities.[50] A few songs paid tribute to the heroism

[47] Hoch, 'Ha'tarbut ha'muziqalit', 177; Fass, 'Theatrical Activities', 70. Also see Fass for a fuller repertoire listing of theatre shows.

[48] The Melody Palace, an old building used for dance and variety shows bordering the ghetto wall, also functioned temporarily as a venue for revue performances. On 6 Sept. 1941 David Zeyderman, Chana Lerner, and Simcha Pustel left the Eldorado in order to set up a new theatre. Operations ceased only two months later. See Hoch, 'Ha'tarbut ha'muziqalit', 92.

[49] Most of these songs can be found in Kaczerginski and Leivick; the remaining few were published in Eleanor Mlotek and Malke Gottlieb (eds.), *We are Here: Songs of the Holocaust* (New York, 1983).

[50] The songs of the Vilna partisans, which fall into the 'defiant' category, are discussed in the following chapter. Similar songs relating to German political prisoners in the camps are discussed in Ch. 3. Music also played an important role within the resistance movement in Warsaw; since the movement's prominent members were drawn in large part from Zionist youth organisations, the repertoire seems to have consisted mainly of pre-existing Hebrew songs. See Yitzhak Zuckerman, *A Surplus of Memory: Chronicle of the Warsaw Ghetto Uprising* (Berkeley, 1993), 37–134.

of certain ghetto characters, while others criticized the corrupt Jewish authorities. Almost half reflected on social inequalities, chronicling the difficulties suffered by certain sectors of the population in comparison with the privileged few. They were particularly focused on issues related to the shortage of food, and to the pervasive problem of begging. With the exception of only a handful, all the songs took pains to acknowledge the horrors of the ghetto; sometimes they documented them in explicit detail. The pervading expression among them was one of loss—of home, livelihood, community, and family—and their spirit was most often one of sadness, despair, and cynicism.

'Di tefile fun khaper' (The prayer of the 'khaper'), written by Irena Gleyzer and composed by Teresa Vaynbaum, focuses on the level of moral degradation to which individuals without means in the ghetto were forced to sink. The speaker is a ghetto 'khaper', a child who would sneak up to passers-by on the street and snatch their food:

> Mayn kerper fun di lekher shaynt,
> Der hunger iz mayn tate,
> Ikh bin a geto-khaper haynt,
> A ganef mit a geler late.
> Fartog . . . men firt shoyn frishn broyt
> A groysn fuln vogn,
> Un s'klemt dos harts fun hunger, noyt,
> Di oygn veynen, klogn.
> To her mikh oys, got,
> Vos du bist in di himlen:
>
> Kh'bin keynmol keyn ganef nit geven,
> Nor ze vi men frest,
> Ven di tsveyte zey shimlen
> Un shiltn dem goyrl dem beyzn.
> To her mikh oys, got,
> Vos du bist bay mir tayer,—
> Ikh vil nokh fun lebn genisn,
> To gib mir hent flinke
> Un oygn vi fayer,
> Kh'zol kenen mir shafn dem bisn.
>
> Men khapt, men shlogt mikh farn broyt
> Mit kantshik un mit shtekn.
> Vos mir lebn, vos mir toyt?—
> Mikh ken shoyn gornit shrekn.
> Baynakht . . . ot geyt a yunge por,

Es dukht zikh, mikh zet kinder.
A shprung, a khap, zey shrayen . . . nor
A bis glaykh mit di tseyner.

Iz dank ikh dir, got, far di fintstere nekht,
Vos du host dem mentshn gegebn,
Ven ale tsum shlofn bakumen dos rekht—
Far mir heybt zikh on ersht dos lebn.
To zay mir, got, moykhl
Di shverste fun zind,
Di velt hot mikh fun got fartribn.
A ganef in geto, an oysvurf atsind
Tsvishn mentshn un khayes farblibn.[51]

My body glows through the holes,
Hunger is my father,
Today I am a ghetto 'khaper',
A thief with a yellow patch.
At dawn . . . fresh bread is already brought
A big, full cart,
And the heart grieves with hunger, hardship,
The eyes weep, lament.
So hear me out, God,
Who is in heaven:

I've never been a thief,
But see how people gorge themselves,
While others grow mouldy
And curse their bitter fate.
So hear me out, God,
Who is dear to me,—
I still want to enjoy life,
So give me nimble hands
And eyes like fire,
So that I'll be able to get myself a morsel.

They catch me, they hit me for the bread
With whips[52] and sticks.
What is my life, what is my death?—
Nothing can frighten me any more.
At night . . . there goes a young couple,
I think I see children.
A leap, a grab, they scream . . . only
A direct bite with the teeth.

---

[51] Kaczerginski and Leivick, 153–4.
[52] A 'kantshik' was a special type of whip made of twisted leather straps.

So I thank you, God, for the dark nights,
That you have given people,
When all are given the right to sleep—
For me, that is when life just begins.
So forgive me, God,
For the heaviest of sins,
The world has banished me from God.
A thief in the ghetto, an outcast now
Left among humans and animals.

This prayer is a mockery of devoutness, an acknowledgement that God no longer wielded power in the ghetto. The 'khaper' prays not for lofty spiritual things, but for the skills to steal from those around him, particularly those who 'gorged themselves' while others withered away. Resorting to this kind of crime was often a necessity for those who had no other means of subsistence in the ghetto. The song portrays these people in a deeply pathetic way, exposing their 'sins' while at the same time showing compassion for their hopeless plight. It also paints a bleak picture of the ghetto, a place of 'humans and animals' where people endured endless hardship, and where some were forced to betray moral principles in order to stay alive.

It is significant that fear of degeneracy was focused specifically on children, since it was on vulnerable groups that ghetto communities bestowed particular attention and care. As we shall see, many ghetto songs and lullabies lamented the fate of young people from the perspective of the older generation, which feared that its descendants might never enjoy the bright future that it hoped for them. We also encounter several songs portraying young, feisty protagonists whose optimism and good cheer was intended as a model to uplift and enliven the community. Part of what makes 'Di tefile fun khaper' so bleak, then, is the suggestion that when children have reached this level of despair and cynicism, things are really lost.

Some of the most harrowing ghetto songs show people struggling to come to terms with death, both their own and that of loved ones. 'Kh'shem zikh' (I am ashamed) and 'Shlof, mayn kind' (Sleep, my child) both saw the composer M. Shenker struggling to cope with the death of his wife and child. In the first, addressed to his wife, he obsessively recounts his guilt at having remained alive while allowing them to go alone to their deaths. His feelings of shame lead to tormenting visions of the pair going up in smoke, the child clinging to its mother and bewailing its father's absence. Disturbing images of this kind pervade both songs. 'Shlof mayn kind' is a macabre lullaby addressed to the dead child, who even in death was given no rest: the 'little mound of ash' in which he slept is scattered by the wind.[53]

Several of the songs also chronicle the widespread food shortage in the ghetto, and its highly developed smuggling industry. Small children were actively recruited for this job, as their size and agility meant that they could more successfully sneak through to the Aryan side of the wall. Songs such as 'Motele fun Varshever geto' (Motele of the Warsaw ghetto) and 'Der kleyner shmugler' (The little smuggler) pay tribute to the bravery of these children, who in many cases became responsible for providing their families with food. The dire situation of the hungry, sick, and frightened inhabitants was often depicted in vivid detail, as were the enormous risks faced by the children as they carried out their tasks.[54]

The Warsaw Ghetto Orchestra

In addition to the theatres, one of the earliest cultural initiatives in the ghetto was the establishment of the Jewish Symphony Orchestra in late 1940. Official permission for the functioning of the orchestra was granted by the authorities on 5 January 1941, on the condition that all programmes be subject to censorship, and that no works by Aryan composers be performed.[55]

Putting a group together proved to be a haphazard affair. String players were easy to come by, but wind and brass players were scarcer. Advertisements were placed in the newspaper, and many jazz and dance band musicians applied on the basis that they could sight-read classical music. Some were co-opted, and instruments substituted where necessary.[56]

During the period of its existence between November 1940 and April 1942, the orchestra had four permanent conductors. The first two, Marian Neuteikh and Adam Furmanski, were its co-founders. Neuteikh had worked with a Jewish symphony orchestra in Warsaw during the mid-1930s, and it is probable that the ghetto orchestra was to some extent a successor to the earlier enterprise. As far as can be gleaned from reviews in *Gazeta Żydowska*, both conductors were fairly well received by ghetto audiences.[57] Szymon Pullman joined the orchestra at the beginning of 1941, and remained its conductor until its activities were

[53] Kaczerginski and Leivick, 234, 236.

[54] Mlotek and Gottlieb (eds.), *We are Here*, 66–7; Kaczerginski and Leivick, 104–5.

[55] Jonas Turkow, *Hayo hayta varsha ha'y'hudit* (Tel Aviv, 1969), 98–9.

[56] Reich-Ranicki, *Mein Leben*, 220–1.

[57] As far as is known, Warsaw was the only ghetto (apart from 'model ghetto' Theresienstadt) to have regular reviews of musical performances. There were six music critics: Aleksander Rosensztein,

terminated. According to Reich-Ranicki, Pullman was committed to maintaining high levels of performance. He enlarged the orchestra, and its quality improved markedly under his leadership. Reich-Ranicki also described him as an extraordinary individual: self-conscious and ambitious, but consistently polite and patient. Israel Hamerman, the youngest of the conductors, first performed with the orchestra in January 1942.[58]

The first concert, conducted by Neuteikh, took place on 25 November 1940 in the Judaica library, under the auspices of ŻTOS. The programme included Beethoven's Coriolan overture and the Piano Concerto in E flat major, and Grieg's *Peer Gynt*. From the outset, no noticeable effort was made to restrict concert programmes to works by non-Aryan composers, and until April 1942 no objection was raised by the German authorities. At least one more ŻTOS concert was held at this venue in late 1940, conducted by Furmanski, with works by Bach, Tchaikovsky, Beethoven, and Mozart. Some of the first concerts were also held in the Melody Palace.

The orchestra performed standard symphonic repertoire, with works by Mozart, Schubert, and particularly Beethoven dominating programmes. However, Pullman's arrival in February 1941 signalled clear changes. Although he continued to include standard programme items, he also enlarged the repertoire to include works by Borodin, Saint-Saëns, and others. In addition, he placed more emphasis on the quality of the orchestra's performance. Reviews of his concerts in *Gazeta Żydowska* were in general more complimentary than they were for the other three conductors. Later, a larger and more modern venue for the orchestral concerts was found in the Femina cinema, which could hold an audience of 900. The last concert by the orchestra, conducted by Neuteikh, was held here in April 1942. In all, the orchestra probably gave around forty performances.[59]

Although the concerts were cheap and relatively well attended, testimonial evidence suggests that most ghetto inmates did not take an interest in them. Moreover, the musicians performed in challenging conditions: with few rehearsals, inadequate lighting, and bad acoustics, in substandard venues, and without sufficient heating in the winter. Performance quality was inevitably affected, and the *Gazeta Żydowska* reviews frequently complained about

Henryk Czerwinski, Wiktor Hart (later confirmed to be a pseudonym for Marcel Reich-Ranicki), and three known only by the names Arwe, A. Ex., and L.A. The reviews seldom made reference to the conditions in which concerts took place. Positive reviews of performances by Neuteikh appeared in *Gazeta Żydowska* on 17 Jan., 4 June, 16 July, and 1 Sept. 1941, and for Furmanski on 30 Sept. 1941. Cited in Hoch, 'Ha'tarbut ha'muziqalit', 67–8.

[58] Reich-Ranicki, *Mein Leben*, 222; Hoch, 'Ha'tarbut ha'muziqalit', 66–70.
[59] Reich-Ranicki, *Mein Leben*, 224; Hoch, 'Ha'tarbut ha'muziqalit', 73, 80.

lack of balance between sections of the orchestra, and the general evidence of too little practice. Hunger was a pressing issue, and Reich-Ranicki recalled that a wealthy doctor would sometimes provide the musicians with a meal before the concerts so that they would have more strength to play. Describing the functions the orchestra fulfilled for its audience, Reich-Ranicki insisted that it was not defiance that drove people to the concert halls, but rather a desire to escape temporarily the gnawing realities of hunger and fear, and to experience 'counter-worlds' (*Gegenwelt*) of musical diversion. He further insisted that the orchestra's establishment was motivated not by a lofty desire to serve art, but rather by the musicians' desperate need to make a living.[60]

On 15 April 1942, the orchestra's activities were suddenly banned for a period of two months. The justification provided was that, contrary to instructions, the orchestra had been performing works by Aryan composers. This was purely a pretext, however, since the German authorities had long been aware of, and yet chose to pay little attention to, the overwhelmingly Aryan content of the orchestra's programmes. No attempt had ever been made to keep the concerts secret, and *Gazeta Żydowska* frequently printed advertisements and reviews with programme information. This convenient excuse nonetheless allowed the authorities to reassert control over community activities. In fact, the ban signalled far more substantial and menacing changes in ghetto life. By the time it was due to be repealed, mass deportations to the death camp Treblinka were imminent. These began on 22 July 1942, and within the space of seven weeks, approximately 300,000 people—75 per cent of the population—were deported. The orchestra never resumed its activities.

Instrumental and vocal concerts on a smaller scale also existed throughout the time of the ghetto. On 2 July 1941 *Gazeta Żydowska* reported the establishment of a patronage committee that would provide public sponsorship for musical groups (among other activities). Concerts were held regularly thereafter, and several were advertised in the newspaper. Piano, violin, and vocal recitals were the most common, and performers included Marysia Eisenstadt, Vera Neumark, Helena Markowitz, Liliana Roman, and Lena Wallfisch. The most prominent and critically acclaimed of these young musicians was the 20-year-old soprano Eisenstadt, who became known as the 'nightingale of the ghetto'. There were also three chamber groups drawn from the ranks of the orchestra; the conductor Pullman was particularly involved with their activities.[61]

---

[60] Reich-Ranicki, *Mein Leben*, 220, 224, 228.
[61] Hoch, 'Ha'tarbut ha'muziqalit', 84; Reich-Ranicki, *Mein Leben*, 226; Turkow, *Hayo hayta*, 84.

The bulk of the chamber repertoire was rooted in the German tradition: alongside works by the non-Aryan composers Mendelssohn, Tchaikovsky, and Dvořák were items by Beethoven, Brahms, Mozart, Bach, Haydn, Weber, Bruckner, and Schubert. But smaller-scale musical activity was also affected by the ban on the orchestra in April 1942. Concerts were restricted, and could include only music by Jewish composers. Repertoire now included works by Mendelssohn, Offenbach, Meyerbeer, and Anton Rubinstein, as well as items by operetta composers Paul Abraham, Leo Fall, and Emmerich Kalman.[62]

Solo and chamber concerts generally took place in the afternoons, in smaller venues such as soup kitchens. Run under the auspices of political parties, the soup kitchens became important sources for underground newspapers and education, as well as social meeting points and sites for cultural activity. They were aimed at those who could not afford café and other entertainments, and as such reached a broader cross-section of the ghetto public than most other centres. Different venues sometimes became associated with particular sectors of the community, and organized correspondingly different types of activities. These included lectures and discussions on topics ranging from Jewish folklore and religious holidays to the work of Yiddish writers such as Sholem Aleichem and I. L. Peretz, chamber music, vocal recitals, and choral singing. The soup kitchens also promoted the activities of several children's choirs, including the 'People's choir' organized by Rachel Auerbach and directed by Ya'akov Gladstein. However, their events were often impeded by considerable practical difficulties. Halls were freezing in the winter, had unsympathetic acoustics, and carbide lamps often had to be used in the absence of electricity. Moreover, musicians and audiences frequently had to deal with the strong smell of cooking vegetables as a backdrop to performances.[63]

Social welfare and other public institutions occasionally organized large-scale events for the community incorporating musical entertainment. On 5 May 1942, the Jewish festival Lag B'Omer, CENTOS organized a 'Jewish children's day'. Festivities were arranged at various venues around the ghetto, and a well-attended rally featuring music and dancing was held at the Femina theatre. On 7 June an orchestra set up by the Jewish Police performed at a ceremony for the opening of the first playground opposite the Community office building on Grzybowska Street. Towards the end of June, with mass deportations imminent, the end of the school year was marked with a solemn

---

[62] Reich-Ranicki, *Mein Leben*, 222, 229–30.

[63] Rachel Auerbach, *Varshever tsavoes: bagegenishn, aktivitetn, goyroles 1933–1943* (Tel Aviv, 1974), 66; Reich-Ranicki, *Mein Leben*, 224.

service at the Moriah synagogue on Dzielna Street. Hundreds of children participated, singing well-known liturgical tunes and concluding with the Jewish national hymn 'Hatikva' (The Hope).[64]

Polish–Jewish Struggles

As earlier accounts suggested, musical life was informed not only by the class status of particular groups, but also by the Polish–Jewish dynamic. The ghetto contained around 2,000 converted and many more assimilated Jews, most of whom were Polish-speaking. As before, this group tended to be better educated, better off materially, and more influential politically than the majority of the population. Ringelblum frequently complained about the luxuries enjoyed by this 'Jewish aristocracy': comfortable accommodation, their own schools, fashionable clothes, and even free lunches from the Catholic charity Caritas. They were a powerful but largely self-concerned group, and found their way into the most important posts in the Judenrat, the police, and similar institutions. Rumours spread that some had converted to Christianity within the ghetto itself so as to avail themselves of these privileges; according to an Oneg Shabbos survey, community leaders feared that conversion would become a growing trend.[65]

The authority wielded by the Polish-speaking Jewish intelligentsia was clearly felt in the realm of cultural life, not only in the cafés. On 30 May 1942 Ringelblum wrote:

Jonas Turkow [a well-known Yiddish actor] acted this season in a Polish repertoire. The reason: There are no good plays in Yiddish. Besides, this is evidence of the marked assimilation so discernible in the Ghetto. The Jews love to speak Polish. There is very little Yiddish heard in the streets. We have had some heated discussions on this question. One explanation advanced is that speaking Polish is a psychological protest against the Ghetto—you have thrown us into a Jewish Ghetto, but we'll show you that it really is a Polish street. To spite you, we'll hold on to the very thing you are trying to separate us from—the Polish language and the culture it represents. But my personal opinion is that what we see in the Ghetto today is only a continuation of the

---

[64] Januz Korczak, *Ghetto Diary* (New York, 1978), 84–5; Michael Zylberberg, *A Warsaw Diary, 1939–1945* (London, 1969), 62–3.

[65] 'Oneg Shabbos' was the code name for the underground archive from the Warsaw ghetto established by historian Emmanuel Ringelblum. The archive attempted to provide a picture of the ghetto independent of the political agendas that shaped 'official' life, was often fiercely critical of the ghetto leadership, and pointed out various forms of social inequality and corruption. Gutman (ed.), *Encyclopedia*, 1607–8; Ringelblum, *Notes*, 214–15; Trunk, *Judenrat*, 218.

powerful linguistic assimilation that was marked even before the war and has become more noticeable in the Ghetto. So long as Warsaw was mixed, with Jews and Poles living side by side, one did not notice it so acutely; but now that the streets are completely Jewish, the extent of this calamity forces itself upon one's attention.[66]

Some of Ringelblum's remarks were exaggerated, particularly those relating to numbers of Yiddish-speakers in Warsaw. Nonetheless, much of what he observed was borne out by contemporary evidence. Only two of the ghetto's five theatres performed in Yiddish. Moreover, the calibre of performance in the Polish theatres was markedly higher, as many of the actors had worked professionally in the pre-war Polish theatre. In the course of time many actors migrated from the Yiddish to the Polish stage, and the latter sunk to a low level as a result. Several Yiddish plays, including the well-known *Mirele Efros*, were even performed in Polish translation rather than in the original.[67] This was in stark contrast to some of the other ghettos, particularly those in Łódź and Vilna, where cultural life retained an identifiably Jewish character.[68]

Nonetheless, a notable effort was also made to promote activities in Yiddish and Hebrew. In December 1940 the clandestine Yidishe Kultur Organizatsye was established in order to raise cultural standards and elevate the status of Yiddish. The group organized courses and lectures, opened a large Jewish library, staged artistic performances, and arranged symposia commemorating Jewish literary figures such as Mendele Moykher Sforim, I. L. Peretz, Khayim Nakhman Bialik, Sholem Asch, and Sholem Aleichem. Prominent Zionists in the ghetto formed a Hebrew cultural group called T'kuma (Resurrection), which included among its many active members the poet Yitzhak Katzenelson.[69]

Some assimilationists even participated in the drive to promote Jewish culture in the ghetto. Prominent among these was the orphanage director Januz Korczak,[70] who made a consistent effort to incorporate Jewish elements in the cultural activities he organized for his children. Several variety pro-grammes were held at the orphanage, which according to former participants

[66] Ringelblum, *Notes*, 289.

[67] Fass, 'Theatrical Activities', 62–3; Ringelblum, *Notes*, 199.

[68] This is revealed in Łódź *Chronicle* entries detailing performances at the House of Culture. Dobroszycki (ed.), *The Chronicle of the Łódź ghetto*, 25, 33, 36, 287, 289, 296. See also Flam, *Singing for Survival*, 19.

[69] Turkow, *Azoy iz es geven*, 249–50; Hillel Seidman, *Togbukh fun Varshever Geto* (Buenos Aires, 1947), 140.

[70] Januz Korczak (aka Henryk Goldszmit, 1878/9–1942), the son of an assimilated Jewish family, was a highly respected physician and educator in pre-war Warsaw. In 1912 he was appointed director of the new Jewish orphanage on Krochmalna Street, where he continued to work during the time of the ghetto. Gutman (ed.), *Encyclopedia*, 816–17.

included performances of Yiddish songs, liturgical tunes, and instrumental works with Jewish themes. Michael Zylberberg, who worked closely with Korczak, also described the pedagogue's insistence on the use of Yiddish at concerts, although he could barely speak the language.[71]

Perhaps the most self-consciously Jewish of the ghetto's musical activities were the songs sung among its religious members. Two of these were collected by Kaczerginski after the war: the 'Varshever geto-lid fun frumer yidn' (Song of religious Jews in the Warsaw ghetto), and 'Oyb nit keyn emune' (If I do not have faith), which survived the war only as a fragment (see Exs. 1.2 and 1.3). Significantly, the former—better known as 'Ani m'amin' (I believe)—has also become by far the most prominent of the Warsaw songs in post-war Jewish awareness, used extensively in Holocaust commemoration ceremonies.

Both songs express the importance of faith. Although neither makes reference to the ghetto, their relevance is obvious. Taking its Hebrew words from Maimonides's Thirteen Articles of Faith, the 'Varshever geto-lid' is a declaration of certainty that ultimate redemption will come:

> Ani m'amin, ani m'amin
> B'emuna shlema,
> B'viat ha'mashi'ach
> Ani m'amin...
> V'af al pi she'yitmahme'a
> Im kol zot, ani m'amin...[72]

> I believe, I believe
> With complete faith,
> In the coming of the Messiah
> I believe...
> And although he may delay
> Nonetheless, I believe...

This was clearly intended as a song of encouragement. As suggested earlier, however, the hope that victims experienced, and to which many made reference, stemmed primarily from an inability to accept or comprehend their imminent fates: in other words, they hoped because their natural instinct was not to believe that what had happened to others would happen to them. With this qualification in mind, I would suggest that songs such as these were first and foremost attempts to construct a context within which the victims' suffering would assume elevated meaning. With its simple, plaintive

---

[71] Korczak, *Ghetto Diary*, 61; Zylberberg, *Warsaw Diary*, 36–7.
[72] Kaczerginski and Leivick, 314.

Ex. 1.2. 'Varshever geto-lid fun frumer yidn'. Kaczerginski and Leivick, 422

Ex. 1.3. 'Oyb nit keyn emune'. Kaczerginski and Leivick, 425

melody and quietly determined lyrics, the 'Varshever geto-lid' suggests a deeply felt resolve to believe, and to hold on to faith, in the face of difficult challenges. The song's points of musical emphasis reinforce this reading: at its climax, the most intense melodic and rhythmic movement coincides with the words 'with complete faith'; a lesser climactic point is reached on the words 'and although he may delay'. Intensity, in other words, is reserved for those moments where the disjuncture between song and reality is most poignantly apparent. The same can be said for 'Oyb nit keyn emune':

> Oyb nit keyn emune
> In got borukh-hu,
> Vos zhe toyg mir ales
> Vos ikh tu?
>
> Oyb nit keyn bitokhn
> In zayn geule,—

Loynt nit tsu lebn
A rege afile.[73]

If I do not have faith
In God blessed be He,
What's the use of everything
That I do?

If I do not have faith
In His salvation,—
It's not worth living
Even for one moment.

The song's rhetorical question has an obvious answer: there is no value to what I do unless I have faith, so let me not waver in my belief now, or life will cease to be worthwhile. The melody is liturgical in style, involving simple movement around the notes of the minor scale. Only the word 'geule' is made to stand out, with a sudden upward leap of a fifth and an extended note value. The musical setting thus emphasizes that which its singers most urgently desire: salvation. Even without knowing that ghetto Jews struggled with issues of religious devotion, we cannot take texts such as these as straightforward evidence of unshaken faith, not least because other contemporary texts, including songs, reveal more questioning stances. These songs advocate a particular approach to the situation: one that involves patience and quiet resolution, rather than the questioning, desperate, angry, and hopeless attitudes expressed elsewhere.

Recording for Posterity

Thus far, we have explored some of the most important ways in which music coloured and enlivened the different layers of ghetto life. In particular, we have seen how the newly composed songs open a window onto the community's emotional world, revealing something of how those trapped in the ghetto understood what was happening to them.

Songs that describe events experienced by Jewish communities were not a new phenomenon. From the sixteenth century onwards, songs with tens and even hundreds of verses documented specific events such as pogroms, plagues, and uprisings.[74] Most included graphic descriptions of the fate that had befallen the Jews, and emphasized the suffering and misery caused by war.

---

[73] Kaczerginski and Leivick, 314.
[74] Ruth Rubin, *Voices of a People: The Story of Yiddish Folksong* (Philadelphia, 1979), 200–8.

Few of the ghetto songs compare to these in either length or detail. Nonetheless, some deliberately follow in this tradition. One of these, entitled 'Treblinka', was written when the Warsaw ghetto inhabitants had begun to discover the fates of those who were being deported during the summer of 1942. It reveals not only their knowledge of what was being perpetrated, but also something of the way in which they had chosen to understand these experiences:

In a kleyn shtetl gants fri nokh fartog,
Men hert a geroysh, a geyomer, a klog,
Mentshn halb-naket, di shrek iz dokh groys,
'Zhides'—shrayt men—'fun der shtub aroys!'
Zhandarmen, politsey, ukrayiner fil,
Tsu mordn di yidn dos iz zeyer tsil.
Men shlogt un men shist, s'iz a moyre, a shrek,
Men firt di yidn tsu der ban avek.
Bashraybn ken es nit keyn feder,
Vi es dreyen zikh di reder,
Di vagones zaynen ful,
Dort firt men yidn oyf kiddush-hashem[75]—
Keyn Treblinka, keyn Treblinka.

Un undzere brider fun yener zayt yam,
Zey kenen nit filn dem bitern tam,
Zey kenen nit hern di bitere noyt,
Az yede sho dervartn mir dem toyt.
Di milkhome vet oykh amol nemen an ek,
Di velt vet derfarn a groyzame shrek,
Ongefilt mit veytog dos yidishe harts,
Ver vet kenen filn undzer shmerts?
Taykhn trern veln rinen
Az men vet amol gefinen
Dem grestn keyver oyf der velt,—
Dort ruen milyonen yidn oyf kiddush-hashem—
In Treblinka, in Treblinka.

Treblinka, dort iz far yedn yid an ort,
Er kumt un blaybt shoyn dort,
Er kumt shoyn nit vider, dos harts tut vey,
Ven men tut zikh dermonen,
Az men tut undzere brider un shvester farsamen
In Treblinka, in Treblinka.

[75] The Hebrew phrase 'kiddush-hashem', translated literally as 'sanctifying the name [of God]', has been invoked in Jewish history since biblical times to denote exemplary ethical conduct. It has become linked in particular with religious martyrdom; a person who chose to surrender his life for the sake of his faith was considered a 'kadosh' (holy one). Gutman (ed.), *Encyclopedia*, 799.

Di yidishe politsey, zey hobn undz geheysn vos shneler geyn:
Ir vet nisht laydn dort keyn noyt.
Ir bakumt dray kilo broyt.
Dos harts tut vey, vi dos kind shrayt tsu der mamen:
'Vi lozstu mikh iber? Farvos nisht beyde tsuzamen
In Treblinka, in Treblinka.'[76]

In a small shtetl soon after daybreak,
One hears a noise, a lament, a cry,
People half-naked, the terror is great,
'Zhides'[77]—they scream—'out of your houses!'
Gendarmes, police, many Ukrainians,
To murder the Jews is their goal.
They beat and they shoot, it is frightening, terrifying,
The Jews are led away to the train.
No pen can describe
How the wheels turn,
The wagons are full,
There Jews are being led in God's holy name—
To Treblinka, to Treblinka.

And our brothers from over the sea,
They cannot feel the bitter taste,
They cannot hear the bitter hardship
As every hour we await death.
The war will also be over one day,
The world will experience a cruel terror,
The Jewish heart with pain is filled.
Who will be able to feel our pain?
Rivers of tears will run
When one day will be found
The biggest grave in the world,—
There rest millions of Jews in God's holy name—
In Treblinka, in Treblinka.

Treblinka, there is a place there for every Jew,
He comes and he stays there,
He does not come again, the heart aches,
When one remembers,
That our brothers and sisters are being poisoned
In Treblinka, in Treblinka.

---

[76] The song presented here is an amalgamation of two similar versions related by survivors of the ghetto, quoted in Kaczerginski and Leivick, 213–16. Other versions are provided in Rubin, *Voices of a People*, 444, and Mlotek and Gottlieb (eds.), *We are Here*, 37–8.

[77] 'Żyd' is the Polish word for Jew. In this context it has pejorative associations that are not conveyed in translation; I have thus left the word as in the original.

The Jewish police, they ordered us to go ever faster:
You won't suffer any hardship there.
You will receive three kilos of bread.
The heart aches, how the child cries to its mother:
'How do you leave me behind? Why not both of us together
In Treblinka, in Treblinka.'

The song's provenance is unknown, but there is evidence that it travelled beyond Warsaw to other east European ghettos, and even as far away as a kibbutz in Romania, where it was heard by one of Kaczerginski's respondents.[78] There is no doubt that those who sang this song intended it as a testimony to what had happened, directed ultimately at those 'brothers from over the sea' who were fortunate enough not to be able to feel their pain. These people clearly no longer believed that they would survive; the only thing they did not know was when their own deaths would come.

In 'Treblinka', people sought not only to chronicle the process of destruction that had engulfed them, but also to bear witness to their own anguished responses. More than anything else, the song described their terror and overwhelming sense of loss. Isolated from the world, goaded on by their own police, and facing certain death, the scope of their tragedy left no room for consolation.

It does seem, nonetheless, that the process of acknowledgement—affirming that they knew what was happening to them—helped the victims in some measure to grapple with their situation. In addition, it allowed them to place their deaths within a larger, specifically Jewish, historical context. After the war, they would not be forgotten: their mass grave would be found and 'rivers of tears' would mourn their loss. Moreover, they would die not as anonymous victims, but 'oyf kiddush-hashem': as holy martyrs for their religion (this phrase is also clearly emphasized in the musical setting). The song reasserts a connection between the Jewish victims and their Diaspora brethren, who by inference will assume the task of preserving their memory. The emphasis on memory, contained within the impulse of the song itself, seems to have given those who sang it at least some measure of solace.

But, as we have seen, solace was only part of what music brought to the inhabitants of the Warsaw ghetto. On one level, it helped the community to restore a sense of stability and familiarity. On another level, it found new life in the rapidly changing social landscape of the ghetto, which it helped

---

[78] Kaczerginski and Leivick, 214; Mlotek and Gottlieb (eds.), *We are Here*, 37.

simultaneously to define and articulate. As a social activity, it was a marker of status, a symbol of the power of some and the helplessness of others. As a creative process, in the newly composed songs, it revealed something of the ways in which people experienced the ghetto: what they witnessed, what they felt, and the varied approaches they took to dealing with loss and uncertainty.

There were also those people, consigned to the lowest ranks of ghetto society, who did not voluntarily hear music of any kind. Embroiled in a constant struggle for physical survival, they simply did not have either the opportunity or the energy to engage with music as entertainment. Receptiveness depended unquestionably on a basic level of health and nourishment. Thus, even the free entertainment provided by social welfare and other ghetto organizations was consumed by a particular category of ghetto inhabitant: those people who still had a place to live, and who sustained 'normal' functioning at least to some extent.

Elsewhere, the case was quite different. In the Vilna ghetto, which forms the subject of the next chapter, people had a much clearer awareness of what was happening. Even if they believed that productive labour might spare the lives of some, the recent slaughter of almost two-thirds of their community by the Einsatzgruppen inexorably coloured their thoughts and responses. If nothing else, they had a vivid sense of the lengths to which the Nazis were prepared to go in solving the 'Jewish Question'. The ghetto's leaders were acutely aware of the need to address the effects of the trauma that the community had suffered, and cultural life proved to be one of the most effective places where this could be done. Even here, however, musical activity was informed by different political trends, the changing circumstances of the ghetto, and not least by the diverse personalities involved in its creation. It is to these activities that we now turn.

2

Vilna: Politicians and Partisans

Jerusalem of Lithuania

In 1939 the Vilna resident A. I. Grodzenski was preparing an almanac documenting Jewish life in the city. The articles he had assembled included reports about literary organizations, sport, religious activities, social institutions, and musical life; many proudly emphasized the glowing reputation that the Vilna community enjoyed among Jews not only in the local area, but also in major Polish cities, and as far away as Paris and New York. The sudden outbreak of war in September prevented publication of the book, but it was recovered after the war by a former community member, Isaac Kowalski. The progress reports that made up the almanac would, in different circumstances, probably have enjoyed no more auspicious a fate than gathering dust along with others of their predictable and prosaic kind. As one of the last vestiges of pre-war Jewish Vilna, however, this almanac bears unique witness to an active and dynamic community life, and in particular to the value and importance afforded by the Vilna Jews to various forms of creative activity.[1]

Vilna's Jewish community did not count among the largest in eastern Europe. On the eve of the Second World War, its population numbered only around 60,000, and waves of simultaneous emigrations and refugee influxes left that figure relatively stable until the time of the German invasion in 1941. Nonetheless, Jews constituted a sizeable proportion of the city's population—almost 30 per cent, according to the last census prior to the Second World War taken in 1931.[2]

Vilna also boasted one of the most historically dynamic and vibrant of the east European Jewish communities. By the middle of the seventeenth century

---

[1] Isaac Kowalski (ed.), *Vilner almanakh* (New York, 1992).

[2] Yitzhak Arad, *Ghetto in Flames: The Struggle and Destruction of the Jews in Vilna in the Holocaust* (New York, 1982), 27–8.

it had become a major centre for Torah study, attracting some of the greatest Jewish thinkers and rabbinic scholars. By the nineteenth century it had established itself as the hub of secular Yiddish and Hebrew culture: some of the most important writers and artists were based there, and it was the home of numerous Zionist and Yiddishist institutions, including the Chibat Tsiyon (Love of Zion) movement, and the literary Pen club. The remarkable quality and scope of cultural life in Vilna earned it the esteemed title 'Jerusalem of Lithuania', a name by which it was known throughout the Jewish world. In the inter-war years, its Jewish life continued to thrive. The vast majority of children attended schools where the language of instruction was Yiddish or Hebrew, and a well-developed school network operated under the Zionist educational organization Tarbut (Culture). There were also youth movements and drama groups, several active publishing houses, and research and cultural institutions including the famous Mefitse-Haskole library and the Yidisher Visnshaftlekher Institut (Jewish Scientific Institute, YIVO).[3]

The vibrant cultural life for which Jewish Vilna was esteemed remained one of its distinguishing features during the war. In the two years of the ghetto's existence, from September 1941 until September 1943, it witnessed a flourishing of artistic activities, including theatrical revues, symphony concerts, vocal recitals, chamber music, art exhibitions, choral singing, competitions, and a successful youth club. An organization founded in early 1942 called the Faraynikung fun Literarn un Kinstler (Association of Writers and Artists, FLK) promoted creativity in the ghetto by providing material assistance of various forms, and organized regular literary evenings, lectures, and discussions. Scores of talented musicians, actors, artists, and writers continued their creative activity in the ghetto until the final months of its existence.

To a large extent, these activities grew directly out of Vilna's pre-war cultural landscape. Most of the people who were to become the ghetto's prominent cultural figures, including Zelig Kalmanovitch, Ya'akov Gershteyn, Avraham Slep, Wolf Durmashkin, Herman Kruk, and others, had long since distinguished themselves as enthusiastic participants in the city's intellectual and artistic life. Some of the ghetto's most important writers, including Shmerke Kaczerginski, Avraham Sutzkever, and Hirsh Glik, had for several years been active in the literary circle Yung Vilne (Young Vilna) and its offshoot Yungvald (Young Forest). The history of cultural life in the ghetto is thus partly the story of how the community was able to re-establish, adapt, and modify its pre-war activities and institutions in the new context.

---

[3] Leyzer Ran, *Vilna, Jerusalem of Lithuania* (Oxford, 1987), 7–8; Arad, *Ghetto in Flames*, 1–2.

Powerful new political currents began to sweep through the ghetto soon after its establishment in September 1941, and our story is equally concerned with the ways in which these shaped the nature and course of the community's creative life. The social structures in question were the Judenrat, particularly from mid-1942, when it was under the leadership of Jacob Gens, and the underground Fareynigte Partizaner Organizatsye (United Partisans Organization, FPO), established in the early part of that year. Although these organizations co-existed peaceably for some months, their relationship became increasingly fraught as the ghetto's situation grew more precarious. Our journey through the ghetto's musical landscape will reveal the powerful mark that both placed on cultural life, and on the ways in which people were encouraged to view the events that had befallen them.

War and the Move into the Ghetto

On 19 September 1939 the Red Army entered Vilna. The city was handed over to the Lithuanians several weeks later, but in June 1940 it once again came under Soviet rule when Lithuania was incorporated into the Soviet Union. The successive changes of authority affected the Jewish community in particular, as Lithuania's frustration with its loss of sovereignty resulted in increased anti-Semitic attacks. In addition, Jewish economic and community life was stifled under the Soviets: many commercial establishments and factories belonging to Jews were nationalized, educational and rabbinic institutions were disbanded, publications ceased, and all schools came under government supervision. The study of Hebrew, Jewish history, and the Bible was forbidden, although Yiddish remained the language of instruction.

In June 1941 the Nazi invasion of the Soviet Union brought Vilna under German occupation. Lithuanian anti-Semitism remained a dominant force in the city: particularly when mass killings began to take place, Lithuanian soldiers, policemen, and others assisted the German authorities, often subjecting Jewish victims to gratuitous violence and humiliation. The German administration intensified the anti-Jewish measures already in place: all Jews were now required to wear a yellow identifying badge; they were banned from public transport, certain streets and public areas; night curfew was imposed; the places and times at which food could be bought were restricted; and telephones were removed from their dwellings. In addition, property was indiscriminately looted and confiscated.[4]

---

[4] Arad, *Ghetto in Flames*, 22, 55–8; Gutman (ed.), *Encyclopedia*, 869–8, 1383.

It did not take long before the mass slaughter of Vilna Jewry began to be implemented. Einsatzkommando 9 arrived in the city in late June 1941, and the shootings began on 4 July. They took place at Ponar, a forest and popular recreation area approximately 8 miles south of Vilna, within easy road and rail access. The Soviet authorities had dug deep pits here for fuel tanks, and these subsequently functioned as mass graves. Some 5,000 Jews were killed at Ponar between 4 and 20 July 1941. On 31 August the second and principal wave of mass killing was inaugurated in preparation for the establishment of the ghettos. Several thousand Jews were incarcerated in Lukiszki prison, and subsequently taken to Ponar. In these *Aktionen* (operations), German killers were assisted by enthusiastic Lithuanian volunteers.[5]

On 6 September 1941 the Jewish population of Vilna was forced into two ghettos. At first they were distributed arbitrarily, depending on their former places of residence in the city. However, it soon became known that Ghetto No. 1, the larger of the two, was reserved for the 'productive' Jews—craftspeople and workers holding permits—while the remainder of the inhabitants were to be incarcerated in Ghetto No. 2. Approximately a week after the sealing of the ghettos, transfers began of orphans, the sick, and the elderly to Ghetto No. 2, and of work-permit holders and their families to Ghetto No. 1. On 7 September separate Judenräte were established in each of the ghettos. While the No. 1 Judenrat was composed primarily of public figures and members of the intelligentsia, the No. 2 Judenrat was made up of ordinary people who had been randomly co-opted. One of the first steps taken by the No. 1 Judenrat was the establishment of a Jewish Police, which was to be headed by Jacob Gens.[6]

By the time the ghettos were established, approximately 20,000 Jews— around a third of the population—had already been killed. The following few months, between September and December 1941, were to see more *Aktionen*. Almost 4,000 people were killed on Yom Kippur, 1 October, and during several more operations later that month Ghetto No. 2 was cleared of its approximately 7,000 remaining inhabitants. It was liquidated on 21 October 1941.[7]

---

[5] Arad, *Ghetto in Flames*, 77, 101–15; Gutman (ed.), *Encyclopedia*, 1572.

[6] Gens was an imposing and highly talented figure. He had served in the Lithuanian army from the age of 16, and later studied at the University of Kovno. In the late 1930s he was called back into the army and promoted to the rank of captain, but was dismissed when the Soviets took over. He then made his living teaching in the Hebrew school at Vilkomir, and at the Jewish school in Juburg. Yahil, *The Holocaust*, 278; Arad, *Ghetto in Flames*, 124–6, 133.

[7] Arad, *Ghetto in Flames*, 134–42.

The most notorious of the *Aktionen* that took place between late October and early November 1941 was known in Yiddish as the 'gele shayn' (yellow *Schein*) operation. *Scheine* were official work permits issued by the Arbeitsamt, printed on coloured cards, that granted temporary immunity from deportation to the holder and three family members: a spouse, and two children aged 16 or under. These permits became the sole guarantee of security. In October 1941 3,000 *Scheine* were issued in Ghetto No. 1, of which 400 were allocated to the Judenrat. Quotas of workers entitled to permits were assigned to authorized factories and workshops, as well as to social services, and the educational and medical professions. People exploited connections, gave bribes, lied about family relations, and forged documents in desperate attempts to acquire permits. Many nonetheless remained without valid passes, and no additional ones could be procured from the authorities. The total ghetto population of around 28,000 was to be reduced to 12,000 (3,000 permit holders and 9,000 dependants); 16,000 ghetto inhabitants were thus condemned to death.[8]

The first major *Schein Aktion* took place on 24 October 1941. The distribution of permits had been completed on 23 October, and after midnight, the ghetto was cordoned off by heavy detachments of German troops and Lithuanian auxiliaries. Close to 4,000 people not in possession of passes were taken to Ponar and shot. Several further *Aktionen* took place between 29 October and 21 December. In total, the number of victims from the time of the German occupation until the end of 1941 is estimated to be 34,000. Several thousand fled to Belorussia or went into hiding outside the ghetto, and only 20,000 remained within the ghetto, around 8,000 of them in hiding.[9]

Calm after the Storm

The end of these *Aktionen* on 21 December 1941 saw the beginning of a long period of relative stability in the ghetto, which lasted until April 1943. The population that remained, having been cleared of its older and less able-bodied members, had a younger and more politicized character than many of the other east European ghettos. At the same time, the patterns of authority that developed in the ghetto were similar: those involved with the Judenrat and the Jewish Police in particular wielded considerably more influence than

---

[8] Ibid. 145–7; Dawidowicz, *The War against the Jews*, 347.
[9] Arad, *Ghetto in Flames*, 149–58.

other inmates; those involved in large-scale food trafficking became some of the community's wealthier members.[10]

Reduced to a third of its original size, the community began slowly to take stock of what had been lost. It also quickly set about re-establishing the footholds of its own existence, which had been so violently disrupted, and which still remained fear-ridden and precarious. Cultural life was one of the most important ways in which this was achieved. With astonishing rapidity, the ghetto community was able to revive some of its cherished institutions, and within a few weeks of the *Aktionen* had already established several new ones.

First priority was given to children and education. Schools were opened and regular teaching began in late 1941; after only a few months, the librarian Herman Kruk noted in his diary the existence of two schools in the ghetto, with a daily attendance of over 700 pupils. A year later, he observed with some pride that the ghetto now boasted three elementary schools, a secondary school, a technical school, a nursery, and boarding schools for orphans. Orthodox groups had also established a *kheyder* (traditional Jewish religious school) and two yeshivas. By the end of 1942 school curricula were organized under five broad headings: Yiddish and Hebrew, religion, Jewish and general history, natural science and geography, and arithmetic.[11]

One of the ghetto's most important cultural centres became the famous pre-war Mefitse-Haskole library, located at 6 Strashun Street. Kruk assumed the task of reorganizing the library within days of the ghetto's establishment—reports suggest that it was vandalized and its contents partially dispersed—and people were soon flocking to borrow books or to spend time in the reading room. In August 1942 it reached a peak membership of nearly 4,000 subscribers. The library building also housed the ghetto archive, statistical authority, and museum. The archive and museum assembled hundreds of valuable documents and artefacts relating to Jewish life in Vilna, some of which were buried in the hope that they would be preserved.[12]

Musical institutions were also quickly re-established. Under the leadership of Avraham Slep and Tamara Girshovitsh, a music school was set up offering tuition in piano, violin, singing, and later music theory.[13] The school was

[10] Arad, *Ghetto in Flames*, 307, 311–12.

[11] Herman Kruk, 'Diary of the Vilna Ghetto', *YIVO Annual of Jewish Social Science*, 13 (1965), 9–78 at 26–7, 52, 32–3, 46.

[12] Avraham Sutzkever, *Fun Vilner geto* (Moscow, 1946), 111; Mark Dworzecki, *Yerushalayim de-Lita in kamf un umkum* (Paris, 1948), 242; Dawidowicz, *The War against the Jews*, 316.

[13] Slep (1884–1942) was a well-known conductor and singing teacher in pre-war Vilna. He was known particularly for his work with the 'Vilbig' choir (acronym for 'Vilner Bildungs-Gezelshaft',

attended by over 100 pupils, and concerts were organized regularly.[14] The well-known conductor Ya'akov Gershteyn revived his popular pre-war student choir, which continued to enjoy great success.[15] In December 1941 a small orchestra was established under the leadership of Wolf Durmashkin, a promising young conductor and accompanist from Warsaw. The first performance took place in March 1942, with under twenty musicians; within a year, the number of members had doubled. During the time of its existence, the orchestra performed some thirty-five concerts. Part of its repertoire consisted of standard concert fare, including solo and symphonic works by Beethoven, Schubert, Chopin, Mozart, and Tchaikovsky. No formal restrictions existed on works by Aryan composers, as they did in Warsaw. In addition, its programmes often included folksongs, 'light' music, and jazz, and interspersed musical pieces with recitations or theatrical sketches on contemporary topics. Many Jews had performed in the Vilna Symphony Orchestra as well as in Jewish orchestras before the war, and they made up the bulk of the new ensemble's members. According to former ghetto inmates, the level of performance was reasonably high.[16]

The ghetto also saw a proliferation of cultural activities centred around Jewish and Zionist themes. Under the auspices of the Brit Ivrit (Hebrew Union), a Hebrew choir with over 100 members was established, also under Durmashkin's leadership. The choir sang pioneer songs, songs with biblical texts, operatic excerpts, Chassidic songs, and folksongs. A smaller Hebrew choir, with fifteen members, was led by Shlomo Sharf from the Vilna Synagogue Choir. Both performed regularly at the conclusion of lecture evenings about Zionist history and other Jewish topics, and were accompanied by Durmashkin's orchestra. The Brit also had a Hebrew theatre, which staged, among other pieces, David Pinski's encouraging *Ha'y'hudi ha'nitschi* (The triumphant Jew) in June 1943. A Yiddish choir led by Slep performed

---

Vilna educational society). He continued to work with the choir in the ghetto, and its performances were enthusiastically received. The repertoire was made up of standard classical works and Jewish folksongs, which he arranged himself. Slep was deported to Estonia a few months before the liquidation of the ghetto, and died there. Girshovitz was a well-known pianist and teacher, and had been an active member of the Jewish Music Institute in Vilna. Kaczerginski and Leivick, 89; Yisaskhar Fater, *Yiddishe muzik in Poyln tsvishn beyde velt-milkhomes* (Tel Aviv, 1970), 172–8, 272.

[14] Dworzecki, *Yerushalayim de-Lita*, 234; Kruk, 'Diary', 244, 376; Zelig Kalmanovitch, 'A Diary of the Nazi Ghetto in Vilna', *YIVO Annual of Jewish Social Science*, 8 (1953), 9–81 at 31.

[15] Yitzhok Rudashevski, *The Diary of the Vilna Ghetto, June 1941–April 1943* (Tel Aviv, 1973), 60; Kruk, 'Diary', 353–4.

[16] Anonymous statement about Wolf Durmashkin, Yad Vashem Archive (hereafter YV), M.1.E/ 1538; Dworzecki, *Yerushalayim de-Lita*, 244; Skurkovitz, *Sima's Songs*, 3; Sutzkever, *Fun Vilner Geto*, 107.

Yiddish folksongs, usually accompanied by the orchestra, while a religious chorus presented liturgical choral music.[17]

The most controversial of the new developments in the ghetto's cultural life was undoubtedly the establishment of the ghetto theatre. The poet Avraham Sutzkever was present at the meeting, attended primarily by the theatre community, where a young director by the name of Viskind proposed the venture in January 1942. According to Sutzkever, although many were taken aback by the suggestion, Viskind convinced them that the theatre would play an important role in uplifting the community. During the twenty months of its existence, the theatre hosted four full-scale dramatic presentations in Yiddish. The first, *Grine felder* (Green fields), a well-known pastoral romance by the Yiddish-American playwright Peretz Hirshbein, opened in August 1942. *Der mentsh untern brik* (The man under the bridge), a Yiddish translation of the play by the Hungarian Otto Indig, was premiered in November of that year. David Pinski's comedy *Der oytser* (The treasure) was staged in March 1943, and *Der mabl* (The flood), a Yiddish translation of Henning Berger's *Syndafloden*, opened during the last weeks of the ghetto's existence in the summer of 1943. A performance of Sholem Aleichem's *Tevye der milkhiker* (Tevye the milkman) was in preparation when the ghetto was liquidated. The actors in these productions were generally able to rehearse only at night, when they had returned from work. The most popular among them were Ya'akov Beregolski, Max Shadovski, Esther Lipovski, Shabsai Blyakher, Yekusiel Rutenberg, Dore Rubin, and the 'ghetto-star' Khayele Rozental.[18]

Shortly after the theatre came the establishment of the Faraynikung fun Literarn un Kinstler under the charismatic leadership of the well-known writer and intellectual Zelig Kalmanovitch. The organization aimed to stimulate creativity in the ghetto and to promote Jewish art and culture. Founded on the initiative of the artists themselves, and representing a wide range of political affiliations, it organized regular literary evenings, lectures, and discussions. Some of the ghetto's leading personalities came to talk on subjects ranging from Barukh Spinoza to the work of the artist Chagall, Yiddish writers such as I. L. Peretz and Mendele Moykher Sforim, and Jewish music. Gatherings would often be concluded with songs in Hebrew or Yiddish. Although musicians were included in this initial group, they established their own association on 10 February 1942, with a membership of fifty.

[17] Dworzecki, *Yerushalayim de-Lita*, 245–6, 253; Trunk, *Judenrat*, 227.
[18] Solon Beinfeld, 'The Cultural Life of the Vilna Ghetto', in Joshua Sobol, *Ghetto* (London, 1989), pp. xxvi–viii; Sutzkever, *Fun Vilner geto*, 105–6; Arad, *Ghetto in Flames*, 323.

The FLK also held three art competitions in the ghetto, with separate categories for literature, music, and painting. These received an enthusiastic response both from the numerous entrants and from the ghetto public.[19]

Apart from organizing these events, the FLK made an enormous effort to provide material help to the ghetto's struggling artists. It assisted them with obtaining work permits, and in some cases was able to support their spouses as well. The organization was also concerned with preserving works by Vilna Jews, both those who had been killed and those who continued with their activities in the ghetto. Material was collected for publication after the war, and some artists were even paid in advance for work-in-progress.

Embracing Jewish Identity

The explosion of cultural life that took place in the early period of the ghetto makes sense when we consider the value and importance that the community had long placed on creative activity. Reduced to a third of its size, and left reeling from the carnage it had witnessed, the traumatized community turned to one of its richest and most trusted resources as a way both of counteracting shock, and of re-establishing its grip on life. A song written shortly after the establishment of the ghetto gives us a sense of how conceptions of what was happening began to be moulded from within the framework of the familiar, as a way of making the new reality more assimilable (see Ex. 2.1). Rikle Glezer was 18 when she wrote 'Es iz geven a zumertog' (It was a summer's day):

> Es iz geven a zumer-tog,
> Vi shtendik zunik-sheyn,
> Un di natur hot dan gehat
> In zikh azoyfil kheyn,
> Es hobn feygelekh gezungen,
> Freylekh zikh arumgeshprungen,
> In geto hot men undz geheysn geyn.
>
> Akh shtelt zikh for vos s'iz fun undz gevorn!
> Farshtanen hobn mir: s'iz alts farloyrn.
> S'hot nit geholfn undzer betn,
> Az s'zol emitser undz retn—
> Farlozn hobn mir dokh undzer heym.

---

[19] Both Sutzkever and Dworzecki date the establishment of the Association to 17 Feb. 1942, while Kruk's diary indicates that it was founded on 20 Jan. of that year. Sutzkever, *Fun Vilner geto*, 107–9; Kruk, 'Diary', 20, 162; Dworzecki, *Yerushalayim de-Lita*, 238–40.

Ex. 2.1. 'Es iz geven a zumertog'. Kaczerginski and Leivick, 364

Getsoygn hot der veg zikh lang.
S'iz shver geven tsu geyn.
Mir dukht, az kukndik oyf undz
Tseveynt volt zikh a shteyn.
Gegangen zaynen zkeynim, kinder,
Vi tsu der akeyde rinder,
Mentshns blut geflosn iz in gas.

Itst zaynen ale mir farshparte,
Farpaynikte, fun lebn opgenarte.
Ver on a tatn, on a mamen,
Zeltn ver es iz tsuzamen.
Der soyne hot dergreykht zayn groysn tsil.

Gevezn zaynen mir tsufil—
Bafoyln hot der har
Tsu brengen yidn fun arum
Un shisn oyf Ponar.
Pust zaynen gevorn shtiber,
Ober ful derfar di griber.
Der soyne hot dergreykht zayn groysn tsil.

Oyf Ponar itst zet men oyf di vegn
Zakhn, hitlen durkhgenetst fun regn,

Dos zaynen zakhn fun korbones,
Fun di heylike neshomes,
Di erd hot zey oyf eybik tsugedekt.

Un itst iz vider zunik-sheyn,
Shmekt prakhtful alts arum,
Un mir zaynen farpaynikte
Un laydn ale shtum.
Opgeshnitn fun der velt,
Mit hoykhe moyern farshtelt,
A shtral fun hofnung dervekt zikh koym.[20]

It was a summer's day,
Sunny and lovely as always,
And nature then
Had so much charm.
Birds sang,
Hopped around cheerfully.
We were ordered to go into the ghetto.

Oh, just imagine what happened to us!
We understood: everything was lost.
Of no use were our pleas
That someone should save us—
We still left our home.

The road stretched far.
It was difficult to walk.
I think that, looking at us,
A stone would have burst out crying.
Old people and children went
Like cattle to be sacrificed,
Human blood flowed in the street.

Now we are all caged in,
Tortured, deceived by life.
Some without fathers, without mothers,
Seldom are they together.
The enemy has achieved his great goal.

There were too many of us—
The master ordered
That Jews from the area be brought
And shot at Ponar.
Houses became empty,

[20] Kaczerginski and Leivick, 7–8.

But graves therefore filled up.
The enemy has achieved his great goal.

At Ponar one can now see on the roads
Things, rain-soaked hats,
These things belonged to the victims [sacrifices],
To the holy souls.
The earth has covered them for ever.

And now it's sunny and lovely once again,
Everything around smells wonderful,
And we are tortured
And all suffer silently.
Cut off from the world,
Blocked by high walls,
A ray of hope barely awakens.

Few of the ghetto songs were so explicit in their descriptions.[21] Glezer painfully chronicled the events she had witnessed: Jews being herded into the ghetto, their futile pleas for help, the slaughter in the streets, and the mass murders that were taking place at Ponar. She also left no doubt as to the emotional state in which this had left the Vilna Jews. They were not only 'cut off from the world' but had been painfully deceived by it. Left alone and helpless, severed from their homes and families, they could not even protect the most vulnerable among them from being sacrificed on the streets 'like cattle'. The imagery of animals being led to the slaughter was frequently invoked during this period, often as a way of condemning the passivity of the victims. The song is suffused with a sense of resignation and helplessness in the face of so much bloodshed. Glezer's words were unambiguous: the enemy had succeeded in what he had set out to achieve, 'everything was lost', and not even a 'ray of hope' glimmered in their future.

But in bearing witness to the devastation of the community and to its deep sense of trauma, Glezer's song also drew on familiar and comforting language and imagery. With Hebrew-derived words such as 'akeyde' and 'korbones'— both meaning 'sacrifice(s)', and bearing distinctly biblical associations (the first referred specifically to the sacrifice of Isaac by his father Abraham)—she brought the narrative of suffering into an explicitly Jewish context. Her use of the words 'heylike neshomes' (holy souls, the second word Hebrew-derived) further suggests a conception of the victims as innocent martyrs for their religion.[22] Religious overtones such as these provided a common conceptual

---

[21] For a listing of newly created songs from Vilna see Appendix, §II.

[22] Most Yiddish words relating to religious or biblical issues are derived from Hebrew; their use thus often elicits particular associations.

framework within which people could try to absorb what had happened. Songwriters during this period frequently turned to earlier episodes in the long history of Jewish suffering, from the Bible to the tsarist pogroms, for analogous reasons. This kind of language provided consolation not only because it gave some meaning to the events within the context of tradition—for example, the incomprehensible slaughter of Ponar becoming a holy sacrifice, an 'akeyde'—but also because it brought with it an affirmation, however faint, that despite its tragic history the Jewish nation had always managed to sustain its existence.

Glezer also constructed her song as the lament not of an individual, but of a community. The use of the first person plural narrative voice—the 'we'—is common in the ghetto songs: the idea that their experiences were shared clearly provided people with some sense of comfort, and served to alleviate their sense of individual aloneness (even though the community remained isolated). Further, the 'we' in this song suggests that Glezer conceived it as a kind of chronicle of the events, which would bear witness to what the group had suffered. Addressing an unnamed listener outside the 'high walls', the narrative voice not only describes the crimes that were perpetrated, but also documents for posterity some of the ways in which the community responded to them.

Finally, we must consider 'Es iz geven a zumertog' as it was sung. We know that it was popular in the ghetto from the fact that it appears in so many postwar testimonies. Since it was not written for a specific performance context (such as the theatre revues), we assume that it was sung in informal contexts such as the youth club, gatherings of the FLK, or similar occasions.

The song was set to the tune of 'Papirosn' (Cigarettes), one of the most popular Yiddish theatre songs, written by Herman Yablokoff in the 1920s. The original described the misery of an orphan peddling his wares on the streets of a nameless European city, struggling to sustain himself alone at a time of enormous deprivation (the context most likely being the period around the First World War).[23] 'Papirosn' retained its popularity among the ghetto Jews, and formed the basis of at least two more ghetto songs. The first, a song from Łódź called 'Nishtu kayn przydziel' (There are no coupons), is a lament on the lack of food in the ghetto, and expresses anger at Rumkowski; the second, from Warsaw, is a song about a starving orphan entitled 'Di broyt farkoyferin' (The bread seller).[24] The familiar melody allowed Glezer to set in

[23] Eleanor Gordon Mlotek and Joseph Mlotek (eds.), *Pearls of Yiddish Song: Favourite Folk, Art and Theatre Songs* (New York, 1988), 267–70.
[24] Flam, *Singing for Survival*, 95; Kaczerginski and Leivick, 110–11.

stark relief 'what happened to us', while at the same time providing some emotional coordinates within which the frightening new reality would perhaps seem less absolute a rupture. It seems likely that such a well-known melody would have reaffirmed a sense of communal identity, once again placing the understanding of these new events within the context of what had come before.

Partisans and the Youth

The ghetto Jews did not—or, more accurately perhaps, could not—view what was happening to them as a radical severance from their past. It was terrifying, unanticipated, and difficult to comprehend, but it was still something that could acquire meaning within the broader narrative of Jewish suffering. David Roskies has argued that the essence of the Jewish commemorative tradition has long been to make sense of contemporary events in terms of ancient texts, and to seize upon the symbols of the past in order to give meaning to the present. He further maintains that in their responses to catastrophe, Jewish communities have almost always sought to define their place along the continuum of the nation's history.[25] This conception of what was happening was evident in a range of writings from the ghetto. The ways in which different people chose to frame and promote it through the framework of cultural activity, however, often depended on their political convictions and aims.

One of the most significant political forces in the ghetto was the underground Fareynigte Partizaner Organizatsye. Established at the beginning of 1942, the FPO was active in armed resistance primarily in the forests surrounding Vilna, in cooperation with the Soviet partisan movement. It was made up of young men and women, mostly in their twenties, of varying political leanings, drawn from Zionist youth organizations including Ha'shomer ha'tsa'ir (The Young Guard), Ha'no'ar ha'tsiyoni (Zionist Youth), and the Revisionist movement Betar. Movements such as these had played an important role in Jewish eastern Europe during the inter-war period, encouraging young people to rebel against the passivity of the older generations. During the war years, they came to play an active role in the various fighting organizations in Warsaw, Białystok, Kraków, and other cities.[26]

[25] David Roskies, *Against the Apocalypse: Responses to Catastrophe in Modern Jewish Culture* (London, 1984), 48, 54.
[26] Gutman (ed.), *Encyclopedia*, 1698–1702.

Relations between the FPO and the Vilna Judenrat remained peaceful for as long as conditions in the ghetto were relatively calm. In the spring of 1943, however, it became apparent that danger was imminent. After a long period of relative quiet, Jews remaining in the smaller ghettos and labour camps around Vilna began to be taken to Ponar, and *Aktionen* continued throughout the summer. The Judenrat's attitude changed as Gens became convinced that contact with partisans in the forests and the smuggling of weapons constituted a threat to the ghetto population. He attempted to send FPO leaders to outlying labour camps, and open clashes resulted. A serious confrontation took place in July 1943 when Yitzhak Vitnberg, the first commander of the FPO, was freed by FPO members while under arrest by the Gestapo. The Gestapo threatened the death of the entire ghetto population if he was not returned, and Gens issued his own further threats. Vitnberg gave himself up under this pressure, and was killed two days afterwards. The Vitnberg affair served as proof for those who argued that the fighters should make their way to the forests rather than fighting in the ghetto, and several FPO members escaped soon after into the Narocz forests to establish a base.[27]

Ultimately, the FPO's main impact was felt in partisan combat in the forests. Nonetheless, the ideologies and convictions of its members left a significant mark in the ghetto as well. One of the most important means through which this was achieved was in the realm of cultural life. FPO members were in fact among the ghetto's most prominent writers: they included, among others, Avraham Sutzkever, Shmerke Kaczerginski, Abba Kovner, Hirsh Glik, and Leyb Opeskin. This was more than a matter of mere coincidence. Creative activity had long been encouraged by the pre-war youth movements, and many had their own literary circles and drama groups. Some of the most significant young writers in the pre-war period, including those involved in Yung Vilne and Yungvald, were also actively involved in political life. This connection between political and literary activity was further intensified in the ghetto.

Some of the partisan writers saw songs as an effective way of promoting their cause, encouraging active resistance, and rousing a spirit of defiance and communal strength. Most of the songs that became associated with the

---

[27] In the last few months of 1942 Soviet paratroopers reached the Vilna area, having been sent to set up a partisan movement. There they encountered the FPO, and as a result of these contacts, the FPO assisted in consolidating, under Soviet auspices, the general underground and the partisan movement. In mid-1943 the Germans succeeded in tracking down the communist organization, and after learning of Vitnberg's presence in the ghetto (he was a communist), demanded that he be handed over. His name was revealed not in his capacity as FPO leader, but as a communist militant. Gutman (ed.), *Encyclopedia*, 1574; Yahil, *The Holocaust*, 467–9.

movement engaged with a common set of themes: the bravery of the partisans, the strength and endurance of the Jewish nation, and the need for revenge. Significantly, these also became some of the most prominent songs with which post-war Jewish communities associated the ghettos. Two young men in particular stood out for their contributions to the partisans' musical legacy. The first was Hirsh Glik, an enthusiastic poet, member of Ha'shomer ha'tsa'ir, and aged only 19 at the time of the German occupation. During the war, in the ghetto and in various labour camps, Glik continued to write prodigiously. Among many other songs and poems glorifying the partisans and strengthening hope in the Jewish future, he was the author of the popular 'Zog nit keynmol az du geyst dem letstn veg' (Never say that you are walking the final road), which became the official hymn of the FPO soon after it was written in 1943. The second was Shmerke Kaczerginski, in his early thirties when the Nazis invaded Vilna, and already an established writer of revolutionary poems and songs. His pre-war political activities were primarily associated with the underground communist youth, and in the ghetto he assisted in the establishment of the FPO.

'Zog nit keynmol' has become perhaps the most emblematic and well known of the ghetto songs (see Ex. 2.2). Glik's writing was influenced by two concurrent events: first, a battle that erupted between a group of Jewish partisans and an SS detachment in the forests near Vilna in 1943, resulting in the deaths of fifteen Jews; and second, the recently received news of the Warsaw ghetto uprising, which made a huge impression on him. The song was based on a melody by the well-known Soviet-Jewish composer Dimitri Pokrass, a rousing and rhythmic march melody in the minor. The defiant and encouraging text goes as follows:

> Zog nit keynmol az du geyst dem letstn veg,
> Khotsh himlen blayene farshteln bloye teg;

Ex. 2.2. 'Zog nit keynmol az du geyst dem letstn veg'. Kaczerginski and Leivick, 361

Kumen vet nokh undzer oysgebenkte sho,
S'vet a poyk ton undzer trot—mir zaynen do!

Fun grinem palmen-land biz vaytn land fun shney,
Mir kumen on mit undzer payn, mit undzer vey,
Un vu gefaln s'iz a shprits fun undzer blut,
Shprotsn vet dort undzer gvure, undzer mut.

S'vet di morgn-zun bagildn undz dem haynt,
Un der nekhtn vet farshvindn mitn faynt,
Nor oyb farzamen vet di zun un der kayor—
Vi a parol zol geyn dos lid fun dor tsu dor.

Dos lid geshribn iz mit blut un nit mit blay,
S'iz nit keyn lidl fun a foygl oyf der fray,
Dos hot a folk tsvishn falndike vent
Dos lid gezungen mit naganes in di hent.

To zog nit keynmol az du geyst dem letstn veg,
Khotsh himlen blayene farshteln bloye teg.
Kumen vet nokh undzer oysgebenkte sho—
S'vet a poyk ton undzer trot—mir zaynen do![28]

Never say that you are walking the final road,
Though leaden skies obscure blue days;
The hour we have been longing for will still come,
Our steps will drum—we are here!

From green palm-land to distant land of snow,
We arrive with our pain, with our sorrow,
And where a spurt of our blood has fallen,
There will sprout our strength, our courage.

The morning sun will tinge our today with gold,
And yesterday will vanish with the enemy,
But if the sun and the dawn are delayed—
Like a watchword this song will go from generation to generation.

This song is written with blood and not with lead,
It's not a song about a bird that is free.
A people, between falling walls,
Sang this song with pistols in their hands.

So never say that you are walking the final road
Though leaden skies obscure blue days.
The hour we have been longing for will still come—
Our steps will drum—we are here!

---

[28] Kaczerginski and Leivick, 3.

Several years after the war, Kaczerginski recalled the context of the song's creation:

'The survivors in the Warsaw ghetto have begun an armed resistance against the murderers of the Jewish people. The ghetto is aflame!' [flashed over the secret radio waves of the partisan organisations]...Two short lines conveyed the flaming news...We knew of no other particulars yet...but we suddenly saw clearly the flames of the Warsaw ghetto and the Jews fighting with arms for their dignity and self-respect. Restless days. Sleepless nights. We armed ourselves. The news of the uprising lifted our spirits and made us proud...and although we were in agony at their unequal struggle...we felt relieved...our hearts became winged...

On the first of May, we arranged an evening on the theme: 'Spring in Yiddish Literature'...Every speaker and every poem which was read aloud was permeated with the spirit of the fighting Warsaw ghetto...Hirshke [Glik] came up quietly beside me. 'Well, what's new with you, Hirshl?'—'I wrote a new poem. Want to hear it?'—'Just like that? Well, read it!'—'Not now, tomorrow I'll bring it to you. It's a poem to be sung.'

On the morrow, Hirshke came to my room bright and early. 'Now listen carefully,' he pleaded, 'I'll sing it for you right away.' He began to sing it softly, but full of excitement. His eyes glowed with little sparks...*Kumen vet noch undzer oysgebenkte sho*...Where did he get his faith? His voice became firmer. He tapped out the rhythm with his foot, as if he were marching...*Dos hot a folk tsevishn falndike vent, dos lid gezungen mit naganes in di hent*...We lived with the spirit of April and the Warsaw ghetto uprising. The partisan staff in the Vilna ghetto decided that the song should become the hymn of its fighters. But the people did not wait for this decision, and the song had already spread to the ghettos, the concentration and labor camps, and into the woods to other partisan brigades.[29]

Glik's message in the song was clearly one of defiant optimism and encouragement, infused with the spirit of the Warsaw uprising that Kaczerginski so passionately described. What is particularly significant is that Glik was able to reconcile this spirit with a forthright acknowledgement of continued Jewish suffering, not only in his own time, but also in the past and probably in times to come as well. Surprisingly perhaps for the theme song of a military organization, 'Zog nit keynmol' was less a battle cry than a defiant affirmation of Jewish endurance. Glik included some hints about the song's context: the 'falling walls' of the ghetto, the fact that it was sung by 'people...with pistols in their hands', a vague acknowledgement that 'leaden skies obscure blue days'. Nonetheless, his writing was directed far more forcefully towards a larger context of Jewish suffering and existence.

[29] Kaczerginski, cited in Rubin, *Voices of a People*, 453–4.

The secret of Glik's optimism lay in its function of collective rather than individual survival. The song's 'we', it was quickly revealed, did not refer only to the partisans. Rather, it was the all-encompassing 'we' of the Jewish people, who had wandered among foreign lands, 'from green palm-land to distant land of snow', arriving each time only with 'pain' and 'sorrow' to shed their blood anew. Invoking the long history of Jewish suffering was of course not unique to Glik, but was common to many other contemporary texts as well. What is interesting, however, is that the partisans chose to identify most strongly with a text that made only oblique reference to their own specific experiences, and then only in order to validate the song's broader message. Only in the fourth stanza did Glik assure his listeners that 'This song is written with blood and not with lead', lest its defiant exhortations be thought overstated. Glik's faith lay in the overriding fact that although individuals would be lost, and although the dawn might be 'delayed'—the ambiguous setting reinforcing the text's applicability to the universal Jewish fate—the nation would always proudly be able to assert, 'Mir zaynen do!' (We are here!)

'Mir zaynen do' was a recurring phrase in Kaczerginski's songs as well. Like Glik, he stressed the idea of Jewish endurance, often in a spirit of rebelliousness and defiance. In his song 'Yid, du partizaner' (Jew, you partisan), he suggested that Jewish continuity would be achieved by casting off shackles and taking up arms.[30] He used the repeated affirmation 'mir zaynen do' to emphasize that the partisans were committed to action, and that they refused to submit anonymously to their fates. The phrase appeared as a veritable battle cry in 'Partizaner-marsh' (Partisan march), written when large numbers of partisans were departing for the forests in August 1943 (see Ex. 2.3):

> Hey F. P. O!
> Mir zaynen do!
> Mutik un dreyste tsum shlakht.
> Partizaner nokh haynt
> Geyen shlogn dem faynt,
> Inem kamf far an arbeter-makht.[31]
>
> Hey F. P. O!
> We are here!
> Boldly and with courage into battle.

---

[30] Kaczerginski and Leivick, 351.
[31] Ibid. 345.

Ex. 2.3. 'Partizaner-marsh'. Kaczerginski and Leivick, 416

> Today partisans
> Are going to beat the enemy,
> In the struggle for workers' power.

Like Glik, Kaczerginski drew primarily on Soviet models in the songs he wrote for the partisans. Interestingly, some of the most important composers of popular Soviet songs during the 1920s and 1930s were Jews, prominent among them Dimitri Pokrass and his contemporaries Matvey Blanter and Isaac Dunayevsky. While their songs included Jewish folk elements, their primary characteristics were 'ideological texts' (usually of a nationalistic kind), and a simple, rhythmic musical style drawing on the tradition of revolutionary Soviet song.[32] Some partisan songs, like 'Zog nit keynmol' and Kaczerginski's 'Itzik Vitnberg', directly appropriated these melodies, but even newly composed ones clearly revealed their influence in their rousing march-like settings, frequent use of dotted rhythms, and their tendency towards short, catchy declamations (as in 'Partizaner-marsh'). In their texts, the partisan writers echoed the 'mood of determination and heroism' expressed in the writings of their Soviet counterparts.[33]

Kaczerginski's songs clearly served as battle hymns, rousing the young partisans to fight. While some made direct reference to what had been perpetrated in the ghetto, and even explicitly mentioned 'Hitler' or 'fascists', they generally chose to document the heroic activities of the partisans. Some of the best known of these documentary songs are his 'Itzik Vitnberg', a song

---

[32] Joachim Braun, *Jews and Jewish Elements in Soviet Music* (Tel Aviv, 1978), 78–81.
[33] Rubin, *Voices of a People*, 420.

recording the story of the FPO commander's capture, escape, and decision to surrender, and Glik's 'Shtil, di nakht iz oysgeshternt' (Quiet, the night is full of stars), which documents a successful diversion staged by partisans Itzik Matskevitch and Vitke Kempner in 1942.[34]

The partisan songs can be distinguished from other ghetto songs in several ways. First, they are generally less cautious in the themes they tackle. They contain frequent calls for revenge and violent action, and paint colourful pictures of the enemy's ultimate defeat by the heroic partisans. The fact that some of the songs were created and sung outside the ghetto, in the forests, of course allowed writers more freedom in their subject matter. A second major difference lies in their approach to the emotional aspects of ghetto life. The partisan songs are usually affirmative and encouraging, and emphasize Jewish bravery and heroism. They do not often deal with other kinds of responses, such as uncertainty, questioning, fear, despair, loneliness, and so on, which feature repeatedly in the songs that circulated at the theatres and the literary clubs. Since discussion of these issues would not have advanced the cause of the partisans, their absence is unsurprising. Finally, as is already evident from the two examples above, the partisan songs can also be distinguished in their musical texts. Those that were based on pre-existing melodies almost always used Soviet songs rather than Yiddish songs, signalling explicit ideological associations. They were usually intended for communal singing, and hence were given memorable, easily sung melodies.

The only other group of songs with which these are comparable are those created by German political prisoners primarily in the pre-war camps in Germany, and sung in camps throughout the war years. As we shall see in the chapter on Sachsenhausen, these songs adopt a similar spirit of encouragement, and were intended to rouse their listeners and raise morale. For the Jewish writers, however, it is clear that much more was at stake than was the case for non-Jewish camp inmates. Their texts are darker and more defiant, and deal more openly with the likelihood of death and need for revenge.

The positive spirit of the partisans entered the bloodstream of the general ghetto population through one particularly important source: the youth. The youth club was a vibrant social centre where teenagers engaged in drama and music-making, studied a variety of subjects under the tutelage of some of the ghetto's leading teachers, and came together in the evenings to amuse themselves. Groups were set up to document the history of the ghetto, and to collect sayings, songs, jokes, and stories that had sprung up relating to ghetto

[34] Kaczerginski and Leivick, 341, 348.

life. A specially designated hall in the club was used for lessons, and there was also a reading hall and a meeting room.[35]

Partisans such as Kaczerginski and Sutzkever were actively involved with the club, providing intellectual guidance, organizing cultural and educational activities, and generally imbuing the children with a mood of hope and encouragement. In a post-war account, Sima Skurkovitz recalled the inspiring meetings she attended at the club, singing Yiddish songs and participating in music and writing competitions.[36] The young diarist Yitzkhok Rudashevski, aged 14 at the time of the German invasion, recorded with great enthusiasm the various club activities in which he participated: dramatic performances, quiz nights, a nature group, history projects, reading groups, and parties. His account suggests that they spent time together on a more or less daily basis, and his observations make clear the spirit of optimism, cheerfulness, and enjoyment of life that was fostered:

11 December 1942: I look around at the crowd, all of our kind teachers, friends, intimates. It is so cosy, so warm, so pleasant. This evening we demonstrated what we are and what we can accomplish. Club members came with songs, recitations. Until late into the night we sang with the adults songs which tell about youthfulness and hope... We sat at the meagre tables and ate baked pudding and coffee and we were so happy, so happy. Song after song resounded. It is already 12 o'clock. We are, as it were, intoxicated with the joy of youth. We do not want to go home. Songs keep bursting forth, they simply will not stop. We disperse late at night... Today we have demonstrated that even within the three small streets we can maintain our youthful zeal. We have proved that from the ghetto there will not emerge a youth broken in spirit; from the ghetto there will emerge a strong youth which is hardy and cheerful.[37]

Rudashevski's comments demonstrate the importance that was attached to providing the youth with support and guidance. The strong partisan presence in the youth club meant that this guidance was often provided in a spirit of optimism and boldness, in preparation for the youth's involvement in active resistance. Kaczerginski's 'Yugnt himn' (Youth hymn), which was dedicated to the club and performed at its official meetings, clearly reveals the ways in which FPO aims and ideologies were modified and adapted for the youth (see Ex. 2.4):

---

[35] Dworzecki differentiates between the various children's clubs in the ghetto and the youth club, suggesting that the latter was the only one of its kind, and that its members were primarily teenagers. Dworzecki, *Yerushalayim de-Lita*, 234–5; Sutzkever, *Fun Vilner geto*, 103; Rudashevski, *Diary*, 80–1.

[36] Skurkovitz, *Sima's Songs*, 21.

[37] Rudashevski, *Diary*, 104–5.

Ex. 2.4. 'Yugnt himn'. Kaczerginski and Leivick, 427

Undzer lid iz ful mit troyer,—
Dreyst iz undzer munter-gang,
Khotsh der soyne vakht baym toyer,—
Shturemt yugnt mit gezang:

  Yung iz yeder, yeder, yeder ver es vil nor,
  Yorn hobn keyn batayt,
  Alte kenen, kenen, kenen oykh zayn kinder
  Fun a naye fraye tsayt.

Ver es voglt um oyf vegn,
Ver mit dreystkayt s'shtelt zayn fus,
Brengt di yugnt zey antkegn
Funem geto a gerus.
    Yung iz yeder...

Mir gedenken ale sonim,
Mir gedenken ale fraynt,
Eybik veln mir dermonen,
Undzer nekhtn mitn haynt.
    Yung iz yeder...

Kloybn mir tsunoyf di glider,
Vider shtoln mir di rey.
Geyt a boyer, geyt a shmider,—
Lomir ale geyn mit zey!
    Yung iz yeder...[38]

Our song is full of sadness,—
Bold is our cheerful step,
Although the enemy stands guard at the gate,—
Young people storm in song:
    Young are all, all, all who want to be,
    Years have no meaning,
    Old people can, can, can also be children
    Of a new and free age.

Whoever wanders on the roads,
Whoever sets his foot down boldly,
The youth will meet him
With a greeting from the ghetto.
    Young are all...

We remember all enemies,
We remember all friends,
We will always recall
Our yesterday with our today.
    Young are all...

Let us gather together our bodies,
And steel the ranks again.
There goes a builder, there goes a blacksmith,—
Let us all go with them!
    Young are all...

Both the song's text and its melody, composed by the ghetto inmate Basye Rubin, mirror the upbeat spirit of the partisan songs. The words that

---

[38] Kaczerginski and Leivick, 325.

Kaczerginski drew from the mouths of his young charges encouraged them to be 'bold' and 'cheerful', and to derive strength from the group; similar words and sentiments encouraged his fellow fighters. Once again we see the importance that was placed on asserting the presence and activity of the group: the young people were encouraged to 'storm' forward with their bold song, and to take courage from the fact that anyone who so chose could participate in the 'new and free age'. It was also important for Kaczerginski to inculcate the idea that 'yesterday' should inform the young people's thoughts and actions as an integral part of their 'today'.

His song was also carefully crafted to frame these attitudes and principles in such a way as to make them attractive to, and appropriate for, young people. There is no mention of fighting or weapons, although the description of 'young people storm[ing] in song' while 'the enemy stands guard at the gate' clearly implies the possibility of future action. The clubs did in fact become important sites of underground activity in the latter part of the ghetto's existence. The song also celebrates the 'youthful zeal' of which Rudashevski wrote, as well as the idea of children as the strong and proud bearers of 'a new and free age', an idea which evidently made its mark on the group's consciousness. The melody, unusually in the major, echoes the march style of the partisan songs, but without taking on their aura of gravity or intensity.

Gens and the Ghetto Theatre

The spirit of hope and defiance invoked by the partisans in their songs obviously served to promote distinct political goals. The songs were sung in informal groups or at meetings, and were intended to rouse the fighters to action and strengthen their sense of solidarity. It is important to remember, however, that these songs did not represent the experiences of the vast majority of the ghetto population. In addition, they constituted only a small proportion of the songs in general circulation, and even then only in the final months before the ghetto's destruction.

The most important site of musical activity was the ghetto theatre. Apart from full-scale dramatic presentations, performances by the Yiddish and Hebrew choirs, and orchestral concerts, the theatre hosted several successful variety shows consisting primarily of songs and theatrical items. The opening performance on 18 January 1942 was celebrated with one of these programmes, including fragments from Ya'akov Gordin's *Mirele Efros* and

I. L. Peretz's *Di goldene keyt* (The golden chain), a choral declamation of Khayim Nakhman Bialik's 'Glust zikh mir vaynen' (I want to cry), performances of folksongs 'Eyli, eyli, lama azavtoni?' (My God, my God, why have you forsaken me?) and 'Zamd un shtern' (Sand and stars) by the cantor Eydelson and Lyube Levitski, and a performance of Chopin's B minor Nocturne by Sonia Rekhtik.[39]

The first few concerts at the theatre were similar to the first, consisting of various unrelated musical and theatrical pieces. Each programme was performed only once. The idea enjoyed such success, however, that beginning in summer 1942 a series of regular revues was staged. These were perhaps the most important musical events in the ghetto. Under the artistic supervision of the theatre director Israel Segal, four revue programmes were put on between mid-1942 and September 1943, each with numerous performances. Although probably no more unified in conception than the initial programmes, these revues consisted primarily of newly composed Yiddish songs, and tackled a variety of subjects related to ghetto life.

The most important people involved in the creation of the revues were Kasriel Broydo, Mishe Veksler, and Leyb Rozental. In his early thirties at the outbreak of war, Broydo was a well-known writer, actor, and director in Jewish Vilna. He became responsible for putting together most of the revues staged in the ghetto. Nine years his junior, Leyb Rozental was after Broydo the most prolific writer of revue texts; many of his songs were written for and performed by his sister Khayele. The composer Mishe Veksler provided music to many of Broydo and Rozental's texts, and also conducted the theatre's resident orchestra. The first revue, called *Korene yorn un vey tsu di teg* (Days of corn and days of woe),[40] had its first performance in June or July 1942. The second, *Men ken gornisht visn* (You can never know), was staged in October of that year. Some time elapsed before the third revue, *Peshe fun Reshe* (Peshe from Rzesza), was first performed in June 1943, and *Moyshe halt zikh* (Moyshe, hold on), the fourth and final revue, began its run shortly before the liquidation of the ghetto in September 1943.

The theatre's opening concert, which was also the first performance of any kind in the ghetto, was organized under the sponsorship of the Ghetto Police and its head, Jacob Gens. From the time that the idea for the theatre was suggested by Viskind early in January 1942, it met with considerable opposition. Writing in his diary the day before the concert, Kruk registered his

---

[39] Sutzkever, *Fun Vilner geto*, 105.

[40] The title was a poignant play on the phrase 'Korene yorn un vaytsene teg' (Days of corn and days of wheat).

disgust at the decision to go ahead with it: while he accepted the fact that other ghettos organized cultural activities, the recent experiences that had befallen the Vilna community—the *Aktionen* had ended barely a month earlier—made them entirely inappropriate. What infuriated him further was the elite complexion of the audience: along with members of the ghetto police and the Judenrat, who were to make up the bulk of the guests, several Nazi officers were to be invited (he even noted with sarcasm that the singer Lyube Levitski had prepared some German songs in case they were demanded). That these people should be celebrating while the remainder of the ghetto was in mourning struck him as immoral and offensive. Angrily, he wrote: 'Oyf a besalmen makht men nisht teater' (One does not stage theatre in a cemetery). The socialist *Bund*, of which Kruk was a prominent member, decided along with several other political groups to boycott the concert, and pamphlets were distributed throughout the ghetto inscribed with this slogan. However, these were removed soon after by a specially deployed police contingent.[41]

The concert was opened by Deputy Police Chief Joseph Glazman with a semi-apology: a memorial tribute to the approximately 34,000 victims that had been killed in the previous months. Observers sent to see whether the mourning of the ghetto was violated reported that the concert was sensitively organized, and in no way insulting to the community's feelings. Dr Lazar Epstein, who had previously expressed in his diary the fear that the evening would be a scandal, remarked instead that 'people laughed and cried. They cast off the depression that had been weighing on their spirits.'[42]

Kruk seems also to have been placated somewhat by the fact that the concert's takings were donated to one of the ghetto welfare organizations. He noted that a sign had been hung at the entrance to the hall reading: 'Zol ayn hungeriker in geto nisht zayn' (There should not be even one hungry person in the ghetto). He reported the concert a success, and although he complained on several further occasions about the offensiveness of the theatre programmes, he gradually came to accept them, if somewhat begrudgingly. Those who had initially opposed the theatre also evidently saw no value in raising further protest, for although the second concert on 25 January was attended by German and Lithuanian dignitaries, among them well-known murderers of Vilna Jewry, no public objection was raised.[43]

[41] Herman Kruk, *Togbukh fun Vilner geto* (New York, 1961), 136.
[42] Cited in Beinfeld, 'Cultural Life', pp. xxiii–iv.
[43] Dworzecki, *Yerushalayim de-Lita*, 248–9; Kruk, *Togbukh*, 146; Sutzkever, *Fun Vilner geto*, 88.

The concerts in fact soon found widespread acceptance among the ghetto population, and the theatre became an important social meeting place. On 8 March 1942, even Kruk conceded:

But life vanquishes all. Again life is pulsating in the Vilna Ghetto. From under the cover of Ponary there emerges a life striving for a better tomorrow. The previously boycotted concerts are gaining acceptance. The halls are crowded. The soirees of the literary association are attended by capacity audiences.[44]

The first concerts took place in the hall of the former Yiddish secondary school on 6 Rudnicka Street, where the Judenrat had its offices. Owing to the increasing demand, however, this venue was soon felt to be inadequate, and the former small municipal hall on Konska Street was renovated for the purpose of creating an official ghetto theatre. The opening of the second theatre took place on 26 April 1942 under the sponsorship of the Judenrat's Cultural Department. Once again, the audience was largely made up of Judenrat members and police officers.[45]

Performances in the theatre were controlled by the Judenrat and its Police Department from the outset. The consequence of this in the first few months, as we have seen, was that it was for the most part the ghetto elite that was able to enjoy them. On several occasions between January and April 1942, Kruk reported concerts, revues, and theatre pieces staged for the benefit of the police, and sometimes for the German authorities.[46]

However, the theatre soon proved useful to the Judenrat in ways pertaining to the general population as well. From the end of December 1941, when the ghetto had begun to settle into a period of relative stability, the Council had adopted a policy of 'work for life', maintaining that the inmates' continued productivity would prolong the ghetto's existence, and subsequently enhance their prospects for survival.[47] At a public address on 15 July 1942, Gens—who

---

[44] Kruk, 'Diary', 24.

[45] Ibid. 33–4; Trunk, *Judenrat*, 226; Gutman (ed.), *Encyclopedia*, 1572.

[46] Kruk, *Togbukh*, 221, 239, 246.

[47] Some sources suggest that the need for Jewish labour at this point was a genuine one. In a document dated 1 Dec. 1941, the Commander of Einsatzkommando 3 Karl Jäger confirmed that all Lithuanian Jews had been eliminated 'apart from working Jews and their families'. He also noted: 'I wanted to eliminate the working Jews and their families as well, but the Civil Administration (Reichskommissar) and the Wehrmacht attacked me most sharply and issued a prohibition against having these Jews and their families shot.' Arad, Gutman, and Margaliot, *Documents on the Holocaust*, 398. The continuing conflict between the need for labour and the racist political goals of the regime make this a more complicated story, however. For a discussion of the factors that led ghetto leaders to employ the 'work-for-life' strategy, and the many struggles—between local and national authorities, on ideological and economic grounds—that marked the development of Nazi policy on this matter, see Christopher R. Browning, *Nazi Policy, Jewish Workers, German Killers* (Cambridge, 2000), 58–88. According to Browning, 'Jewish leaders were not deluded in believing

had now been appointed to the head of the Judenrat in addition to his position as Chief of Police—declared: 'The basis of existence in the ghetto is *work, discipline and order.* Every resident of the ghetto who is capable of work is a pillar on which our existence rests' (emphasis in original).[48] The importance of the policy and its underlying reasoning were revealed in a June 1943 article published in Gens's mouthpiece, *Geto Yedies* (Ghetto News):[49]

The most remarkable new development in the life of the ghetto is the growth of the ghetto industry. Our industry was still on a very small scale last year and today it has become the main source of employment in the ghetto. About 3,000 persons now work in ghetto industries and efforts are being made to increase this number to 4,000 and even 5,000. Both in the ghetto industries and in the work in small units we have been obliged to prove that, contrary to the accepted view that we will not succeed in any craft, we have in fact proved very efficient and they cannot find a replacement for us. Under the present war conditions the work in general and the work for the Wehrmacht in particular are absolutely the need of the hour. It is a fact, the Head of the Ghetto said, among other things, that the clouds of recent days have begun to be scattered, and economic factors alone influence this issue. Because of this we are obliged, and in the future as well, not to drop away from the working plan.[50]

During his tenure, Gens sought constantly to increase the numbers of those in employment, and by April 1943 more than 10,000 Jewish labourers were counted. Most worked in factories outside the ghetto, primarily in the heavy timber and metal industries. Within the ghetto, about 3,000 worked in workshops and light industry. Gens's commitment to this policy made him a controversial figure, not least with regard to his willingness to hand over 'undesirables' such as criminals, the old, and the ill in order to save those capable of working.[51]

Gens also soon realized that the theatre could play an important role in furthering the 'work for life' agenda, much as it was doing for Chaim

---

that many local German authorities had a strong interest in the productive exploitation of Jewish labor'; they were mistaken, however, in the desperate hope that the vested interests of these local authorities could ultimately save a remnant of the community.

[48] Arad, Gutman, and Margaliot, *Documents on the Holocaust*, 438.

[49] *Geto Yedies* was the Judenrat newspaper, a Yiddish-language bulletin that appeared weekly on Sundays, beginning in Sept. 1942, until the final phase of the ghetto's existence. It was distributed among ghetto institutions and posted on public billboards. Reports were included about ghetto events, places of employment, cultural life, health, education, and social welfare; notices from the ghetto administration were also included. Shmerke Kaczerginski, *Khurbn Vilne* (New York, 1947), 331–2; Arad, *Ghetto in Flames*, 331.

[50] Arad, Gutman, and Margaliot, *Documents on the Holocaust*, 455–6.

[51] Gutman (ed.), *Encyclopedia*, 555–6; Yahil, *The Holocaust*, 445; Arad, *Ghetto in Flames*, 159–60; Dawidowicz, *The War against the Jews*, 350.

Rumkowski in Łódź.[52] On several occasions, he took the opportunity to present speeches after concerts. He also occasionally incorporated his propaganda about the value of work into the performances themselves. An article printed in *Geto Yedies* on 11 October 1942 about the revue *Men ken gornisht visn* indicated that at least one number was explicitly intended to emphasize the importance of productivity.[53] In October 1942, a series of Sunday concerts was instituted for workers who could not attend performances during the week. This was on the initiative of David Kaplan-Kaplanski, a well-known businessman in the ghetto and a close affiliate of Gens. The programmes, held at the theatre, usually consisted of an introductory address by Kaplan-Kaplanski, a lecture on a cultural theme, and recitations or singing in Hebrew and Yiddish.[54]

In a public address on 15 January 1943 commemorating the first anniversary of the theatre, Gens justified his continued support for the institution, and presented his conception of its role in the community:

Last year they said that the theatre was just a fad of mine. 'Gens is amusing himself.' A year has passed and what do we see? It was not just a fad of Gens. It was a vital necessity... For the first time in the history of Vilna we were able to get a curriculum of studies that was all Jewish. A big Jewish Writers' association, big children's homes, a big Day Home, a wide Jewish life. Our care for children has reached a level never seen before in the Jewish life of Vilna. Our spiritual life reaches high, and we have already held a literary competition. A musical competition will be held in another few weeks. All this was achieved by artists who mounted the stage. How did the idea come up? Simply to give people the opportunity to escape from the reality of the ghetto for a few hours. This we achieved. These are dark and hard days. Our body is in the ghetto but our spirit has not been enslaved. Our body knows work and

---

[52] The relationship of the Łódź Judenrat to music raises interesting issues in parallel to the case of Vilna, although its context is distinct. Łódź had a wide-ranging and active musical life, which included an orchestra, several choruses, the revue-theatre Avant-Garde, a children's theatre, as well as many solo performers. Cultural activities initially developed on public initiative, but in early 1941, independent cultural institutions were abolished by the Judenrat chairman Rumkowski, and all cultural work subsequently came under his strict supervision. On 1 Mar. 1941 the official House of Culture was inaugurated, and it was here that both symphony concerts and revues were presented. Rumkowski frequently used performances there as a platform for delivering political speeches. The extent of Rumkowski's control over cultural life has serious implications when it comes to the interpretation of music's functions. Programmes had to pass his rigid censorship: entire shows were rarely permitted to be performed, and unwelcome political criticism could result in a venue being closed down. In this sense, it is likely that officially sanctioned musical activities aided in the larger deceptive maintenance of order for which Rumkowski has been retrospectively condemned. They were not a place for challenging commentary on the internal political workings of the ghetto, let alone the victims' attitudes towards their oppressors. Rather, they seem on the whole to have provided 'politically correct' entertainment, as well as a forum for Rumkowski's own agendas.

[53] Kruk, *Togbukh*, 559–60, 368–9.

[54] Dworzecki, *Yerushalayim de-Lita*, 244.

discipline today because this maintains the body. The spirit knows of tasks that are harder. Before the first concert they said that a concert must not be held in a graveyard. That is true, but the whole of life is now a graveyard. Heaven forbid that we should let our spirit collapse. We must be strong in spirit and in body.[55]

The theatre performances were certainly intended by Gens to comfort the population, and to allow them to escape temporarily from the ghetto reality. However, his motives were also more pragmatic than his speech suggested. Because they could calm ghetto audiences, performances were a way of ensuring greater manageability and enhanced productivity. They also helped to discourage the desire for active resistance, and to promote instead the value of emotional fortitude. There are numerous indications among contemporary writings that Gens's support for and frequent initiation of cultural activities stemmed directly from this objective. In mid-November 1942, for example, rumours had been spreading in the ghetto causing widespread fear and alarm. Kruk reported that many people had begun to sleep, fully clothed, in the *malines* (hideouts). In order to combat this situation, Gens ordered the arrest of those believed to have spread the rumours. In addition, he ordered that theatre performances be staged in order to divert and reassure the population. With his usual caustic disdain for Gens and his policies, Kruk responded: 'In sum, one is amused in these days of woe.'[56]

Gens was by no means as heavy-handed in his policies as was Rumkowski. In Łódź, Rumkowski's workshops were some of the most important sites of cultural activity, particularly after 1942 when the first mass deportations to Chełmno took place. Revues that included lively sketches and songs about life in the workplace were performed. Flam collected at least two songs from the factories that seem to have served explicitly propagandistic aims, expressing enthusiasm about the daily labour that people were expected to perform, and thanking the 'President' for supporting their activities.[57] While Gens only presented speeches in the theatre on occasion, Rumkowski spoke at the conclusion of almost all concerts performed at the House of Culture; he also censored public events, and frequently banned songs that were too open in their descriptions of Nazi crimes or the despair of the Jewish victims.[58] Although most of the Vilna theatre songs did not make any mention of the perpetrators of the crimes, they did confront some of the more difficult social

---

[55] Arad, Gutman, and Margaliot, *Documents on the Holocaust*, 449–50.
[56] Kruk, 'Diary', 45–6; Gwynne Schrire, *In Sacred Memory: Recollections of the Holocaust by Survivors Living in Cape Town* (Cape Town, 1995), 102.
[57] Flam, *Singing for Survival*, 26, 162–6.
[58] Kaczerginski and Leivick, 93.

and emotional aspects of life in the ghetto, without Gens's objection. What principally concerned the head of the Judenrat was the defiant attitude, associated primarily with the FPO, that promoted active resistance as the only viable response to the situation. This attitude threatened to compromise his 'work for life' policy, and he sought to combat it on all fronts.

Thus, while many of the theatre songs dealt directly with the reality that the ghetto inmates were facing, they also promoted approaches and responses that accorded with Judenrat attitudes. In some cases, these were openly advocated. Broydo's 'Es shlogt di sho' (The hour strikes), for example, in some ways mirrors the partisan songs in its optimistic text, and particularly in its march-like melody (see Ex. 2.5). However, the writer qualified his affirmative 'mir zaynen do' not with incitement to action, but with the suggestion that hope and *patience* would ultimately bring the hour of victory:

> Es shlogt di sho,
> Mir zaynen do,
> Mir kukn in di vaytn.
> S'vert der himl vider blo,
> S'kumen naye tsaytn.
> Un khotsh dervayl iz fintser-shtok,
> Vartn mir geduldik,
> Es kumt der tog, es shlogt di sho—
> Dan falt der, ver s'iz shuldik.[59]

> The hour strikes,
> We are here,
> We look into the distance.
> The sky becomes blue again,
> New times are coming.
> And though it is pitch dark now,
> We wait patiently,
> The day will come, the hour strikes—
> Then he who is guilty will fall.

Other songs promote this ideology in less explicit ways. Some approach ghetto life with light-hearted satire and humour, or make light of difficult issues, perhaps as a way of diverting temporarily from the gravity of the situation. Some suggest that a strong sense of character and a confident attitude will help people to confront adversity. But the predominant sentiment among the songs is one of acceptance, whether despairing and resigned or cheerful and light-hearted.

---

[59] Kaczerginski and Leivick, 354.

Ex. 2.5. 'Es shlogt di sho'. Kaczerginski and Leivick, 429

The darker sides of ghetto life were confronted more frequently in the earlier revues than in the later ones. Even here, though, descriptions of what people were experiencing were usually mild, and sometimes made only vague reference to the ghetto itself. 'Es vet zikh fun tsvaygl tsebliyen a boym' (From a twig will grow a tree), written by Broydo and composed by Yankl Trupyanski, was performed as part of the first revue, first as the introduction and later in the finale (see Ex. 2.6). It is typical of its type in the way it approaches ghetto life:

> Vi shver s'iz tsu gloybn—
> Farbay aza vinter
> Farnuret in shmates un kelt.
> A shtral hot tseshmoltsn
> Dem ayz fun mayn fentster,

Ex. 2.6. 'Es vet zikh fun tsvaygl tsebliyen a boym'. Kaczerginski and Leivick, 368

Gebrakht a gerus fun der velt.
A velt hot tseblit zikh
Mit vaysinkn tsvit,
Un feygelekh hobn
Getsvitshert a lid.
  Nor bay undz iz
  Gro un fintster,
  S'hengt der umet oyf di vent,
  Varft di zun undz karge shtraln—
  Klaybn mir zey mit di hent.
  Varemt undz di shpits fingerlekh on,
  Trogn mir aheym shtralekhlekh zun,
  Un es vert undz epes gringer,
  S'vilt zikh zingen, shpringen fray.

A vintele hot zikh
Farganevet durkh shpares,
A sod ayngeroymt mir derbay:
Es hot zikh haynt hinter
Dem hiltsernem parkan
Tsevaksn der roziker may.
Un vintele zogt,
Az di grezelekh grin
Zey shikn grusn
Un rufn ahin.
   Nor bay undz iz . . .

Avek iz der tate
In shtot oyf der arbet,
Er muz azoy vayt nebekh geyn,
Er vet mir haynt brengen
A frishinkn tsvaygl
Mit bletelekh grininke sheyn.
Nu, vet es in reyninkn vaserl shteyn
Un s'vet zikh fun tsvaygl tsebliyen a boym.
   Nor bay undz iz . . . [60]

How difficult it is to believe—
That such a winter is past
Wrapped in rags and cold.
A ray has melted
The ice from my window,
Brought a greeting from the world.
A world blossomed
In white bloom,
And birds twittered a song.
   Only with us
   It is grey and dark,
   Misery hangs on the walls,
   The sun throws us meagre rays—
   We gather them with our hands.
   They warm up our fingertips,
   We carry home little rays of sun,
   And it becomes somewhat easier for us,
   We want to sing, jump freely.

A little wind
Sneaked through crevices,

---

[60] Kaczerginski and Leivick, 28–9.

And whispered a secret to me:
Today, behind
the wooden fence
The rosy May grew freely.
And the little wind says
That the little green grasses
Send greetings
And beckon.
　　Only with us...
Father has gone
To work in town,
He has to go so far, poor thing.
Today he is going to bring me
A fresh little twig
With beautiful green leaves.
So, it will stand in clean water
And from a twig will grow a tree.
　　Only with us...

Broydo's lyrics characterize the ghetto by juxtaposing it with the outside. While the world beyond 'the wooden fence' is a place of freshness and natural beauty, the inside remains cold, gloomy, and dark. Trupyanski reinforced the starkness of the contrast by setting the verses in a lively 6/8 metre, and the chorus in a more sombre 4/4. Songs such as Rozental's 'Shotns' (Shadows), Broydo's 'Bay undz iz shtendik fintster' (It is always dark with us), and his 'Es benkt zikh' (Longing), performed in the first and second revues, similarly describe the ghetto's feeling of aloneness and isolation from the world, depicting 'withering' people enclosed in narrow rooms, and a world enshrouded in endless fog and night.[61]

The use of natural imagery in these songs was a common way of conveying the ghetto atmosphere: the moon is often 'pale', flowers 'withering', and the sun's rays 'meagre'. But the theatre songs seldom stray into the perilous territory of Glezer's 'Es iz geven a zumertog', with its explicit images of death and destruction, and its intensely pained sentiment. Instead, they often conform to a model not unlike that of 'Es vet zikh fun tsvaygl': descriptions (of varying length) of the gloominess in the ghetto, concluding with verses that are more hopeful and encouraging. This brand of optimism presented consolation in the fact that things would not always be this way; that 'one day', this terrible time would come to an end. Like Broydo's twig 'with beautiful green leaves', many of the theatre songs suggest that the hope

---

[61] Kaczerginski and Leivick, 5, 50, 63.

of a better future might in time grow beyond the grey and gloomy ghetto into something big and strong.

As life in the ghetto grew increasingly fraught, the revues became more encouraging and optimistic. As elsewhere, these shifts bore a direct relationship to the inhabitants' successive phases of shock and adaptation: shock, experienced immediately after violent events, was often expressed through direct description; adaptation was revealed in the gradual return to defensive coping strategies. As conditions worsened, the need for hope and solace unsurprisingly grew stronger. *Peshe fun Reshe* was staged in June 1943, at a time when many of the labour camps on the outskirts of Vilna were being liquidated, and some of the inmates sent back into the ghetto (Rzesza was one of these camps). The title song is the defiantly cheerful story of a girl who, despite being left homeless and lonely, refuses to allow her spirit to be broken. Theatre audiences enjoyed several more uplifting songs about the courageous and feisty ghetto children, popular among them 'Fun Kolkhoz bin ikh' (I am from Kolkhoz), 'Dos transport-yingl' (The transport boy), and 'Yisrolik', a song about an orphaned cigarette pedlar who greets his dire fate with 'a whistle and a song'.[62]

Moyshe halt zikh, the final revue, was performed during the last phase of the ghetto, when the remaining Jews were being deported to labour camps in Estonia. Broydo himself, who was directing the show, was arrested and deported during its preparation. The revue's title song was sung by a boy concerned for his brother Moyshe, who was terrified that he would not be able to hide or escape from the ghetto. The song is rousing and full of spirit, encouraging Moyshe not to give up, to hold his head high, and to believe that freedom will come.[63] 'Mir shpannen tsum bessern morgn' (We are striding towards a better tomorrow) expresses the hope that a better future is on its way, while Rozental's 'Mir lebn eybik' (We live forever) asserts the tenacity and strength of the Jewish people, especially through times of hardship and suffering.[64]

[62] Ibid. 106, 112, 114, 168. Children were a problem in the ghetto, as many had been orphaned during the *Aktionen*. A boarding home was opened on 8 Mar. 1942, but it failed to solve the problem of the many orphans who roamed the ghetto and were prone to juvenile delinquency (stealing food primarily). Thirteen children were in ghetto jail at the beginning of Mar. 1942, out of a total of forty youngsters who had been caught committing criminal acts. It was decided to seek suitable employment for them, and they were organized in May 1942 by Police Officer Joseph Muszkat in the Transport Brigade, which forms the subject of 'Dos transport-yingl'. Their job was to transport foodstuffs in handcarts from the Judenrat stores to distribution centres—the public kitchen and boarding houses. They were paid for their work in food and clothing. Arad, *Ghetto in Flames*, 319.

[63] Kaczerginski and Leivick, 300.

[64] Ibid. 350, 357.

Apart from consoling people with assurances that a better future was on its way, the theatre revues also fulfilled the simple function of entertainment, distracting people temporarily from the difficulties of the present. 'Rozinkes mit mandlen' (Raisins and almonds), which served as prologue and epilogue to *Moyshe halt zikh*, made explicit that this is what the revues were ultimately intended to achieve:

Nu, zaynen mir shoyn itst baym sof—
A bisele farbrakht,
Un lomir hofn s'nemt an ek
Oykh tsu der shverer nakht.

Mir hobn aykh gegebn haynt
Fun hakl bakl kol,
Alts mit vos mir zaynen raykh,
Gegebn aykh in moyl.

Rozinkes mit mandelekh—
Dos iz dokh gornit shlekht,
Es hoybt dem mut, es shtarkt dem gayst,
Nu zogt, tsi hob ikh rekht.

Rozinkes mit mandelekh,
Tsu gezunt zol es aykh zayn,
A bisele fargesn haynt
Fun undzer layd un payn.[65]

Well, we're now already at the end—
We've enjoyed ourselves a little,
And let's hope that an end will also come
To the difficult night.

Today we have given you
All of everything,
Everything with which we are rich
We gave you, directly.

Raisins and almonds—
It's not bad
It lifts the courage, it strengthens the spirit,
Well tell me, have I got it right.

Raisins and almonds,
May it be good for your health,
To forget a little today
Of our suffering and pain.

---

[65] Kaczerginski and Leivick, 302. Quoted here are four verses from the epilogue.

The phrase 'Raisins and almonds' was a reference to a pre-existing lullaby of the same name, a long-time Yiddish favourite written by Abraham Gold-faden, the founder of the modern Yiddish theatre, as part of his opera *Shulamis* in 1880. The gentle lyrics of the original told of a boy being rocked to sleep; the little goat that stood under his cradle had gone to market and would return with raisins and almonds.[66] Goldfaden's classic was the basis for several ghetto songs. In Łódź, Isaiah Shpigl and David Beyglman wrote 'Nit keyn rozhinkes, nit keyn mandlen' (No raisins, no almonds), a poignant lament about a father who had not gone to market, but left his home and gone away to the end of the world. Another song entitled 'In Slobodker yeshiva' (In the yeshiva of Slobodka), based on Goldfaden's melody, was a desperate plea from Kovno that the memory of Jewish suffering and death in the ghetto be passed on to future generations.[67] The phrase 'Raisins and almonds' itself evoked the richness of Jewish tradition, and the song, used in these new circumstances, highlighted the extent to which Jews had been severed from familiar communal existence. At the same time, particularly in its Vilna manifestation, the allusion to this beloved cultural model encouraged people to take comfort in the legacy of their cultural heritage.

The hope that the theatre songs expressed was not a simple one, and did not stem from a refusal to face the reality at hand. Instead, it was a way of making that reality somewhat easier to bear. The artists and writers hoped that the little enjoyment their audiences derived helped to hearten and uplift them, and allowed them to forget their 'suffering and pain', if only for a while. In addition, however, it is clear that consolation came not only from forgetting the situation temporarily, but also from confronting it and talking about it—even if in muted terms—within a group framework. The revue songs recognized and endorsed a range of emotional responses to the situation: uncertainty, questioning of fate, longing for the past, a sense of separation from the world. Like Glezer's 'Es iz geven a zumertog', they also frequently addressed the communal 'we', rather than depicting the experiences of isolated individuals. The revues thus fulfilled an important role in making people feel part of a group in their suffering. Finally, they tried to provide some meaning and comfort by construing ghetto life in terms of familiar concepts and attitudes. For the most part, this was achieved through the assertion of Jewish identity, and through the assurance that the Jewish nation would endure, as it had done for centuries. The songs

---

[66] The refrain of Goldfaden's song was itself an adaptation of the folksong 'Unter Yankeles vigele' (Under Yankel's cradle). Eleanor Gordon Mlotek (ed.), *Mir trogn a gezang: Favourite Yiddish Songs of our Generation* (New York, 2000), 4–6.

[67] Kaczerginski and Leivick, 93, 306.

encouraged people to take comfort from the fact that the Jewish people had suffered before, and that they had always lived to see the end of their most trying episodes.

Beyond the Theatre

The nature of the Judenrat's influence on the material produced by the revue writers is impossible to determine precisely. While there is no doubt that Gens used the theatre as a means of reassuring the ghetto population, and of disseminating his own propaganda, it is difficult to take an entirely cynical view. We know that people enjoyed the revues, and that performances were often filled to capacity. It is also apparent that the theatre functioned as an important social space, where people came together voluntarily to restore some sense of normality, and to seek emotional support within the community framework. Those who initially opposed the theatre were not silenced into submission, but rather became reconciled to the idea because of the positive response of the population.

Evidence suggests that the revue songwriters had a reasonable degree of freedom to choose which themes they would address. At the same time, however, the context within which their songs would be performed had a perceptible influence on the issues they chose not to tackle. Many of the songs created outside of the theatre framework confronted serious issues such as the fear of death, the crisis of faith, or the devastation of families through death and deportation. They also heeded the historical imperative to record what had been witnessed with a sense of great weight and urgency. Flam identifies a similar trend in Łódź, where songs performed away from Rumkowski's censorship and the demands of the street audience allowed people to express 'helplessness and the lack of hope' more openly.[68] The theatre songs avoided sombre tones of this kind in their portrayals of ghetto life. It remains unclear whether this was a factor of deliberate restriction on Gens's part, or whether it was more a matter of self-censorship on the part of the writers, who genuinely identified with the idea of encouraging and entertaining their audiences. Whatever the case, it is clear that although Gens's control over performance material was far from absolute, most of the events staged at the theatre carried the unmistakable signs of his influence.

The songs that circulated outside the theatre are some of the most harrowing to have emerged from the ghetto. The song 'Aroys iz in Vilne a nayer

---

[68] Flam, *Singing for Survival*, 126.

bafel' (A new command has been issued in Vilna), for example, documents the liquidation of the shtetls around Vilna during spring 1943. Under the pretext of transferring the inhabitants of these shtetls to Vilna and Kovno, the Gestapo loaded them in trains and transported them to Ponar. When they realized what was happening, several of the victims mounted a spontaneous resistance, and even managed to kill some of the guards. The song describes these events in detail, with understated emotion.[69] There were also several new lullabies that witnessed the phenomenon of children left parentless by the *Aktionen*. 'Dremlen feygl oyf di tsvaygn' (Birds doze on the boughs) was dedicated by Lea Rudnitski to a 3-year-old boy whose parents were murdered during the April 1943 deportations (see Ex. 2.7):

> Dremlen feygl oyf di tsvaygn,
> Shlof, mayn tayer kind.
> Bay dayn vigl oyf dayn nare
> Zitst a fremde un zingt:
> Lu-lu, lu-lu, lu.
>
> S'iz dayn vigl vu geshtanen
> Oysgeflokhtn fun glik,
> Un dayn mame, oy dayn mame
> Kumt shoyn keynmol nit tsurik.
> Lu-lu, lu-lu, lu.
>
> Kh'hob gezen dayn tatn loyfn
> Unter hogl fun shteyn,
> Iber felder iz gefloygn
> Zayn faryosemter geveyn.
> Lu-lu, lu-lu, lu.[70]

Ex. 2.7. 'Dremlen feygl oyf di tsvaygn'. Kaczerginski and Leivick, 387

---

[69] Kaczerginski and Leivick, 32–3.
[70] Ibid. 87.

Birds doze on the boughs,
Sleep, my precious child.
By your little cradle, on your cot,
A stranger sits and sings:
   Lu-lu, lu-lu, lu.

Your little cradle stood
As if woven with happiness.
And your mother, oh your mother
Is never coming back.
   Lu-lu, lu-lu, lu.

I saw your father running
Under a hail of stones,
Over fields flew
His orphaned cry.
   Lu-lu, lu-lu, lu.

Lullabies had long been one of the most popular Yiddish song genres, and had formed part of the Yiddish theatre tradition since its inception in the mid-nineteenth century. Many followed a common model: a mother singing to her child about better times to come, and dreaming about her ambitions for him. Often the father would be away, working in town in order to provide food and money for the child's education. In Rudnitski's lullaby, as well as many others created in the ghettos, this model was turned on its head: mother was 'never coming back', and father left the child with only an 'orphaned cry'.[71] 'Dremlen feygl' was based on the Yiddish melody 'S'iz keyn broyt in shtub nishto' (There is no bread at home), written by Izi Charik and composed by Leyb Yampolski. The tension between the subverted text and the familiar, soothing melody serves to emphasize the poignancy and pain of the new reality, where a child has to be lulled to sleep by a stranger.

A series of original ghetto songs was also premiered at the small arts theatre Di Yogenish in Fas (The rush into the barrel, a pun on the name of the philosopher Diogenes), located in a café on Rudnicka Street. This venue seems not to have been subject to Judenrat control, and the material performed there often reflected more searching and distressed responses to the ghetto than were evident in the theatre songs. Some of the most moving among them are Sutzkever's 'Unter dayne vayse shtern' (Under your white

---

[71] Other examples are 'Her, mayn kind, vi vintn brumen' (Listen, my child, how winds roar), and the well-known 'Makh tsi di eygelekh' (Close your little eyes), written by Isaiah Shpigl and David Beyglman in Łódź. In Shpigl's text, 'father will never come home'. Flam notes that when Rumkowski heard a performance of the latter song, he forbade it on the grounds that it 'manifested a pessimistic point of view of his "kingdom"'. Flam, *Singing for Survival*, 148; Kaczerginski and Leivick, 122.

stars) and Kaczerginski's 'Friling' (Spring), written after the death of his wife Barbara in April 1943.

As we have already seen, musical activity occurred not only in the context of the theatre or the partisan groups, but also at the youth club, FLK meetings, and informal gatherings. Some of the newly composed theatre songs continued to circulate at these venues after the revues had finished their runs. Broydo's uplifting 'Efsher vet geshen a nes' (Perhaps a miracle will happen) and 'Men ken gornisht visn' (You can never know) were popularly sung outside the theatre, as were Leyb Rozental's 'Tsu eyns, tsvey, dray' (One, two, three) from the third revue, and a sequence of optimistic songs from *Moyshe halt zikh*.[72]

In addition to the new compositions, people continued to sing melodies that they had sung before the war, and developed new appreciation for old folksongs and Zionist songs. As many fretted over the fate of their beloved city, nostalgic songs such as the famous 'Vilna, Vilna', written by the Americans V. L. Wolfson and A. Olshanetski, became popular. The sentiments expressed in songs like 'Eyli, eyli, lama azavtoni?' (My God, my God, why have you forsaken me?), 'Zamd un shtern' (Sand and stars), and 'Hulyet, hulyet, beyze vintn' (Frolic, frolic, evil winds) acquired fresh meaning and potency. Children's groups gave choral renditions of Bialik's 'Glust zikh mir vaynen' (I want to cry) and Peretz's 'Ale mentshn zaynen brider' (All men are brothers). Both Soviet and Zionist songs were circulated widely, as they provided visions of a more hopeful future. The former had become popular among the youth particularly during the 1939–41 Soviet occupation, and many were translated into Yiddish. Some of the most popular Hebrew songs, sung by the Hebrew choirs, bore titles such as 'Anu ohavim otakh moledet' (We love you, homeland) and 'Y'rushalayim, y'rushalayim!' (Jerusalem, Jerusalem!). Also popular were Mordekhai Gebirtig's prescient elegy 'Es brent' (It is burning),[73] and a series of well-known nostalgic songs and love songs.[74]

Although we have focused on the activities of the FPO separately from those that took place under the auspices of the Judenrat, in reality their relationship was complicated and changeable, and it was impossible to draw a strict line

[72] Dworzecki, *Yerushalayim de-Lita*, 278–9.

[73] Gebirtig wrote this song following a pogrom in the Polish town Przytyk in 1938. It became popular in many of the east European ghettos (Gebirtig was interned in Kraków), and is often performed at commemoration ceremonies. Mlotek and Gottlieb (eds.), *We are Here*, 12–13.

[74] Dworzecki, *Yerushalayim de-Lita*, 281, 245–6; Franz Ruttner, 'Die jiddischen Lieder aus dem Wilnaer Getto', in Florian Freund, Franz Ruttner, and Hans Safrian (eds.), *Ess firt kejn weg zurik: Geschichte und Lieder des Ghettos von Wilna, 1941–1943* (Vienna, 1992), 124.

between them. The partisan Sutzkever, for example, was recruited as the first literary adviser to the theatre. In addition, the Judenrat often subsidized the work of the FLK, in which partisans were prominently represented.[75]

Ultimately, no unified or essential spirit typified the ghetto's cultural life. On one level, pre-war institutions helped to restore familiar coordinates, and to re-establish an environment that gave the community a sense of identity and meaning. At the same time, new musical creations captured the varied flavours of the ghetto, and the new currents that marked its social and political life. They also actively endorsed a range of attitudes and emotional responses, helping people to construct a more communal narrative of the new reality that was engulfing them.

The ghetto after October 1941 was a radically different place than its counterparts in the Generalgouvernement and the Warthegau.[76] The massacres that had preceded its establishment left a largely young and able-bodied but tiny population of around 20,000 people. Almost everyone in the ghetto had lost someone close to them. In addition, after witnessing several waves of *Aktionen* they had a clear sense of what fate could have in store for them. They thus had a more conscious need for optimism and community support. The politicized among them further promoted the importance of morale-raising and active resistance.

We also know that attempts to draw reassurance and stability from musical activity could have only a limited measure of success. For all the constructive roles music played, people ultimately had physical needs that outweighed their emotional ones. Nonetheless, as we have seen, in the ghettos physical and emotional endurance were still relatively closely linked. People were in a mental and physical position to derive benefit from cultural activity, and under the assumption that normal life would one day resume, they devoted energy to sustaining their communities, and particularly to supporting and nurturing the youth.

The camps, by contrast, presented an infinitely harsher set of circumstances. Here, as we shall see, the needs of the body often overwhelmed even the most basic of emotional and moral functions. In the following two chapters, we shall explore the ways in which music surfaced in these establishments, hostile on so many levels to human existence.

---

[75] Kruk, *Togbukh*, 254, 325–6.

[76] Warthegau referred to a territorial administrative unit established in the Polish territories annexed to the Reich in Oct. 1939 (the name originated from the river Warthe). Generalgouvernement (General Government) referred to those parts of Poland that had not been incorporated into the Reich. Gutman (ed.), *Encyclopedia*, 549, 1633.

3

Songs Confront the Past: Life in Sachsenhausen

Biography of the Camp

In April 1936 the Inspector of Concentration Camps and SS Guard Units Theodor Eicke authorized the establishment of the Sachsenhausen concentration camp near Oranienburg, 35 kilometres north of Berlin. Sachsenhausen held a special importance in the camp system, particularly when the Camp Inspectorate was transferred from Berlin to Oranienburg in 1938. In Himmler's 1941 classification, it fell into the same 'moderate' category as camps such as Dachau and Auschwitz I.[1]

The establishment of Sachsenhausen came at a time when the camp system was undergoing fundamental restructuring. The earliest camps, rather than being organized centrally by the new government in Berlin, came under the authority of state agencies or local party groups, and some facilities were totally shielded from state supervision. During a phase of consolidation and expansion from 1934 to 1936, the camp bureaucracy was centralized and structured according to a uniform scheme, and the detention system to some extent standardized. New facilities were constructed that were to remain in place until the end of the war: Sachsenhausen in 1936, Buchenwald in 1937, Flossenbürg and Mauthausen in 1938, and Ravensbrück in 1939. These were to have substantial absorption capacity, and would be used to deploy inmates

---

[1] In Jan. 1941 Himmler gave his approval to the idea that camps be classified according to the categories of prisoners for which they were primarily intended. Living conditions corresponded in degrees of severity to the types of prisoners and the danger they represented to the state. A decree issued by Heydrich on 2 Feb. laid down three categories: the first type of camp was intended for less dangerous prisoners who could easily be made to 'mend their ways'; the second was for those who had longer criminal records, but were still likely to be 'corrected'; and the third was for prisoners considered 'non re-educable'. In practice, living conditions depended on a range of additional factors, and changed markedly during the course of the war. Aharon Weiss, 'Categories of Camps: Their Character and Role in the Execution of the "Final Solution of the Jewish Question" ', in Yisrael Gutman and Avital Saf (eds.), *The Nazi Concentration Camps* (Jerusalem, 1984), 115–32 at 125.

as labourers in SS enterprises. With the exception of Dachau (which from its inception was under state supervision), all of the camps from the first phase were disbanded, and their prisoners relocated.[2]

The first prisoners sent to Sachsenhausen came from Esterwegen, established in 1933 and situated close to the Dutch border in north-west Germany. At the end of June 1936, three prisoners were brought to work in the site office, and building of the camp began with the arrival of a further fifty prisoners on 12 July. Nine hundred additional prisoners had been brought in by the end of September. On 5 November the concentration camp Columbia-Haus (Berlin) was closed down, and the remaining prisoners sent to Sachsenhausen. In 1937, more political prisoners were transported from jails and camps in Germany.[3] While adherents of opposition political movements were the primary targets for 'protective custody' (*Schutzhaft*) in the early years of the regime, the net soon widened to include groups that the SS considered harmful or socially unacceptable: in particular, homosexuals, criminals, Jews, and so-called 'asocials'.[4]

Inequality was manifest in all aspects of life in Sachsenhausen. Depending on their designation (as political, criminal, etc.),[5] nationality, particular skills, camp connections, and additional random factors, inmates received widely varying treatment. Some of the most significant differences were felt in the areas of food rationing and distribution, accommodation, assignment to work commandos, allocation of free time, permission to receive letters and packages, and physical treatment. Although all inmates suffered from the ordeal of incarceration, it is clear that certain groups—primarily Gypsies, Jehovah's Witnesses, homosexuals, and Jews—were targeted with particular brutality. In comparison, German and Scandinavian[6] prisoners were granted

---

[2] Wolfgang Sofsky, *The Order of Terror: The Concentration Camp* (Princeton, 1997), 29–33.

[3] Johannes Tuchel, *Die Inspektion der Konzentrationslager 1938–1945: Das System des Terrors* (Berlin, 1994), 124; Klaus Drobisch and Günther Wieland, *System der NS-Konzentrationslager 1933–1939* (Berlin, 1993), 262.

[4] The growth of the camp's prisoner population was as follows (figures as of the end of December of each year): 1936: 2,000; 1937: 2,523; 1938: 8,309; 1939: 12,168; 1940: 10,577; 1941: 10,709; 1942: 16,577; 1943: 28,224; 1944: 47,709. Georg Wolff, alendarium der Geschichte des KZ Sachsenhausen: Strafverfolgung (Oranienburg, 1987), 5–35.

[5] Inmates were classified according to the nature of the 'crime' that had led to their internment. Often this grouping was haphazard and arbitrary. Different categories of inmates were commonly named according to the coloured triangles they were forced to wear: red for politicals; green for criminals; black for 'asocials', etc.

[6] Norwegians in particular had a wealth of advantages in Sachsenhausen: they were generally not subjected to brutal treatment, remained in regular contact with family and friends, and received well-stocked food parcels from home as well as from the Red Cross throughout the war.

far more freedom to pursue leisure activities, maintain contact with the outside world, and 'organize' necessities.[7]

Inmates were also divided on the basis of an SS-imposed prisoner hierarchy, common to most of the larger camps. The hierarchy was dominated by a system of functionaries, made up almost exclusively of German political and criminal inmates. There were various ranks of functionaries, from *Lagerälteste* (camp leader) to *Blockälteste* (block leader), *Stubenälteste* (room leader), *Kapo* (leader of work commandos), and those working in the *Schreibstube* (administration office). Their positions gave them control over fellow prisoners, contact with the authorities or at least with a wider circle of prisoner functionaries, power to change the composition of blocks and work commandos, and access to useful information and necessities. Responsibilities were carried out in widely diverging ways. Some *Blockälteste*, for example, chose to assist the prisoners under their command with the 'organization' of provisions, or had them assigned to relatively tolerable work commandos; others were more willing to assist the SS in order to ensure their own survival. According to the reports of former inmates, criminals were more likely to fall into the latter category, politicals into the former. The leaning of the prisoner hierarchy towards 'green' or 'red' at any given time depended on the relative numbers from each group in functionary positions, and could significantly alter the nature of life in the camp.

Recreation in Sachsenhausen could generally take place only during free time in the evenings or on Sundays, when most inmates were not required to work. They used this time to talk among themselves, rest, read, perform chores such as cleaning their clothes and shoes, or to engage in creative activities. However, only a tiny minority of prisoners consistently experienced leisure time in this way: opportunities for participation differed substantially according to an inmate's place within the hierarchy. As we shall see, there were also several prerequisite conditions to carrying out musical activities: a measure of free time; a stable physical condition;[8] the leniency of the *Blockälteste* or *Stubenälteste*; and, sometimes, the leniency of the guards.

The most substantial voluntary music-making generally took place within groups united by national, political, or religious affiliation. In this chapter,

---

[7] 'Organizing' was a euphemistic camp term used to describe the means—honest or otherwise—through which inmates obtained all kinds of necessities, ranging from bread and soap to more extravagant items.

[8] While some prisoners had enough access to basic necessities to sustain 'normal' functioning, many were utterly depleted by the constant brutality, cramped living conditions, exhaustion, and starvation.

I explore the activities of German, Czech, Polish, and Jewish prisoners, although Russian and French prisoners also organized musical activities of varying quality and scope.[9]

German Politicals, Czech Artists, and Degrees of Privilege

German political prisoners were a strong and prominent presence in Sachsenhausen. Those who belonged to political organizations in particular came to the camps with several advantages: connections with comrades from all over Germany, professional experience of working in organized groups, and the unifying potential of distinct political goals. Many had by the late 1930s already been incarcerated for several years, and had experience of organizing resistance activity. They shared a common opposition to Nazism, and often a commitment to advancing their political causes from within the camp. The communist prisoner Harry Naujoks, a former *Lagerälteste*, recounted how groups of inmates found secret ways to meet in order to discuss political strategies, or to exchange information about recent international developments.[10] Prisoners such as Gypsies, Jehovah's Witnesses, homosexuals, and Jews—interned for who they were rather than for any ideologies they held—lacked the same kind of group framework for effective communal resistance. If they felt anger towards the regime, they lacked the channels to mobilize their sentiments into action. In addition, and most significantly, they did not

[9] Documentary evidence relating to the activities of Russian and French inmates is relatively scarce. Kulisiewicz documented the work of Russian POW Alexej Sazonow, who wrote three songs before his death in Sachsenhausen in 1942 ('Scharla-Tiuga!', 'Sonia', and 'Hekatombe 1941'): research materials relating to Sachsenhausen (Kulisiewicz Collection), United States Holocaust Memorial Museum Archive (hereafter USHMM), RG-55.003.89. Testimonies have also documented how Russian prisoners performed at international gatherings on the *Appellplatz*: see interview with Bruno Meyer, Akademie der Künste, Berlin, Arbeitlerliedarchiv (hereafter AdK), 6; interview with Helmut Bock, AdK, 37; responses to a questionnaire about cultural activities in Sachsenhausen, AdK, 44; interview with Ernst Harter, AdK, 80. The activities of Soviet prisoners are also briefly discussed in Emil Ackermann and Wolfgang Szepansky (eds.), ... *denn in uns zieht die Hoffnung mit: Lieder, gesungen im Konzentrationslager Sachsenhausen* (Berlin, n.d.), 14–15. Several songs by French inmates are held in the Gedenkstätte und Museum Sachsenhausen, Depot (hereafter GMSD), IV 163; IV 172.

[10] Harry Naujoks, *Mein Leben im KZ Sachsenhausen 1936–1942: Erinnerungen des ehemaligen Lagerältesten* (Cologne, 1987), 45. Naujoks was a boilermaker from Hamburg (b. 1901). He joined the German Communist Party (*Kommunistische Partei Deutschlands*, KPD) in 1919, and was arrested by the Nazis in 1934. After two years and three months in various jails, he was taken to Sachsenhausen, interned there until 1942, and then taken to Flossenbürg. He served as *Lagerälteste* in Sachsenhausen from 1939 until his transfer. His account of his experiences is particularly valuable because of the high office he held: he is able to reveal privileged insights about the inner workings of the camp and the dynamics of the prisoner hierarchy.

have the same access to the influential network of politicals in the prisoner hierarchy, and they were not allowed to assume functionary positions themselves.[11]

The greatest opportunities for music-making in Sachsenhausen were enjoyed by these political prisoners. This was the case in most of the larger camps as well, although in the case of Dachau it concerned German prisoners who were 'prominent' but not necessarily politically affiliated.[12] In addition, organized music-making across the camp spectrum owed its existence, in large part, to the willingness of German political prisoners to help other inmates in the organization of events. Their assistance could be provided in a number of ways: securing instruments or venues, providing information regarding the safest concert times, or simply turning a blind eye to illegal activities. Naujoks's account reveals the extent to which powerful prisoners were able to facilitate musical performances. First, the sheer presence of the *Lagerälteste* would often be enough to make them 'safer' from the SS. He had the power to prevent SS officers from attending an event, and could success-fully persuade them that certain activities were not subversive or threatening. Illegal musical activities among non-political prisoners could usually be held with the knowledge of a political *Blockälteste*, but prisoners under the com-mand of criminal functionaries were more at risk of being given away. Thus inmates who enjoyed relatively little leniency from the SS authorities as far as leisure activities were concerned relied heavily on superior prisoners in the hierarchy.[13]

The prisoners who benefited most in this regard were the 1,200 Czech students who had arrived in Sachsenhausen in November 1939. From the outset, they established close relationships with high-ranking communists in

[11] The gradual internationalization of the camp population after the outbreak of war led to increased social differentiation between nation groups: Germans quickly rose to the top of the pecking order, while non-Aryans—principally Jews, Poles, and Russians—were at the bottom. Sofsky, *The Order of Terror*, 35.

[12] Sonja Seidel has shown, for example, that cultural life in Buchenwald was driven largely by German communist prisoners, who drew on pre-war KPD traditions in the ways they found to adapt music to the camp conditions. Sonja Staar has also shown that several members of resistance organizations were active in Buchenwald's cultural life, among them communist Rudi Arndt. Sonja Seidel, 'Kultur und Kunst im antifaschistischen Widerstandskampf im Konzentrationslager Buchenwald', *Buchenwaldheft*, 18 (1983), 23–40; Sonja Staar, 'Kunst, Widerstand und Lagerkultur: Eine Dokumentation', *Buchenwaldheft*, 27 (1987), 5–79 at 7. See also Guido Fackler, *'Des Lagers Stimme'—Music im KZ: Alltag und Häftlingskultur in den Konzentrationslagern 1933 bis 1936* (Bremen, 2000), 371. On Dachau, see Václav Vlach, cited in Milan Kuna, *Musik an der Grenze des Lebens: Musikerinnen und Musiker aus böhmischen Ländern in nationalsozialistischen Konzentrationslagern und Gefängnissen*, trans. Eliška Nováková (Frankfurt am Main, 1993), 135.

[13] Naujoks, *Mein Leben*, 295–300; Aleksander Kulisiewicz, *Adresse: Sachsenhausen. Literarische Momentaufnahmen aus dem KZ*, ed. Claudia Westermann (Gerlingen, 1997), 19.

the hierarchy, including Naujoks. They were housed in blocks 50, 51, 52, and 53, and 'prominent' prisoners Edgar Bennert, Paul Gmeiner, Christian Mahler, Fritz Meissner, and Martin Schöler were among those assigned as *Blockälteste*.[14] Thanks to these block leaders, the students were able to maintain to some degree their contact with cultural and intellectual life. They pursued energetic artistic activities, were allowed to borrow books from the camp library, and some were placed in work assignments as land surveyors, architects, and doctors.[15]

In January 1940 an outbreak of scarlet fever in the Czech blocks led to the imposition of a quarantine. Because of the persistent recurrence of the disease, the camp command continued the quarantine for several months; the inmates had no contact with the rest of the camp, and their barracks were sealed. Despite the prohibitions, however, Naujoks and several other political prisoners were able to maintain some contact with the students. This period of isolation in fact afforded them remarkable freedom and autonomy, particularly as far as artistic life was concerned. Thanks to the assistance of the politicals, they were able to organize a wide-ranging programme of musical activities, which included numerous formal and informal concerts, and the establishment of three successful ensembles.[16]

The first ensemble, a string quartet, was put together in early 1941 with the help of political functionaries in the *Schreibstube*. The first violinist was the well-known virtuoso Bohumír Červinka; the remaining musicians were Karel Štancl (violin), Jan Škorpík (viola), and the German prisoner Eberhard Schmidt (cello, included in the group because there were no cellists among the Czechs). Instruments were not permitted in the barracks before 1942, but the functionaries helped the students to find ways around the prohibitions.[17] It was arranged that Červinka be allowed to send for his violin from home, and instruments were obtained for the other players. Pieces were specially arranged for performance by František Marušan; later, scores were obtained for works by Beethoven, Brahms, Schumann, Borodin, Grieg, and Dvořák.[18] The first performance took place at Easter 1941 in the delousing barracks, but the quartet's unanticipated popularity meant that larger performance venues had to be organized for subsequent concerts. The group continued to

---

[14] František Marušan, AdK, 49; Wolff, alendarium, 15.
[15] Arnold Weiss-Rüthel, *Nacht und Nebel: Aufzeichnungen aus fünf Jahren Schutzhaft* (Munich, 1946), 73–9.
[16] Karel Štancl, AdK, 46.
[17] Bohumír Červinka, AdK, 77.
[18] Karel Štancl, AdK, 46.

perform for approximately three years, until Škorpík was transferred to another camp.[19]

The second ensemble, which probably only performed in the Czech blocks, was a choir of forty singers established in Block 51 by Marušan. Works by the Czech composers Smetana, Dvořák, Janáček, Křížkovský, Nešvera, and others were arranged for the choir, and the level of performance was apparently high.[20]

The best-known of the ensembles was an eight-voice a cappella group called 'The Sing-Sing Boys', established in block 52 at the initiative of Mirek Pilar.[21] Initially, its repertoire consisted mainly of songs from the pre-war period: dance songs, popular songs from films, folk songs, and in particular the works of jazz composer Jaroslav Ježek. The group's style was jazzy and improvisatory, and its members became well known for being able to imitate the sounds of instruments with their voices. In the course of time the repertoire expanded to include German and Polish dance melodies, as well as songs in Spanish, English, and French.[22]

Performances by 'The Sing-Sing Boys' were frequently attended by German political prisoners. The close connections between the two groups are confirmed by the choir's inclusion in its repertoire of some of the politicals' most popular songs, such as 'Moorsoldatenlied' (Moor soldiers' song), 'Grüne Kolonnen' (Green columns), and 'Die Gedanken sind frei' (Thoughts are free). In a gesture of reciprocity, the politicals also learnt some Czech songs and included them in their concerts. During free time in the evenings and on Sunday afternoons, the Czech singers would go from block to block to perform for the prisoners. They often sang at birthday celebrations, and would occasionally be called in by Naujoks to raise the morale of a particular block.[23] According to Karel Štancl, who sang bass with and later directed 'The Sing-Sing Boys', the group took its work seriously:

[19] Kuna, *Musik an der Grenze*, 258–9; Bohumír Červinka, AdK, 77.

[20] Karel Štancl, AdK, 46; František Marušan, AdK, 49.

[21] Kuna suggests that the name could have been both an allusion to the notorious American Sing Sing prison, and a derivative of the German word 'singen'. Kuna, *Musik an der Grenze*, 126. Another account quotes Pilar as saying that the name was created spontaneously at the premiere performance. The group's name at the time, 'Sängerknaben', was announced in English as the 'Singing Boys'. Someone from the audience shouted out his disapproval, and suggested they call themselves 'Sing-Sing' instead; the new name was then adopted. Wolfgang Muth, 'Musik hinter Stacheldraht: Swing in Ghetto und KZ', in Bernd Polster (ed.), *Swing Heil: Jazz im Nationalsozialismus* (Berlin, 1989), 211–20 at 215.

[22] Muth, 'Musik hinter Stacheldraht', 215. The songbook used by this group was preserved by the former leader of the group, Karel Štancl. A copy is held in AdK, 138.

[23] Wolfgang Szepansky, AdK, 10; responses to a questionnaire about cultural activities in Sachsenhausen, AdK, 42, 44, 45; Karel Štancl, AdK, 46; Bohumír Červinka, AdK, 77.

None of us had studied art professionally, but we were held together by our common fate, and by our common love of music and singing. We also wanted to express our contempt and our resistance towards the bestiality and tedium that surrounded us. We were bound by the endeavour 'to do something' against the monotonous ill-treatment, the sadness and the misery of camp life, to raise ourselves every day over the wall with the barbed wire. I always see us in my mind's eye, the way in which we—bald-headed, dressed in striped rags, in wood-soled shoes with our numbers on our breasts and our trousers—gave gala concerts. It is almost unbelievable what power there was in our singing, and how it helped us to humanize relations in an inhuman milieu and an inhuman time.[24]

For the Czech students, music was a way of affirming connections both to a pre-war national identity, and to a sense of community within the camp. They not only sang the fashionable, youthful songs of their pre-war days, but also—once the quarantine had ended and they could circulate more widely—made gestures towards other national groups. On this point, Štancl emphasized that although music had a certain significance, its prominence in camp life should not be exaggerated. His observation suggests that, like others in his position, he was aware that the opportunity to use music in this way was a privilege denied to most other prisoners. As such, he felt it important to keep in mind the context that allowed them to express themselves, to demonstrate their contempt, and 'to do something' about the events they were witnessing.[25]

German political prisoners shaped the musical life of Sachsenhausen not only in the valuable support they offered other groups, but even more so in the regular musical events they organized themselves. The first gathering to inspire what later became a permanent arrangement was put together by the communist Bernhard Bästlein on Christmas Eve 1936. This was the first time since the establishment of the camp that a large group of political prisoners had met in such a context. Initially intended to be a meeting of KPD comrades from Hamburg, it ultimately attracted a host of members from regional communist groups as well. A short address by Bästlein was followed by enthusiastic singing. Thereafter various occasions, from international remembrance days to birthday celebrations, were used for similar spirit-building sessions.[26]

---

[24] Štancl, cited in Muth, 'Musik hinter Stacheldraht', 215–16.

[25] Karel Štancl, AdK, 46. Regarding the activities of Czech prisoners, see also the discussion of Jan Vala in Kuna, *Musik an der Grenze*, 290–5. Vala was active as a singer in the camp, and was housed in Block 26 with fellow Czechs and veteran German prisoners. He sang not only pre-existing Czech songs, but also some of his own newly composed verses. He also learnt songs in several languages, and visited numerous blocks (including the infirmary) to entertain the inmates.

[26] Wolff, alendarium, 9; Naujoks, *Mein Leben*, 48–9.

Accounts of these musical evenings recur frequently in the testimonial literature.[27] Throughout the time of the camp's existence, inmates arranged regular communal sing-songs or *Schallerabende*, the primary purpose of which was to boost prisoner morale. Evenings would typically begin with a short address, followed by recitation of poems and singing. According to Naujoks, despondency and hopelessness were dangerous in the camp, and those in a position to organize these events hoped to ease prisoners' dispositions by giving them the opportunity to 'switch off' for a few hours. Participatory singing was popular because it was technically accessible to all, did not require preparation, regular practice, or music-reading skills, and did not require instruments or any other incriminating evidence to be hidden away. Naujoks emphasized, however, that only a small minority of Sachsenhausen's prisoners was able to participate in these gatherings.[28]

The *Schallerabende* were explicitly political events, and played an important part in the work of the illegal resistance organization in the camp (run primarily by communists). Political discussion and education could take place in small groups, but song evenings helped to 'awaken and strengthen the power of resistance' within the greater prisoner community. Because of their popularity, the *Schallerabende* also became a way of cementing communal relations. Naujoks wrote about the important *Schallerabend* that took place on 16 April 1939, shortly after the news was received that 1,400 prisoners, including approximately 250 politicals, were to be freed. The occasion was used to secure the bonds between those who were leaving and those who would be coordinating underground activities inside the camp. The first meeting between German and non-German anti-fascists was also

---

[27] Many accounts contain at least some reference to the politicals' communal musical evenings. See e.g. Ackermann and Szepansky, ... *denn in uns zieht die Hoffnung mit*; interview with Karl Schirdewan, AdK, 36; responses to a questionnaire about cultural activities in Sachsenhausen, AdK, 43, 44, 45; Werner Staake, AdK, 47; Kulisiewicz, *Adresse: Sachsenhausen*, 19, 26–8; Fritz Lettow, *Arzt in den Höllen: Erinnerungen an vier Konzentrationslager* (Berlin, 1997), 179; Odd Nansen, *Day after Day* (London, 1949), 444.

[28] Naujoks, *Mein Leben*, 300. Communal singing had long played a role in the activities of communist and social democrat parties in Germany. In the aftermath of the 1848 revolution, hundreds of workers' choral societies were established by amateur musicians, who saw them as a means of strengthening communal sentiment. Although membership of these societies dropped after 1867, when unification began to be realized, they continued to pursue their activities; during the Weimar years, they were still popular. They were overtly political organizations, and their repertoire generally reflected a nationalist, left-wing agenda. It is likely that the prominence of choral singing among political prisoners, not only in Sachsenhausen but in other camps as well, was a direct extension of the long-standing importance choruses held for these political groups. See Richard Harold Bodek, 'We Are the Red Megaphone!: Political Music, Agitprop Theater, Everyday Life and Communist Politics in Berlin during the Weimar Republic' (Ph.D. diss., University of Michigan, 1990), 44, 49.

held during a song evening intended to strengthen international solidarity, at Christmas 1939.[29]

The *Schallerabende* were exceptional in the context of the camps both for the enthusiasm with which they were pursued, and for their sheer scope. However, perhaps their most valuable legacy—also a powerful marker of the influence held by political prisoners—lay in the many songbooks specially created to be used at these evenings. The books, many of which survived the war, began to be created during the Czech student quarantine in January 1940. Taking advantage of the time and relative freedom afforded the students, as well as the existence among them of many artists, Naujoks approached them regarding putting together a songbook. He brought them the texts the politicals had been singing, and asked if they would provide illustrations. Initially, Naujoks had simply envisioned the songbook for himself, but it was admired by so many of the prisoners that more were created.[30]

The songbooks that survive paint a vivid picture of musical life among political prisoners.[31] On average, they were approximately 12 × 10 cm in size; the smallest contained eight songs; the largest contained 150 or more. The plain, checked, or lined notebooks were probably 'organized' by prisoners working in the *Schreibstube*. Although some were neater and more carefully notated than others, prisoners clearly put great effort into creating them. Most were neatly handwritten, with song titles and first letters of songs in decorative script. Some were decorated with colourful shadings and detailed patterned borders; others had elaborate and beautiful illustrations on separate pages. The drawings had diverse subjects: landscapes and houses, ships and planes, tanks, weapons, animals, and images of camp life.

---

[29] Naujoks, *Mein Leben*, 115–16; Wolff, alendarium, 17.

[30] Naujoks, *Mein Leben*, 175.

[31] At least sixteen songbooks related to the activities of German political prisoners in Sachsenhausen have been preserved. The originals of four are in the GMSD: 'Und wenn wir marschieren', III 628; songbook of Emil Wieden, V8; songbook of Gregorz Schulz, III 202; songbook of Joop, 96.00063. A further four are in the Gedenkstätte und Museum Sachsenhausen, Archiv (hereafter GMSA): 'Wo ein Lied erklingt, da laß Dich nieder, Böse Menschen singen keine Lieder', NL 6/72; 'Liederbuch der bündischen Jugend', NL 6/73; 'Ein Lied auf den Lippen', NL1-17-S.1–155; Songbook of Otto Troitzsch, R24/8. The AdK holds one original songbook, published as Günter Morsch (ed.), *Sachsenhausen-Liederbuch: Originalwiedergabe eines illegalen Häftlingsliederbuches aus dem Konzentrationslager Sachsenhausen* (Berlin, 1995); and copies of six additional songbooks, the originals of which are presumably held in private collections: 'Liederbuch aus dem KZ Sachsenhausen', 117; 'Lager-Lieder von Sachsenhausen', 121; 'Das Lagerliederbuch I. Teil' (1940), 125; 'Das Lagerliederbuch I. Teil' (1941), 133; 'Lager-lieder und Lieder die gesungen werden im Schutzhaftlager Sachsenhausen', 140; 'Was wir sangen und singen', 119. A songbook belonging to the prisoner Willy Feiler was published as *Das Lagerliederbuch: Lieder, gesungen, gesammelt und geschrieben im Konzentrationslager Sachsenhausen bei Berlin 1942* (Dortmund, 1983).

The songbooks drew on a repertoire of at least 285 songs, most of which had existed prior to 1936, and had no connection with Sachsenhausen.[32] Many were songs with which prisoners were familiar from school, the military, and particularly workers' youth movements. This makes it clear that, as far as musical activity was concerned, German political prisoners benefited not only from the freedom afforded them by the authorities but also from a long-established tradition of how music could be used in a communal setting. We have already explored how in the ghettos, music often helped inmates to establish continuity with pre-war life, and to sustain elements of their tradition even while its functions and implications were modified. These German political prisoners were among the few groups who were able to effect this process in a comparably substantial way in the camps. The vast majority of their songs had similar and easily identifiable musical qualities: they were strophic, syllabic, and made use of straightforward rhythmic patterns. They also had singable melodies, usually in the diatonic major and with limited ranges, suitable for singing by large groups.

The songs fell under a variety of thematic banners, some of which were indicated in the organization of the books themselves. There were soldiers' songs (emphasizing military victory and group camaraderie), hiking and travel songs, songs of encouragement (although unrelated to the camp, these assumed particular significance), songs glorifying the beauty of youth, love songs, and songs of spring and nature. In contrast to the songs of other prisoner groups, there was a distinct absence of critical texts, no anger or calls for revenge, no mention of the Nazi party, and nothing approaching tragedy or grief. In fact, although their living conditions were arguably the most conducive of any prisoner group to artistic creation, German politicals boasted few original compositions. Considering the purposes the evenings were intended to fulfil, however, the choice of repertoire is not surprising. The songs helped to lift spirits and raise morale, and also to sustain inmates' connections with home and community.

The songbooks also included a number of songs that had been written in the moor camps,[33] other concentration camps, or Sachsenhausen itself. Sachsenhausen had received large transfers of inmates from other camps,

---

[32] Detailed repertoire listing is given in the Appendix, §III.

[33] The term 'Moorlager' (moor camps) refers to the labour camps established from 1933 in the marshy Emsland area of northern Germany, west of Bremen between the Ems River and the Dutch border. Inmates of these camps were to be deployed as labourers to drain the nearby marshes. The best known were Börgermoor and Esterwegen. Prisoners from these camps were later employed to build concentration camps, including Sachsenhausen, to which they were subsequently transferred. See Sofsky, *The Order of Terror*, 30.

particularly in the early years of its establishment, and these men had brought with them many of the new songs they had created. The opening items in the songbooks were almost always drawn from these songs. They included the 'Moorsoldatenlied' (Moor soldiers' song), 'Den Spaten geschultert' (Spades on our shoulders), 'Grüne Kolonnen' (Green columns), 'Esterwegen', 'Wir sind Moorsoldaten' (We are moor soldiers), 'Auf, Jungens, auf!' (Up, boys, up!), 'Sachsenhausenlied' (Sachsenhausen camp song), 'Im Walde von Sachsenhausen' (In the forest of Sachsenhausen), 'Buchenwalder Lagerlied' (Buchenwald camp song), 'Graue Kolonnen' (Grey columns), 'Und wenn wir marschieren' (And when we march), and 'Lichtenburger Lagerlied' (Lichtenburg camp song). Many of these songs were also popularly sung amongst political prisoners in Buchenwald, Ravensbrück, and elsewhere.[34]

The songs were popular for their rousing and encouraging qualities. 'Moorsoldatenlied' and 'Und wenn wir marschieren' in particular assumed the status of unofficial camp hymns, and were often sung at the conclusion of gatherings. Many songs were set to triumphant, cheerful march melodies, and their texts, like 'Grüne Kolonnen' cited below, promoted optimism, comradeship, and solidarity (see Ex. 3.1):

Ex. 3.1. 'Grüne Kolonnen'. Lammel and Hofmeyer (eds.), *Lieder aus den fashistischen Konzentrationslagern*, 21–2

[34] See e.g. Wolfgang Schneider, *Kunst hinter Stacheldraht: Ein Beitrag zur Geschichte des faschistischen Widerstandes* (Leipzig, 1976), 75; Projektgruppe Musik in Konzentrationslagern, *Musik in Konzentrationslagern* (Freiburg, 1992), 67–8, 76.

Was uns auch begegnet hier,
Kameradschaft sei's Panier!
Keinem wirklich gut es geht,
Übt drum Solidarität!
Grüne Kolonnen rücken aus
Bei Sonne, bei Regen und Sturmgebraus.
Und geht dann die Fahrt durch den Stacheldraht,
Kopf hoch, Moorsoldat!...[35]

Whatever we encounter here,
Comradeship be our motto!
Nobody is really fine
So practise solidarity!
Green columns move out
In sun, in rain, and roaring storms.
And when we go through the barbed wire,
Chin up, moor soldier!...

Most of these songs included images of camp life: descriptions of marching columns, forced labour, living conditions, and feelings of isolation or homesickness. However, their descriptions were almost always mild enough to be counterbalanced with encouraging refrains. This is the case in the 'Moorsoldatenlied' (see Ex. 3.2):

Ex. 3.2. 'Moorsoldatenlied'. Lammel and Hofmeyer (eds.), *Lieder*, 18

[35] Inge Lammel and Günter Hofmeyer (eds.), *Lieder aus den faschistischen Konzentrationslagern* (Leipzig, 1962), 21–2. Quoted here is the first verse of 'Grüne Kolonnen'.

Wohin auch das Auge blicket,
Moor und Heide nur ringsum.
Vogelsang uns nicht erquicket,
Eichen stehen kahl und krumm.
  Wir sind die Moorsoldaten
  Und ziehen mit dem Spaten
  Ins Moor!

Hier in dieser öden Heide
Ist das Lager aufgebaut,
Wo wir fern von jeder Freude
Hinter Stacheldraht verstaut.
  Wir sind die Moorsoldaten...

  ...
Doch für uns gibt es kein Klagen,
Ewig kann's nicht Winter sein.
Einmal werden froh wir sagen:
Heimat, du bist wieder mein.
  Dann ziehn die Moorsoldaten
  Nicht mehr mit dem Spaten
  Ins Moor![36]

Wherever the eye looks
All around only moor and heath.
No birdsong to comfort us,
Oaks stand bare and crooked.
  We are the moor soldiers,
  And march with our spades
  Into the moor!

Here on this barren heath
The camp is built,
Where, far from any joy,
We are packed behind barbed wire.
  We are the moor soldiers...

  ...
But there is no complaining for us,
It can't be winter for ever.
One day we will cheerfully say:
My country, you are mine again.
  Then the moor soldiers
  Will *no* longer march with their spades
  Into the moor!

---

[36] Inge Lammel and Günter Hofmeyer (eds.), *Lieder*, 14–15, 18. Quoted here are the first, second, and final verses of the 'Moorsoldatenlied'.

Most of the new song texts were based on existing melodies, and prisoners often drew on songs with particular political associations. 'Grüne Kolonnen', for example, was based on 'Arbeitsmann, du lebst in Not' (Worker, you live in hardship), one of the most popular workers' songs of the 1920s and 1930s, made famous by the agitprop troupe 'Kolonne Links'. Other new camp songs were based on workers' songs that were themselves popular items in the repertoire. 'Graue Kolonnen' was a modification of 'Wilde Gesellen' (Wild fellows), changing the verses but retaining the original encouraging refrain 'Uns geht die Sonne nicht unter' (The sun will not go down for us). Similarly, unmodified old workers' songs such as 'Wir sind des Geyers schwarze Haufen' (We are Geyer's black troops), 'Fichtemarsch' (Fichte march, named after the philosopher Johann Gottlieb Fichte), 'Die Gedanken sind frei' (Thoughts are free), and 'Seeräuberlied' (Pirates' song) acquired new associations of defiance and resistance. These well-known songs became some of the most popular in the repertoire.[37]

One of the most important newly created songs, the 'Sachsenhausenlied' (see Ex. 3.3), was based on the workers' melody 'Die Bauern wollten Freie sein' (The peasants want to be free). In the winter of 1936/7 the camp commandant Weissenborn decided that Sachsenhausen needed its own official song, and the communist inmates Bästlein, Karl Wloch, and Karl Fischer obliged by writing the following text:

> Wir schreiten fest im gleichen Schritt,
> Wir trotzen Not und Sorgen
> Denn in uns zieht die Hoffnung mit
> Auf Freiheit und das Morgen.

Ex. 3.3. 'Sachsenhausenlied'. Lammel and Hofmeyer (eds.), *Lieder*, 51

[37] Ackermann and Szepansky,... *denn in uns zieht die Hoffnung mit*, 6–7, 20–1; Inge Lammel, 'Das Sachsenhausen-Liederbuch', in Morsch (ed.), *Sachsenhausen-Liederbuch*, 18.

Was hinter uns, ist abgetan,
Gewesen und verklungen.
Die Zukunft will den ganzen Mann,
Ihr sei unser Lied gesungen.

Aus Esterwegen zogen wir leicht,
Es liegt verlassen im Moore,
Doch bald war Sachsenhausen erreicht—
Es schlossen sich wieder die Tore.

Wir schaffen hinter Stacheldraht
Mit Schwielen an den Händen
Und packen zu und werden hart,
Die Arbeit will nicht enden.

So mancher kommt, kaum einer geht,
Es gehen Mond' und Jahre,
Und bis das ganze Lager steht,
Hat mancher graue Haare.

Das Leben lockt hinter Drahtverhau,
Wir möchten's mit Händen greifen,
Dann werden unsre Kehlen rauh
Und die Gedanken schweifen.

Wir schreiten fest im gleichen Schritt,
Wir trotzen Not und Sorgen,
Denn in uns zieht die Hoffnung mit
Auf Freiheit und das Morgen.[38]

We march firmly with equal strides,
We defy hardship and worries
Because we carry in us the hope
Of freedom and the morrow.

What is behind us is dismissed,
Been and faded away.
The future requires man to give all of himself,
Let's devote our song to it.

We marched easily out of Esterwegen,
It lies deserted in the moors,
But soon we reached Sachsenhausen—
The gates were closed again.

We labour behind barbed wire
With callused hands
And knuckle down and become hard,
The work won't end.

---

[38] Lammel and Hofmeyer (eds.), *Lieder*, 51–2.

Many arrive, hardly any go,
Months and years go by,
And by the time the entire camp is built up,
Some will have grey hair.

Life beckons beyond the wire fence,
We want to grab it with our hands,
Then our throats become raw
And our thoughts wander.

We march firmly with equal strides,
We defy hardship and worries
Because we carry in us the hope
Of freedom and the morrow.

The authors concurred that the song should be used as a means of strengthening the unity of the prisoners. After the war, Wloch remarked that it aptly reflected 'the spirit of the anti-fascists' in its sense of optimism, determination to 'defy hardship', and hope for the future. Although it was impossible to misinterpret this spirit, he claimed that the SS were 'too stupid' to understand that it might be used in this way, and Weissenborn initially raised no objection to it. As Hans-Ludger Kreuzheck has shown, however, the SS at many of the larger camps deliberately used official songs of this kind—most of which reflected a similar spirit of defiance and longing for freedom—as a tool for demonstrating their control over the inmates, to mock them as they marched to and from work, or at forced singing sessions.[39]

Wloch also observed that 'Die Bauern wollten Freie sein' was chosen deliberately in a spirit of resistance as a basis for the text. For Bästlein, it met the authors' requirements by being a melody that was well known and had 'fighting character' (*Kampfcharakter*), but would nonetheless not be recognized as a workers' song by the SS. However, once again the choice was less subversive than the authors might have thought. In fact, this and many other songs had ceased to be the exclusive store of left-wing political groups long before the establishment of the camps, and had appeared in Nazi publications from the 1930s onwards.[40]

---

[39] Wloch, cited ibid. 53; Hans-Ludger Kreuzheck, ' "Unsere Kuhle": Musik im KZ Neuengamme und in anderen Lagern', in Peter Peterson (ed.), *Zündende Lieder, verbrannte Musik: Folgen des Nationalsozialismus für Hamburger Musiker und Musikerinnen* (Hamburg, 1988), 55–68 at 61–4. Eckhard John has also suggested that these songs were part of a control tactic used by the SS, who wanted prisoners to continue to harbour the illusion that freedom would come. Eckhard John, 'Musik und Konzentrationslager: Eine Annäherung', *Archiv für Musikwissenschaft*, 48 (1991), 1–36 at 30.

[40] 'Die Bauern wollten Freie sein' appeared in these official Hitlerjugend songbooks: Hugo W. Schmidt (ed.), *Uns geht die Sonne nicht unter: Lieder der Hitler-Jugend* (Cologne, 1934); and

Some of the overlap in repertoire is easily explained by the fact that hostile political groups drew on a common core of eighteenth- and nineteenth-century German folk songs. However, as the historian Vernon Lidtke has demonstrated, the Nazis also deliberately appropriated songs by social democrats and communists during the 1930s in an attempt both to undermine their political rivals and to attract workers to their ranks.[41] Some of the most popular songs among political prisoners were appearing in Nazi songbooks around the same time as they were being sung in the camps, such as 'Und wenn wir marschieren', 'Wir sind des Geyers schwarze Haufen', 'Wilde Gesellen', 'Die Gedanken sind frei', 'Wir sind jung' (We are young), 'Brüder, zur Sonne, zur Freiheit' (Brothers, to the sun, to freedom), 'Wann wir schreiten Seit an Seit' (When we march side by side), and 'Wenn die Arbeitszeit zu Ende' (When work has ended). Most required only minor modifications to conform with Nazi ideology; others were appropriated whole. The first verse of 'Brüder, zur Sonne, zur Freiheit', for example, appeared in all Nazi versions exactly as it did in the politicals' songbooks. The melody of the same song was also used as a basis for the popular Nazi ditty 'Brüder in Zechen und Gruben' (Brothers in the pits and mines). 'Wann wir schreiten' had long since been sung by Nazis in its original form.[42]

The Nazi habit of appropriating songs for their own purposes continued during the war years. Both political and folk songs were similarly 'Nazified' in what was probably an attempt to rid them of their positive communal associations and political potency. At forced singing exercises and other

Reichsjugendführung (ed.), *Unser Liederbuch: Lieder der Hitler-Jugend* (Munich, 1939); as well as in Thilo Scheller (ed.), *Singend wollen wir marschieren: Liederbuch des Reichsarbeitsdienstes* (Potsdam, n.d.). Gisela Probst-Effah has suggested that the authors of the 'Sachsenhausenlied' were in fact aware that this song had been appropriated by the Nazis, and that they had nonetheless chosen to use it in order to camouflage the content of the new text. However, apart from their above-cited remarks to the contrary, the fact that this was intended to be an official song, and thus openly sung by the prisoners, makes this explanation unlikely. Gisela Probst-Effah, 'Das Lied im NS-Widerstand: Ein Beitrag zur Rolle der Musik in den nationalsozialistischen Konzentrationslagern', *Musikpädagogische Forschung*, 9 (1989), 79–89 at 82.

[41] Vernon L. Lidtke, 'Songs and Nazis: Political Music and Social Change in Twentieth-Century Germany', in Gary D. Stark and Bede Karl Lackner (eds.), *Essays on Culture and Society in Modern Germany* (Arlington, 1982), 167–200 at 172–3.

[42] Hitlerjugend and other Nazi songbooks contained dozens of songs which were also used by left-wing groups in the camps. See e.g. Gerhard Pallmann (ed.), *Wohlauf Kameraden! Ein Liederbuch der jungen Mannschaft von Soldaten, Bauern, Arbeitern und Studenten* (Kassel, 1934); Scheller (ed.), *Singend wollen wir marschieren*; Schmidt (ed.), *Uns geht die Sonne nicht unter*; Erwin Schwarz-Reiflingen (ed.), *HJ singt: Die schönsten Lieder der Hitler-Jugend* (Leipzig, n.d.); Wolfgang Stumme (ed.), *Liederblatt der Hitlerjugend: 1. Jahresband* (Berlin, 1936); id. (ed.), *Liederblatt der Hitlerjugend: 2. Jahresband* (Berlin, 1938); Reichsjugendführung (ed.), *Unser Liederbuch*.

punishments, camp prisoners would often be ordered to sing one of a number of well-known folk songs, all of which appeared in the *Schallerabend* song-books as well. As with the official camp hymns, songs of this kind mocked the prisoners' grim reality by forcing them to sing about cheerful, carefree themes. Among the most common were 'Hoch auf dem gelben Wagen' (High up on the yellow wagon), 'Steht ein Häuslein mitten im Walde' (In the middle of the forest stands a little house), 'Schwarzbraun ist die Hasel-nuss' (The hazelnut is blackish-brown), and 'Sängergruss' (Singers' greeting):

> Wilkommen frohe Sänger,
> Seid gegrüsst vieltausendmal,
> Den heutigen Tag zu ehren
> Lasst uns singen, dass es laut erschallt,
> Trallala, trallala, trallala, trallala,
> Drum lasst uns singen und fröhlich sein . . . [43]

> Welcome, merry singers,
> Thousands of greetings
> To honour this day
> Let our song ring out loudly,
> Trallala, trallala, trallala, trallala,
> Thus let us sing and be merry. . .

Their tendency to employ the same kinds of songs points to a remarkable congruity between Nazi and communist conceptions of music's social and political functions. In ideological terms, both privileged the music of the 'common people'; in pragmatic terms, they realized that music, especially participatory singing, could communicate basic political ideas and assist in group integration. A comparative look at pre-war songbooks from both groups reveals a shared emphasis on camaraderie and solidarity, particularly in a military context, and with reference to a common enemy.[44]

Wloch's insistence on the subversive nature of the politicals' activities, and the incapacity of the SS to grasp this, was echoed by others. Describing a 1941 Christmas celebration dedicated to the murdered Soviet POWs, Wilhelm Girnus told of how the prisoners took the song 'Unsterbliche Opfer' (Im-mortal victims) as a theme for variations; he claimed that the SS were too stupid to realize their intentions. Karl Schirdewan confirmed that although the SS often attended and enjoyed the performances, they luckily did not understand the deeper meaning of some of the songs. Heinz Hentschke also

[43] GMSA, NL1–17–S.1–155. Quoted here is the first verse of 'Sängergruss'.
[44] Carl Hoym, *Proletarier singe! Ein neuzeitlich Liederbuch für jung und alt* (Hamburg, 1919); Pallmann, *Wohlauf Kameraden*; Schmidt, *Uns geht die Sonne nicht unter.*

maintained that the practice of appropriating songs worked in the opposite direction: some camp songs were sung to the melodies of old military and Nazi melodies, usually for reasons of camouflage, but also because inserting or subverting lyrics became a way of demonstrating opposition to the regime. Hentschke gave the example of 'Wir sind Moorsoldaten', which aside from being set to a unnamed Nazi tune had two versions of its final verse. The first was the 'official' version included in the songbook, the second was sung only when they were among themselves:[45]

Version 1

Wir stehen verwegen
Und halten's mutig aus;
Die Tage vergehen,
Auch wir gehn bald nach Haus.

We stand boldly
And endure it with courage;
The days go by,
We, too, will go home soon.

Version 2

Wir stehen verwegen,
Solang' der Zwang uns hält,
Sobald sich Kräfte regen,
Die kämpfen, bis Hitler fällt.[46]

We stand boldly
As long as we are forced to,
As soon as powers stir,
That will fight until Hitler falls.

All these remarks point to a common conception among political prisoners of the role singing could play. With their music, these prisoners maintained, they demonstrated their commitment to resistance, however dangerous. Whatever they endured at the hands of the SS, their political convictions and hope for freedom were not quashed. These assertions may afford the victims a certain retrospective moral victory. However, the overlap in reper-

---

[45] Interview with Karl Schirdewan, AdK, 36; testimonies, interviews with former camp prisoners, AdK, 81; interviews with former camp prisoners, AdK, 103; manuscript about cultural life in the camps by Kulisiewicz, and interview, AdK, 2. Hentschke cited in Inge Lammel and Günter Hofmeyer, *Lieder*, 25, 33–4. The suggestion that the SS were 'too stupid' to understand the inmates' jokes and hidden allusions is also echoed in some secondary writing; see e.g. Inge Lammel and Günter Hofmeyer (eds.), *Kopf hoch, Kamerad!: Künstlerische Dokumente aus faschistischen Konzentrationslagern* (Berlin, 1965), 89.

[46] Lammel and Hofmeyer (eds.), *Lieder*, 23–4.

toire outlined earlier meant, on a more practical level, that the Nazis would have been familiar with at least some of the songs the politicals were singing. For this reason, their continued tolerance for their extensive musical activities cannot be ascribed to mere ignorance.

There are many indications that it was not in fact necessary for the politicals to be secretive about their activities. By all accounts, the SS knew about and tolerated their regular song evenings. They were generally more lenient about how the politicals chose to entertain themselves in the camp, perhaps because of their position in the racial hierarchy of the prisoners, or because of the prominent role they played in running the camp. Numerous testimonies describe how SS officials walked in on politicals' performances, and allowed them to continue without punishment. In addition, a few of the songbooks were inscribed with prisoner and block numbers, implying that concealment was not a serious issue.[47]

Thus, although the SS knew about the politicals' activities, and were sometimes familiar with the content of what was being sung, they saw no need to prohibit or even restrict them. This suggests that they fulfilled a function that was of some value: at the very least, they were a way of keeping prisoners calm and occupied. These song evenings were some of the most enthusiastically pursued musical activities in any camp. From knowledge of their sheer scope and from the many accounts of former prisoners, we know that they played a role in raising spirits and communal sentiment, and that to some extent they assisted the cause of underground resistance. However, it is important to acknowledge that the politicals would not have been granted this freedom if the SS had perceived their activities as a serious threat. The Nazis held ultimate control, and subversion was possible only if they allowed the means to pursue it. As we shall see, they were perfectly capable of denying the freedom of other prisoner groups, and had no difficulty discerning subversive activities even when they did not exist. The observations of the former prisoner G. Wackernagel serve to temper our understanding of music's potential significance in the camp. While recognizing that the song evenings engendered palpably higher morale and commitment to the anti-fascist cause, he emphasized that they were primarily a means of easing the pressures of daily life in the camp, and could ultimately make only a limited contribution to the struggle against fascism.[48]

---

[47] Responses to a questionnaire about cultural activities in Sachsenhausen, AdK, 42, 44.
[48] Responses to a questionnaire about cultural activities in Sachsenhausen, AdK, 45.

Cynicism, Nationalism, and the Polish Experience

Afforded considerable power in the prisoner hierarchy and freedom to engage in leisure activity, German political prisoners were able to apply music to constructive communal ends. Polish prisoners, by contrast, encountered music on a more restricted scale, and of a radically differing nature. Poles began to arrive in Sachsenhausen within weeks of the outbreak of war in September 1939. The first groups to be transported were minorities with Polish citizenship who had been living in Germany, among them 900 Jews. During 1940, transports of over 7,000 Poles accounted for the bulk of new arrivals to the camp; many of these men were clergymen, intellectuals, army officers, and other prominent public figures.[49]

In 1940, the newly arrived Polish musician Aleksander Kulisiewicz wrote the song 'Koncentrak' (Concentration camp). Here he described the 'equality' enjoyed by Sachsenhausen inmates, maintaining with sarcasm and much vitriol that although the camp was the 'home of the devil', it was also, ironically, a place where everyone was equal (see Ex. 3.4):

Ex. 3.4. 'Koncentrak'. USHMM, RG-55.004.18

---

[49] Wolff, *alendarium*, 1.

Koncentrak wredny, wredny pies,
Diabelska jego sława,
Ach, na cóż trupom pański gest,
W pasiaku wszystko chała!
Dyplomu tu nie trzeba i biskup scheisshaus zamiata—
Czyś ciura, czy generał, nie będziesz pępkiem świata!
La la-la-, la-la, la-la, la, i biskup scheisshaus zamiata...
I ja też zamiatam! Jum-pą dididą dididą dididą jum-pą!
Czyś ciura, czy generał, nie będziesz pępkiem świata.[50]

Concentration camp, disgusting, disgusting dog,
Devilish is his glory,
Ah, why does a corpse need gentle gestures,
In the camp jacket everything is shit-equal!
No need for diplomas here, and the bishop sweeps the shithouse—
Whether you are a slave or a general, you won't be the centre of the world!
La la-la-, la-la, la-la, la, and the bishop sweeps the shithouse...
And I am also sweeping! Jum-pa didida didida didida jum-pa!
Whether you are a slave or a general, you won't be the centre of the world!

Most of Kulisiewicz's songs depict the camp experience with similar anger and cynicism. His approach also reflects that of the vast majority of Polish songs from Sachsenhausen, in terms of both content and style. Unlike their German counterparts, Polish songs confronted difficult issues relating to camp life: they frequently included descriptions of death and suffering, and relentlessly parodied the Nazi regime and its ideologies, targeting specific personalities for criticism. Using sarcasm and black humour, they displayed their contempt for the regime, and openly expressed the desire for revenge. For the most part, they were based on pre-existing melodies, including popular dances such as czardas, tangos, foxtrots, and marches.[51]

Although the German prisoners' repertoire consisted largely of songs composed before the establishment of Sachsenhausen, even their camp compositions were far milder in tone, and politically more tactful. This was unsurprising: not only were they unlikely to jeopardize their relative security through offending behaviour, but they were also not in a position to want to be unduly subversive. By contrast, the Poles' lowly position in the prisoner hierarchy left them largely powerless, and subject to numerous hardships.

[50] Songs with notation from Sachsenhausen (Kulisiewicz Collection), USHMM, RG-55.004.18.
[51] At least sixty-two original Polish songs have been preserved from Sachsenhausen, of which around three-quarters had either music or lyrics written by Kulisiewicz. In several cases these consisted of words written by fellow prisoners which he set to music. See the Appendix, §IV for a list of the repertoire.

They thus had not only the motivation but also, in their language, a certain degree of freedom to vent their emotions regarding their fates.

The crucial difference between the German and Polish songs, however, was informed by musical context. For the political prisoners, singing was almost always communal, a means of promoting solidarity and raising morale. Opportunities for Poles were more limited. Usually they were only able to attend performances by individuals or small groups, or occasionally to initiate spontaneous group sessions themselves. The prisoners who gave clandestine performances would generally move from block to block during free time in the evenings or on weekends, singing for small groups of fellow prisoners in exchange for extra food or cigarettes, which were a valuable bartering item. They always had to be on the lookout for SS guards, and generally avoided the criminal functionaries, who were unlikely to tolerate them. These types of secret performances were commonplace in other camps, and although we have limited knowledge about how they worked in Sachsenhausen, it seems that the ultimate aim of remuneration was still there, even if it was only partly what motivated the singers. As a result, unlike their German counterparts, the Polish songs constituted expressions of a more personal nature, although they frequently addressed issues of common significance to the inmates: camp conditions, love for Poland, and the prospect of freedom.

Despite the zeal of his claims in 'Koncentrak', Kulisiewicz was not blind to the fact that the treatment of prisoners was far from equal. In fact, it was towards the camp's 'prominent' prisoners that he consistently directed much of his anger, and he purposefully premiered the song in one of their barracks.[52] Kulisiewicz's provocative tone, both in his songs and in his post-war writings on cultural life in the camp, drew censure during the 1970s from former German political prisoners. In correspondence with the Akademie der Künste, Berlin, many criticized his relentlessly negative emphasis, maintaining that his dark and troubling songs would have found few listeners. One argued:

These are not songs that were made for performances in the camp. They represented an absurd threat to prisoners who performed or heard them, because they could give the prisoners no moral strength . . . they are deeply negative and present a distorted picture of camp life. They are untrue and therefore unsuitable for popularization.

Another unnamed correspondent, evidently advising on the suitability for publication of Kulisiewicz's writing, complained that the account was distorted and subjective. Most striking was the fact that

---

[52] Song texts in German (Kulisiewicz Collection), USHMM, RG-55.007.01.

The fraternal international solidarity exercised in Sachsenhausen as in all other concentration camps, and the anti-fascist resistance struggle in Sachsenhausen with its countless victims, also as far as cultural activity in the camp is concerned, does not find expression in the manuscript. In particular, the unity of the prisoners against fascist terror, without regard to worldview, origin or belief, that was reached to a high degree in Sachsenhausen, is disregarded by K.

The most frequent point of defensiveness in these correspondences was Kulisiewicz's portrayal of hierarchy and privilege, and his emphasis on what separated the prisoners rather than on what united them. The writers insisted that German politicals fought to assist fellow inmates wherever possible, and to stop others from abusing positions of power. Moreover, they condemned Kulisiewicz's neglect of the integral part played by music in the resistance struggle. While his own songs sought gloatingly to teach prisoners a lesson, 'cultural performances staged by the anti-fascist resistance fighters always served to provide moral strength, impart optimism and fighting spirit among the prisoners'.[53]

These accusations have obvious political implications, in particular what seems to be an over-defensive readiness to label as defamatory any statement that threatens the memory of German political prisoners. However, while they reflect a conception of music appropriate to the experiences of a certain sector of the camp population, their aptness with regard to the Polish prisoners' context is questionable. Accounts by witnesses suggested, in fact, that singing activity among Poles was intended to have quite different effects. This description of a concert by Kulisiewicz was given by the former inmate André Gouillard:

Two camp nurses led a soloist to a so-called podium, that had been improvised out of a straw sack. The man, called Alex, was blind. The sockets of his eyes were yellow and the eyes were stuck together with pus. I did not know him. He had an old Polish camp number, but people said that he was supposedly a Hungarian Jew from Kecscemet. He was young and terribly emaciated. He sang. He raised his hands and a threatening fist. His voice was full of madness and hatred, then again pleading and often like the crying of a sick child. The audience gazed upon the soloist as if upon a statue of revenge. Several sick prisoners became powerless. I understood only two words: 'choral' and 'attention'. When the word 'attention' sounded for the second time... I lost consciousness.[54]

---

[53] Correspondence of former prisoners with the Akademie der Künste, Berlin regarding Kulisiewicz, GMSA, 13919.

[54] Gouillard, cited in Carsten Linde (ed.), *KZ-Lieder: Eine Auswahl aus dem Repertoire des polnischen Sängers Alex Kulisiewicz* (Sievershütten, 1972), 9. Kulisiewicz was only temporarily blinded: he caught an infection while working in the kennels, but regained his sight approximately six weeks later.

The comment about Kulisiewicz's 'supposed' origins reveals that people had in fact heard about him, and that his singing was attracting cautious attention even though the precise nature of his activities could not be widely publicized. Gouillard's account, however, is a far cry from descriptions of *Schallerabende*. This was clearly a highly charged performance that deeply affected its audience—whose poor state, significantly, is included in the description. From both their subject matter and their performance context, it is clear that the Polish songs were not intended for widespread popularity or communal morale-raising. Their musical texts, too, were not suitable for group singing: most encompassed relatively wide ranges, made use of chromaticism, and demanded liberal use of rhythm (*rubato*). Instead, they seem to have provided a framework within which the experience of victimization could be confronted, and where opposition to the regime could be expressed. After the war, Kulisiewicz stated explicitly that his intent had been to sing not the camp 'hits', but rather the 'songs of suffering'.[55] The fact that people continued to attend his performances under dangerous conditions suggests that these were sentiments with which they identified, or through which they were able to derive feelings of solace in shared experience.

More so than any of their counterparts, the Polish writers insisted on confronting the horrors of camp life in graphic detail. Their subject matter included descriptions of victims of gassing ('Spalona matka': The burnt mother), individual murders ('Le Crucifié': The crucified), and the execution of rebellious prisoners, as in the song 'Egzekucja' (Execution) by Kulisiewicz (see Ex. 3.5). The latter's explicit descriptions of physical torture were common to many other songs of its kind:

> Na szubienicy cień człowieka.
> Oczy przekorne wyszły z orbity
> I świecą jeszcze jak dwa guziki...
> Szyja oślizgła, żółta, długa—
> Nogi bestialsko skatowane—
> Gdzie jesteś ludzkie zmiłowanie?!!...
> I nikt nie krzyknie: Ecce homo!...[56]

> On the gallows a shadow of a man.
> Defiant eyes have left their sockets
> And shine, like two buttons...
> The neck slippery, yellow, long—

---

[55] Kulisiewicz, cited in Linde (ed.), *KZ-Lieder*, 11.

[56] Songs with notation from Sachsenhausen (Kulisiewicz Collection), USHMM, RG-55.004.18. Quoted here are the first seven lines of 'Egzekucja'.

Ex. 3.5. 'Egzekucja'. USHMM, RG-55.004.18

> The feet horribly tortured—
> Where are you, human pity?!!...
> And nobody cries: Ecce Homo!...

The biblical reference 'Ecce Homo' was to become a recurring theme. A citation from John 19: 5 meaning 'behold the man', and referring to Jesus wearing the crown of thorns, the phrase encapsulated Kulisiewicz's rage at the Nazis' inhumanity, and the silence with which the outside world responded to their crimes. Similar trends, particularly the distressed appeals to human compassion from silent bystanders, surfaced in the writings of other Polish prisoners as well. Writing in 1942, the 24-year-old Warsaw poet and journalist Leonard Krasnodębski expressed despair at the apathy of the world in his 'Chorał z Piekła Dna' (Chorale from the depths of hell; see Ex. 3.6):

> Słyszcie nasz chorał z piekła dna!
> Niech naszym katom w uszach gra
> Chorał! Chorał! Z piekła dna
> Niech naszym katom, niech naszym katom gra
> Słyszcie nasz chorał, słyszcie nasz chorał z piekła dna!
> Attention! Attention!
> Tu ludzie giną—tu ludzie są! Tu ludzie są![57]

---

[57] Songs with notation from Sachsenhausen (Kulisiewicz Collection), USHMM, RG-55.004.18.

Ex. 3.6. 'Chorał z Piekła Dna'. USHMM, RG-55.004.18

Hear our chorale from the depths of hell!
May it echo in the ears of our killers
Chorale! Chorale! From the depths of hell
In our killers' ears, in our killers' ears may it echo
Hear our chorale, hear our chorale from the depths of hell!
Attention! Attention!
Here, people are dying—Here, there are people! Here, there are people!

Gouillard's account of Kulisiewicz's performance in the hospital, which refers
to 'Chorał', confirms—contrary to the suggestions we encountered earlier—
that songs such as these were in fact performed, and that they elicited
powerful responses from their audiences. Even more explicitly than 'Egzekucja', Krasnodębski's song was an appeal to be heard. In the musical settings
of both songs, desperation is expressed with dramatic emphasis on the words
'Ecce Homo' and 'Attention'. The setting of 'Chorał' is particularly affecting,
its stagnant, dirge-like melody pierced only twice by these futile cries for help.
Many of the Polish songs reveal a similar sense of frustration and powerless-
ness. They also indicate that the idea of having their suffering acknowledged
by the outside world was one that preoccupied Polish inmates: it was
expressed frequently and with great intensity.

In many of the Polish songs, portrayal of the camp world is framed by vitriolic and often macabre sarcasm. Kulisiewicz's 'Maminsynek w Koncentraku' (Mummy's boy in the concentration camp), for example, uses euphemistic Nazi language to describe the ordeal of a young prisoner. Greeted by the 'angel' of the Gestapo with a kick in the teeth, the man is sent off in an 'elegant' goods train with corpses, and later returned to his mother 'silently and with resignation', as ashes in an urn. A song entitled 'Erika' (after the daughter of the SS Sturmbannführer[58] Oscar Maurer, supervisor of Sachsenhausen's work commandos) similarly describes the 'wonderful' treatment of prisoners, and the young girl's indifferent presence at their torturous marching sessions. Kulisiewicz noted that the sarcasm and gallows humour so characteristic of these songs was felt among the community to be a useful coping mechanism.[59]

Another common theme is outspoken criticism of Nazi ideologies and officials. The tone of these songs is consistently hateful, sardonic, and irreverent, and their subject matter confirms that they could only have been performed at clandestine gatherings. A song entitled 'Heil Sachsenhausen' satirizes the Nazi idea of *Rassenschande* (the perceived defilement of the Aryan race through sexual relations with non-Aryans). 'Czarny Böhm' (Black Böhm) takes as its subject the self-satisfied head of Sachsenhausen's crematorium, who would boast constantly of the people he had burned. 'Germania' ridicules the 'imbecilic' Führer, while 'Pożegnanie Adolfa ze Światem' (Adolf says farewell to the world) characterizes Hitler as 'impotent' and 'homeless', in comparison to 'Stalin of Steel'.[60]

In his post-war writings, Kulisiewicz acknowledged the widely felt need for sentimental, nostalgic, religious, and love songs which would allow prisoners to forget camp life for a while.[61] Nonetheless, Polish songs that fall into this category once again diverge from their German counterparts in that they almost always maintain a connection to the camp. Songs of nostalgia such as 'Pod Berlinem Płynie Woda' (Near Berlin flows water) juxtapose the grim reality in Sachsenhausen with memories of home, while 'Była u Mnie Matka Boska' (The mother of God came to me) expresses longing for Poland's freedom on the explicit background of suffering in the concentration

---

[58] Major. For detailed listing of SS ranks, see Mark C. Yerger, *Riding East: The SS Cavalry Brigade in Poland and Russia 1939–1942* (Atglen, Pa., 1996), 217.

[59] Song texts in German (Kulisiewicz Collection), USHMM, RG-55.007.01; *Przegląd Lekarski* articles in German translation (Kulisiewicz Collection), USHMM, RG-55.019.09.

[60] Songs with notation from Sachsenhausen (Kulisiewicz Collection), USHMM, RG-55.004.18.

[61] *Przegląd Lekarski* articles in German translation (Kulisiewicz Collection), USHMM, RG-55.019.09.

camp.[62] While religious songs from other camps, particularly Dachau, are sincerely devout, those from Sachsenhausen are cynical castigations of God for remaining quiet in the face of his subjects' suffering.[63] Even songs considered optimistic adopt a distinctly different slant. Unlike the German songs, which tend to refer in milder tones to abstract concepts such as 'the future', 'going home', or 'attaining freedom', encouragement in the Polish songs is usually based on the idea of Nazi defeat, and expressed with strong feelings of desperation and defiance. 'Hej, pod Berlinem!' (Hey, near Berlin!) was written in 1944 by Freund von Marcinek and Zbigniew Kossowski, based on the melody of a Ukrainian revolutionary song (see Ex. 3.7):

> Nasza ziemia krwawo płacze, krematoria dymią . . .
> Wasze brzuchy nienażarte—nasze wargi sine.
> Hej, pod Berlinem nasze słońce wstaje! . . .
> Niewolniczy zrzucim pasiak—słuchaj, podła zgrajo! . . . [64]

Ex. 3.7. 'Hej, pod Berlinem!'. USHMM, RG-55.004.18

---

[62] Songs with notation from Sachsenhausen (Kulisiewicz Collection), USHMM, RG-55.004.18.

[63] This disparity is almost certainly a consequence of the large numbers of Polish clergy incarcerated at Dachau (almost 3,000, more than in any other camp). Manuscripts that were preserved include songs written by the priests Aleksander Szymkiewicz and Jan Kaprzyk, and scores used by the Polish camp choir, which consisted primarily of Christmas entertainments: *kolędy* (carols) and music from *szopki* (Nativity plays). Songbook of the Polish camp choir in Dachau 1943–4 (Kulisiewicz Collection), USHMM, RG-55.002M.07; research materials relating to Dachau (Kulisiewicz Collection), USHMM, RG-55.003.30. For Polish religious songs from Sachsenhausen, see songs with notation from Sachsenhausen (Kulisiewicz Collection), USHMM, RG-55.004.18.

[64] Songs with notation from Sachsenhausen (Kulisiewicz Collection), USHMM, RG-55.004.18. Quoted here is the first verse of 'Hej, pod Berlinem!'

Our earth cries with blood, the crematoria are smoking...
Your stomachs are never satisfied—our lips are blue.
Hey, near Berlin our sun is rising!...
We are chucking our slave jackets away—listen, you vile bunch!...

The fervency of the anger and sarcasm with which Polish writers approached their subject matter confirms that their songs were not intended to fulfil the same communal functions as were the German songs. It was important that people could have their experiences and responses acknowledged within a communal setting, but beyond this the songs could not serve as a vehicle for overcoming those experiences, or construing them optimistically. A former German political prisoner cited earlier criticized Kulisiewicz for the relentless negativity of his work and the 'distorted picture of camp life' it provided. But 'distorted' from whose point of view? Unlike Germans, Poles were low down in the prisoner hierarchy; they had no 'privileged' status to maintain and few political goals to advance. The clandestine nature of their gatherings and, more decisively, the language factor, meant that to some degree they had more freedom to broach subversive topics: they referred directly to Hitler, and openly expressed anti-fascist sentiment. However, their isolation from other groups in the camp—a result both of language and fierce nationalism—meant that their opportunities for engaging in creative activity in the first place were limited.[65]

German politicals drew on a long-standing tradition of using music to build solidarity; in fact, the bulk of their repertoire consisted of the very songs with which this tradition had been established. In emphasizing the importance of resistance in their song texts, they avoided more detailed engagement with camp life. Even their newly created camp songs had been written in the mid-1930s, when the camp experience was far milder than it was to become after 1939. It is telling that they saw no need to change the texts, or to write new ones describing the worsening situation. All this suggests that they were encouraged to view the period of incarceration not as a radical break from their pre-war lives, but merely as a temporary interruption. Their struggle in the camps was thus subsumed into a larger, ongoing struggle that would continue upon their release.

By contrast, the camp world with which the Poles engaged was not characterized by this kind of solidarity and optimism. It follows, therefore, that encouraging these sentiments would not be a primary motivation for

[65] Manuscript about cultural life in the camps by Kulisiewicz, and interview, AdK, 2; correspondence of former prisoners with the Akademie der Künste, Berlin regarding Kulisiewicz, GMSA, 13919; *Przegląd Lekarski* articles in German translation, USHMM, RG-55.019.09.

music-making. In reality, Poles had little power or freedom to act, and feared that their plight had been forgotten by the outside world. Considered in this light, and as the songs themselves suggest, music was not only a place where they could document their suffering, but was also a medium through which strong feelings of anger, hatred, and bitterness could be vented, and where the unpleasant realities of the camp experience could begin to be confronted.

The Orchestra, Forced Music-Making, and Jews

Apart from these voluntary activities, Sachsenhausen also had a musical life that was initiated by the SS authorities. This was represented most prominently by the official orchestra, established in 1942 and led by the military conductor Peter Adam.[66] Orchestras of this kind existed in most of the larger camps, including Buchenwald, Dachau, Flossenbürg, Mauthausen, and Auschwitz.[67] As was the case elsewhere, musicians made use of the combination of instruments available in the camp (appropriated from the belongings of new arrivals), or those they were allowed to receive from home. They had the privilege of receiving additional bread rations for their playing, and worked almost exclusively inside the camp. Performances were mostly for the SS, or for important visitors; the repertoire consisted mainly of German marches and popular melodies, and the musicians usually had to write their own arrangements. The orchestra was made up of forty inmates from various countries. It began as a wind band, but by the following year had grown into a fully-fledged symphony orchestra with up to eighty members.[68]

One of the orchestra's tasks was to give concerts for the entertainment of SS and fellow prisoners. Extant programmes and concert tickets reveal that these

---

[66] Although there is consensus among post-war accounts that Adam led the orchestra for most of its existence, some former prisoners mentioned different conductors. Because most accounts lack both specific details and corroboration, it is difficult to construct a precise chronology of the orchestra's leadership. See the interview with Karl Schirdewan, AdK, 36; responses to a questionnaire about cultural activities in Sachsenhausen, 43, 44. For more on Adam, see Naujoks, *Mein Leben*, 299, and Kulisiewicz, *Adresse: Sachsenhausen*, 17.

[67] On Dachau, see Krzysztof Dunin-Wąsowicz, *Resistance in the Nazi Concentration Camps* (Warsaw, 1982), 291. A study by Paul Cummins entitled *Dachau Song: The Twentieth-Century Odyssey of Herbert Zipper* (New York, 1992) documents the establishment of a clandestine orchestra in the camp in May 1938, although no additional sources confirm the existence of an orchestral group at this point in the camp's history. On Buchenwald, see Seidel, 'Kultur und Kunst', 9, and Vlastimil Louda, cited in Schneider, *Kunst hinter Stacheldraht*, 78–82. See also Kuna, *Musik an der Grenze*, 48–55, 67–95 (Kuna's emphasis is on Czech musicians in these ensembles).

[68] Henri Michel, *Oranienburg-Sachsenhausen: KZ-Erinnerungen und Hungermarsch in die Freiheit eines politischen Gefangenen* (Eupen, 1985), 83; Lettow, *Arzt in den Höllen*, 172; Kulisiewicz, *Adresse: Sachsenhausen*, 17.

were officially sanctioned, formal, and well-organized affairs. Concerts were held in prisoners' blocks or in the *Trockenbaracke* (the barracks that usually served for the drying of the prisoners' washing). The seven existing programmes date from 25 April 1943 to 8 April 1945, suggesting that the concerts were not frequent or regular events. Three were scheduled on the occasion of Easter celebrations; another was held at Christmas.[69]

The performances were generally divided into two parts, with an interval, and consisted of between eight and ten short items. The repertoire was drawn largely from operettas and 'light' works by composers such as Johann Strauss, Franz von Suppé, Franz Lehár, Paul Lincke, and others. Almost half were marches, operetta overtures, and dance melodies. There were also a substantial number of pieces by 'serious' composers, almost always drawn from well-known works: Beethoven's *Egmont* overture, Mozart's *Eine kleine Nachtmusik*, fragments from Bizet's *Carmen*, Brahms's Hungarian Dance No. 6, and selections by Dvořák, Grieg, Wagner, Schubert, Haydn, Verdi, and Tchaikovsky. Kulisiewicz maintained that works by Jewish and Polish composers were 'smuggled' into the orchestra's programmes, although the SS probably knew about this. The choice of repertoire broadly mirrored that of orchestras in other camps.[70]

The prisoners who would have been able to attend these concerts were probably those in the upper echelons of the hierarchy. This suggestion is borne out by the testimonial literature, as descriptions of orchestral concerts were almost always given by political prisoners or those belonging to other protected groups. The Norwegian prisoner Odd Nansen attended several concerts during his incarceration, although he was generally unimpressed by the standard of performance. The Belgian prisoner Henri Michel, by contrast, attended an 'unforgettable' concert on Christmas Eve 1943, where the 'outstandingly good' performance 'sent the thoughts of the audience wandering into a world of art, nobility and culture not experienced by many for years'.[71]

---

[69] Admission ticket for concert in Sachsenhausen, GMSD, III 7; concert programme 26 Apr. 1943, GMSD, III 626; concert programme 25 Apr. 1943, GMSD, III 627; concert programme 1 Apr. 1945, GMSD, III 418; concert programme 8 Apr. 1945, III 419; songs, drawings, and concert programmes from Sachsenhausen, AdK, 29; Michel, *Oranienburg-Sachsenhausen*, 83. Testimonies indicate that Easter and particularly Christmas were occasions for festivity that the SS tolerated and even encouraged. Extra food rations would sometimes be provided, work would be suspended, and inmates would be allowed to organize and attend special events. The SS also exercised relative leniency on these occasions with regard to the material the prisoners were allowed to perform. See also Nansen, *Day after Day*, 457–8; Naujoks, *Mein Leben*, 287; Hartmann in AdK, 44, Schmellentin in AdK, 42, and Wackernagel in AdK, 45 (responses to a questionnaire about cultural activities in Sachsenhausen).

[70] Kulisiewicz, *Adresse: Sachsenhausen*, 17. See the Appendix, §V for a list of the repertoire.

[71] Nansen, *Day after Day*, 458, 506; Michel, *Oranienburg-Sachsenhausen*, 84–5.

The orchestra was to some extent a matter of pride for the SS authorities, and it existed to provide them with entertainment on appropriate occasions. However, it was more frequently used to serve punitive purposes. For example, the musicians were often made to play cheerful German dance tunes and marches as a background to public floggings and executions. This kind of musical punishment was not unique to Sachsenhausen, and indeed had many other manifestations: primarily forced singing sessions, and numerous other musical tortures.[72]

The prisoners who most frequently formed the target of these punishments were Jews, who were housed in a cordoned-off section of the camp known as the *Sonderlager* (special camp). In contrast to most other inmates in Sachsenhausen, the music that the Jewish prisoners encountered was more often forced than voluntary, and it was not counterbalanced by the activities they were able to organize themselves. These were necessarily restricted and covert, and always accompanied by the fear of discovery. The situation was similar in most of the larger camps: Jews were afforded more restricted opportunities than their counterparts, and for the most part experienced only spontaneous, clandestine singing sessions; they were also subjected more frequently to musical torture.[73]

Shortly after his release from Sachsenhausen in 1941, the former inmate Eric Goodman gave an account of his experiences as a forced labourer. Along with approximately 1,800 other Jewish men, he had been brought to the camp after *Kristallnacht* on 9–10 November 1938.[74] One of Goodman's most enduring memories was a particular type of punishment to which his group was regularly subjected:

Late in the evening, when we were already tired and longed for the little bit of rest that remained for us in the day, we were made out of pure abuse to remain standing in the courtyard and to sing, sing continuously, into the depths of the night. The

---

[72] Michel, *Oranienburg-Sachsenhausen*, 217; Alec Le Vernoy, *No Drums, No Trumpets* (London, 1988), 186; G. Sverrisson, *Wohnt hier ein Isländer? Erinnerungen von Leifur Muller* (Bremerhaven, 1997), 217. For other camps, see Kuna, *Musik an der Grenze*, 31–6.

[73] Testimonial accounts confirm that this was the case; we can also infer this from the fact that Jews produced relatively little musical material in the camps (as compared with the ghettos). It is also well known that Jews were generally subjected to more brutal treatment than other camp inmates. On Buchenwald, see Projektgruppe Musik in Konzentrationslagern, *Musik*, 67–8; and John, 'Musik und Konzentrationslager', 10. Bergen-Belsen posed a slight exception: see Thomas Rahe, 'Kultur im KZ: Musik, Literatur und Kunst in Bergen-Belsen', in Claus Füllberg-Stolberg, Martina Jung, Renate Riebe, and Martina Scheitenberger (eds.), *Frauen in Konzentrationslagern: Bergen-Belsen Ravensbrück* (Bremen, 1994), 193–206.

[74] *Kristallnacht* (Night of broken glass) was the name given to the pogrom conducted throughout Germany and Austria on these dates. The name refers to the broken shop windows of Jewish stores. Gutman (ed.), *Encyclopedia*, 836.

1. Musical performance in the Kovno ghetto. Reproduced by permission of USHMM, courtesy of George Kadish/Zvi Kadushin

2. Musicians performing on Mazowiecka street in Warsaw. Reproduced by permission of USHMM, courtesy of Hans-Joachim Gerke

3. Child beggar playing the harmonica, Warsaw. Reproduced by permission of USHMM, courtesy of Hans-Joachim Gerke

4. Jewish partisan unit operating in the Lithuanian forests. Reproduced by permission of USHMM, courtesy of Eliezer Zilberis

5. Violinists in the Kovno ghetto orchestra. Reproduced by permission of USHMM, courtesy of George Kadish/Zvi Kadushin

6. Aleksander Kulisiewicz sings 'Chorał z Piekła Dna' (Chorale from the depths of hell). Reproduced by permission of USHMM, courtesy of Aleksander Kulisiewicz

7. Sachsenhausen prisoners stand in columns under the supervision of camp guard.
Reproduced by permission of USHMM, courtesy of National Archives

8. Sunday concert for the SS at Auschwitz performed by the men's prisoner orchestra.
Reproduced by permission of USHMM, courtesy of the Main Commission for the
Prosecution of the Crimes against the Polish Nation

same happened when, now and then, someone tried to escape. Then the sirens howled eerily through the night, until the victim had been seized, but in the meantime all the prisoners had to remain standing on the big square, without food, without pause to rest, and had to sing. During this singing many perished, exhausted.[75]

Many of the Jews interned in Sachsenhausen had similar memories. Like prisoners in the main camp, they followed a stringent daily routine: an early wake-up call (around 4.30 a.m. in the summer, a little later in winter), as many as twelve hours of forced labour at factories in the vicinity, and strict roll-calls both in the mornings before they departed for work and when they returned at night. The evening sessions were often particularly distressing, and could last for several hours. Those who had died during the day had to be laid out on the *Appellplatz* (roll-call square) in order that prisoner numbers would balance with those taken in the morning. Delays would be caused if they did not tally, and some inmates recalled standing on the *Appellplatz* for over twenty-four hours waiting for escapees to be retrieved. The evening roll-call was also used as a time for carrying out punishments: the public flogging or execution of rebellious prisoners, and the meting out of group punishments such as 'sport' or military drills.[76]

It was at these sessions on the *Appellplatz* that forced singing exercises of the kind described by Goodman took place. A song would be announced, and the men would be required to sing together in precise, military fashion, often for hours at a time. Aside from the physical torment of having to sing after an exhausting day's labour, often in the cold and without having eaten, many found it difficult to bear the frivolous, upbeat German songs they were forced to sing. The repertoire consisted of the same well-known folk songs demanded from prisoners in the main camp, among them 'Sängergruss', 'Schwarzbraun ist die Haselnuss', 'Steht ein Häuslein mitten im Walde', and 'Hoch auf dem gelben Wagen'. The length of the singing sessions depended on the whim of the officer in charge, and the same songs would often have to be sung repeatedly. Inmates were beaten or punished who did not sing along, or whose singing was deemed unsatisfactory. If the group was judged to have performed badly, all would be forced to endure further punishment drills.

---

[75] Eric Goodman, Wiener Library Archive (hereafter WL), Eyewitness Testimony P.II.d. No. 528.
[76] Manuela R. Hrdlicka, *Alltag im KZ: Sachsenhausen bei Berlin* (Leske and Budrich, 1992), 67; Gutman (ed.), *Encyclopedia*, 1321–2. 'Sport' euphemistically described a common activity where prisoners would be made to perform strenuous training exercises, often until they collapsed from exhaustion.

Inmates in the main camp sometimes experienced sessions such as these, but in the *Sonderlager* they were more frequent, and the accompanying torture more severe. They were also not the only type of musical punishment to which Jews were subjected. Religious men in particular would often be made to sing psalms and liturgical melodies in degrading situations, sometimes while being beaten. Naujoks recalled a Jew being made to sing a self-mocking song about his enormous nose.[77]

Only in few reports by Jewish inmates did music feature in more positive ways. Hans Reichmann, writing after his release from the camp in summer 1939, insisted that Jews did not sing in the camp unless commanded to. He did recall, however, that on one of the nights of Hanukkah Adolf Burg had sung for his fellow inmates the traditional song 'Ma'oz Tsur'. Reichmann described the emotional response to the song, in particular that of one of the oldest prisoners, who unprompted began to recite his Barmitzvah portion, which he had learnt forty-five years earlier. Leon Szalet, who arrived in Sachsenhausen in September 1939, recounted a moving incident on Yom Kippur, which fell shortly after he arrived in the camp. Knowing the significance of the day for the Jewish prisoners, the SS guards had subjected them to particularly brutal treatment. Szalet described what happened once the guards had left them for the night:

All at once the oppressive silence was broken by a mournful tune. It was the plaintive tones of the ancient 'Kol Nidre' prayer. I raised myself up to see whence it came. There, close to the wall, the moonlight caught the uplifted face of an old man, who, in self-forgetful, pious absorption, was singing softly to himself the sorrowful melody with the familiar, deeply moving words... We sat up very quietly, so as not to disturb the old man, and he did not notice that we were listening. As if transported into another world, he chanted the prayer to the end, so softly that the words were scarcely distinguishable to those who did not know them by heart. His old, quavering voice held us in a spell. When at last he was silent, there was exaltation among us, an exaltation which men can experience only when they have fallen as low as we had fallen and then, through the mystic power of a deathless prayer, have awakened once more to the world of the spirit.[78]

Music related to Jewish occasions was evidently meaningful not only for the devout, but also for prisoners of varying degrees of religious observance. Szalet also described the events of Hanukkah 1939, which included an

---

[77] *Przegląd Lekarski* articles in German translation (Kulisiewicz Collection), USHMM, RG-55.019.09; Naujoks, *Mein Leben*, 40.

[78] Hans Reichmann, *Deutscher Bürger und verfolgter Jude: Novemberpogrom und KZ Sachsenhausen 1937 bis 1939* (Munich, 1998), 214, 228; Leon Szalet, *Experiment 'E': A Report from an Extermination Laboratory* (New York, 1945), 70–1.

emotional rendition of the Jewish hymn 'Hatikva'. This trend was manifest in many ghettos and camps, as people sought to re-establish connections with pre-war identities and to foster a sense of group belonging. Paradoxically, as we shall see later, the experience of victimization led many Jews to return to their roots with a renewed sense of significance, and awakened the need to reclaim their Jewish heritage. Impromptu sessions such as these occurred only infrequently, however. The Jewish men in the isolated *Sonderlager* suffered harsh ill-treatment compared with those incarcerated in the main camp, were denied even more basic necessities than their non-Jewish counterparts, and were subject to severe restrictions on their movement.[79]

The opportunities for organizing illegal musical activity in *Sonderlager* were consequently limited, and the few events that did take place almost always relied on the intervention of non-Jewish political prisoners. The former inmate Johann Hüttner reported that *Schallerabende* were occasionally held there, and recalled a particularly memorable evening shortly after Christmas 1941. Programme items included 'Grüne Kolonnen', a performance of Beethoven's canon 'Freundschaft ist die Quelle wahrer Glückseligkeit' (Friendship is the source of true happiness) with the modified text 'Freundschaft, Kameradschaft, Solidarität' (Friendship, comradeship, solidarity), 'Und wenn wir marschieren', and an address by a prominent German political prisoner. In addition to sharing some common repertoire, Jewish and non-Jewish politicals evidently had close links in the camp. According to Hüttner, approximately 250 men from the main camp attended this clandestine performance.[80]

The only permanent musical group to exist among the Jewish prisoners was a four-part choir led by the Polish-born inmate Rosebery d'Arguto (aka Martin Rosenberg). Already before the war d'Arguto had been a well-respected musical figure and political activist. In 1905 he became involved in revolutionary activity in Poland, and fled from the Polish police to Austria, later to Italy, and settled in Berlin during the First World War. There he successfully conducted several choirs, particularly children's groups. He was well known for his progressive and experimental activities, and was active in the communist-affiliated Deutsche Arbeiter-Sängerbund (German workers' choral union). It was for his leadership of a large mixed workers' chorus in Berlin during the 1920s and 1930s that he achieved the highest critical acclaim. The Gesangsgemeinschaft Rosebery d'Arguto (Singing community

---

[79] Szalet, *Experiment 'E'*, 20–2, 168–71; Naujoks, *Mein Leben*, 146–8.
[80] Responses to a questionnaire about cultural activities in Sachsenhausen, AdK, 43.

of Rosebery d'Arguto) was a huge and highly successful enterprise, with almost 400 members. It was also politically active, performing at demonstrations and rallies particularly for the KPD, and in support of proletarian organizations such as the Interessengemeinschaft für Arbeiterkultur (Workers' culture syndicate), the Internationale Arbeiterhilfe (International workers' relief), and the Rote Hilfe (Red relief). With Hitler's rise to power in 1933, d'Arguto's activities with the choir were banned. He returned to Poland in 1934, and remained there until 1939. On a short trip to Germany to settle some personal matters in September 1939, he was arrested by the Gestapo, and with approximately 900 Jews of Polish extraction taken to Sachsenhausen on 13 September.[81]

The choir was established in April 1940 with between twenty and thirty members. According to reports, d'Arguto worked tirelessly with his singers during free time: he was obsessed with his work not only from an artistic point of view, but because he saw the choir as a vehicle for conveying urgent political imperatives and expressing opposition to the regime. The continued existence of the group in fact depended on his political commitment, and on his close connections with political prisoners in the main camp. Whereas the leadership of block 38 (d'Arguto's block) was made up of criminals, the *Blockälteste* and *Stubenälteste* of block 39 were German politicals who supported the choir's activities, allowing it to rehearse and perform there. In addition, Block 39 contained a relatively large number of Jewish politicals prepared to lend their support to d'Arguto's endeavours. D'Arguto was also able to call on pre-war friends in the camp, and relied on several 'prominent' inmates for the organization of the choir's activities: notably Naujoks, August Baumgarte, Antonín Zápotocký (later to become President of Czechoslovakia), and the Polish camp doctor Stanisław Kelles-Krauz.

Information about the choir's activities is scant, since most of those who came into contact with it did not survive. Because it was illegal, rehearsals and performances had to be carefully secured if they were to remain undetected. This meant that most prisoners were probably unaware of its existence. In addition, at least at the outset, it could probably only perform in the Jewish blocks. The non-Jewish prisoner Werner Havemann recalled asking d'Arguto shortly after his arrival whether he would be prepared to lead a choir in the camp (Havemann obviously held a powerful position in the hierarchy, as he

---

[81] Peter Andert, 'Rosebery d'Arguto: Versuche zur Erneuerung des proletarischen Chorgesangs', in Klaus Kändler, Helga Karolewski, and Ilse Siebert (eds.), *Berliner Begegnungen: Ausländische Künstler in Berlin 1918 bis 1933* (Berlin, 1987), 340–5 at 344; Ernst Lindenberg, 'Rosebery d'Arguto— Vorkämpfer der Arbeiterchorbewegung', *Musik und Gesellschaft*, 4 (1971), 231–40 at 236.

could seek out newcomers that interested him). D'Arguto refused. After the war, Havemann expressed surprise at never having encountered the illegal choir that d'Arguto later founded, observing that either it was so illegal that news of its existence never reached him, or that it was founded after he had left the camp. That Havemann, a 'prominent' prisoner interned in Sachsenhausen until November 1940, did not come into contact with the choir suggests the limited extent to which it was able to impact on the general inmate community at this time. Later, when the SS had begun to focus their attention on other groups such as the Soviet POWs, who began to arrive in the summer of 1941, the choir had more freedom to perform in other barracks outside the *Sonderlager*. Hüttner reported that it was sometimes able to perform in 'political' blocks in the main camp on the days between Christmas and New Year, when the SS were less vigilant.[82]

References to the choir's repertoire are also limited. Hüttner remembered only two of its songs: 'Es war ein König in Thule' (There was a king in Thule), based on a text by Goethe, and a German song based on the Yiddish folk melody 'Tsen brider' (Ten brothers). Kulisiewicz, who developed a close friendship with d'Arguto during his incarceration,[83] also recalled the latter song, which he called the 'Jüdischer Todessang' (Jewish death song). The original Yiddish song recounts the pitiful fates of ten brothers, traders in cargo and flax, who die one by one until only one is left; in keeping with the tragi-comic spirit of Yiddish song, the refrain playfully reads: 'Oy, Shmerl with the fiddle, Tevye with the bass, / Play a little song for me in the middle of the street!'[84] Quoted here is the song's German camp adaptation (see Ex. 3.8):

Zehn Brüder waren wir gewesen, haben wir gehandelt mit Wein
Einer ist gestorben—sind wir geblieben neun.
   Oj-oj! Oj-oj!
Jidl mit dem Fiedel, Mojsche mit dem Bass,
   Singt mir mal ein Liedel, müssen wir ins Gas!
Ein Bruder bin ich nur geblieben; mit wem soll ich nun weinen?
Die and'ren sind ermordet! Denkt ihr an alle neun!
   Oj-oj! Oj-oj!

---

[82] Interview with Johann Hüttner, AdK, 40; responses to a questionnaire about cultural activities in Sachsenhausen, AdK, 42.

[83] Although they were housed in separate areas of the camp, Kulisiewicz and d'Arguto were able to spend time together when Kulisiewicz came to the *Sonderlager*. The two found common ground not only in their love of music but also in their political convictions. See the manuscript about cultural life in the camps by Kulisiewicz, and interview, AdK, 2.

[84] 'Oy, Shmerl mit dem fidl, Tevye mitn bas, / shpilt zhe mir a lidl, oyfn mitn gas!' Mlotek and Mlotek (eds.), *Pearls of Yiddish Song*, 121–3.

Ex. 3.8. 'Jüdischer Todessang'. USHMM, RG-55.004.23

Jidl mit dem Fiedel, Mojsche mit dem Bass,
Hört mein letztes Liedel; ich muss auch ins Gas!
Zehn Brüder waren wir gewesen
Wir haben keinem Weh getan.[85]

---

[85] Songs in German (Kulisiewicz Collection), USHMM, RG-55.004.23. D'Arguto used the
pluperfect tense in his German text ('We had been ten brothers', etc.), probably in order to keep
the sound and rhythmic structure of the German close to the Yiddish original (rather than to change
the sense of the words). For this reason, I have used the past tense rather than the pluperfect in my
translation.

We were ten brothers, we traded in wine
One died—we were left nine.
   Oy-oy! Oy-oy!
   Yidl [little Jew] with the fiddle, Moyshe with the bass,
   Sing a little song for me, we have to go into the gas!
I am the only brother left; with whom shall I now cry?
The others have been murdered! Think of all nine!
   Oy-oy! Oy-oy!
   Yidl with the fiddle, Moyshe with the bass,
   Listen to my last little song; I also have to go into the gas!
We were ten brothers,
We never hurt anyone.

According to Kulisiewicz, d'Arguto and the choir found out in late 1942 that a transport would soon be taking Jewish prisoners to Auschwitz-Birkenau or Majdanek. In the three weeks before it was due to depart, d'Arguto wrote the new song, shortening 'Tsen brider' from ten stanzas to two, modifying the words, and translating it into German so that a larger number of prisoners in the camp would be able to understand it. This applied not only to German Jews in the *Sonderlager*, but also—perhaps more importantly—to non-Jewish political prisoners in the main camp. The German version played sardonically on the word 'gas'; in the new version, the Jewish minstrels no longer sang for the brothers 'in the middle of the street', but because they were now being forced 'to go into the gas'. This phrase is emphasized in the new musical setting.

In drawing on a well-known Yiddish folk source and adapting it to the new conditions, d'Arguto was following in an age-old Jewish tradition. This song had in fact previously been the subject of several revisions and modifications, expressions of the changing circumstances of successive Jewish communities.[86] It is interesting that the experience of incarceration led someone like d'Arguto—a non-practising Jew who had gone so far as to de-Judaize his name—to write an explicitly Jewish lament. Kulisiewicz, who had spoken with him at length about the song, explained that the original refrain ('Shmerl mit dem fidl...') had been specifically modified in order to make clear to listeners who were not familiar with the song that it was referring to Jews.[87] D'Arguto even emphasized to the point of caricature the quintessential Jewish exclamation 'oy' with which the refrain opened. That d'Arguto

---

[86] Mlotek and Mlotek (eds.), *Pearls of Yiddish Song*, 121, 258.
[87] This story was corroborated by Max Sprecher, a theologian who had been with d'Arguto in Sachsenhausen. Kulisiewicz, *Adresse: Sachsenhausen*, 22; transcription of a lecture by Max Sprecher, AdK, 55.

and his fellow inmates chose to sing about the communal Jewish fate—even if only at this desperate juncture—suggests that, as in the ghettos, Jews found meaning in forging links with their past, and situating their experiences within a Jewish historical trajectory. This phenomenon is all the more striking here because German Jews, who made up the bulk of Sachsenhausen's Jewish population, were historically more assimilated than their east European counterparts in the ghettos.

The dearth of source material makes it difficult to construct a more detailed history of the choir's activities. Nonetheless, the not inconsiderable number of witness accounts describing d'Arguto himself give a clearer indication of what he hoped to achieve with the group, and its resulting character. Szalet wrote of d'Arguto's uncompromising integrity, explaining that despite his 'privileged' work placement, he never succumbed to the atmosphere of moral degradation around him. Other surviving inmates spoke of him with veneration, recalling his energy and dynamism, and in particular the inspiration that those around him drew from him.[88]

It is apparent that d'Arguto saw his music as a powerful means of strengthening group morale and solidarity, and that he pursued these aims with integrity and conviction. Furthermore, the 'Todessang' suggests that while reaffirming Jewish identity was one way in which d'Arguto felt Jewish inmates could construe what was happening to them, it was equally important to him that they gain the sympathy of non-Jewish prisoners. Musical activity was thus not only a way of consoling the group in the *Sonderlager*, but was also a way of communicating their experiences to those outside, and perhaps also of ensuring that what they had suffered would be witnessed and remembered.

Jewish prisoners were granted little respite from the realities of Sachsenhausen, however. Subjected to a combination of hard labour and gratuitous violence, they inhabited a world where the struggle for life took precedence over everything else. Within such a context, music simply could not flourish for long. Indeed, the absence of songs is a more telling testament to the Jewish experience in the camp than the few songs that remain. Opportunities for voluntary music-making were limited at best, and were marginalized increasingly as camp conditions worsened. As time progressed, people's mental and

---

[88] Through the influence of a musician working in the camp office who regarded him highly, d'Arguto was placed in the indoor commando, which performed comparatively light work such as food distribution or overseeing of the washrooms and toilets. Szalet, *Experiment 'E'*, 111. See also interviews with former members of the Gesangsgemeinschaft Rosebery d'Arguto, AdK, 3; interview with Johann Hüttner, AdK, 40; Kulisiewicz, *Adresse: Sachsenhausen*, 23; research materials relating to Rosebery d'Arguto (Kulisiewicz Collection), USHMM, RG-55.003.93.

physical states gradually deteriorated. Kulisiewicz recalled d'Arguto's rapid decline during the latter period of his incarceration, when he began to tell the same stories about his choir in Berlin over and over again. A description of the choir's last rehearsal in October 1942 serves to confirm the authorities' astonishing lack of tolerance for Jewish activities, and to remind us just how little latitude Jews were afforded within the framework of Nazi control. According to Kulisiewicz, who witnessed the event, several SS men stormed into the block and took the entire choir outside to perform punishment exercises. Half-naked, they were made to do 'sport' while singing the refrain of the 'Todessang'. Many died there and then; the others had to remain standing through the night on the *Appellplatz*. Later that month, a transport of Jews, including d'Arguto, was sent to Auschwitz.[89]

Remembering Sachsenhausen

Like many other topics pertaining to the Nazi camps, music has been subject to the politics of memorialization. In the case of Sachsenhausen, which for most of its post-war lifetime fell under the jurisdiction of the GDR, public memory unsurprisingly has been informed by communist thought. Research projects concerned with music have focused on the activities of German political prisoners as if they were broadly representative, despite the fact that documentary material relating to other groups was equally obtainable (if not as plentiful). Where the activities of other prisoner groups have been considered, discussions tend to be framed in terms of the German political prisoners' conception of the role of music: that is, as a powerful tool in the resistance struggle, and a means of building morale and group solidarity.[90]

A move beyond these limiting paradigms is needed in order to achieve a more accurate understanding of the camp's internal dynamics. As we have seen, variables such as nationality, religion, position in the prisoner hierarchy, and work or block placements could radically alter an individual's experience

---

[89] Kulisiewicz, *Adresse: Sachsenhausen*, 24; Linde (ed.), *KZ-Lieder*, 15.

[90] See in particular the writings of Inge Lammel, introduction to *Lieder*, and 'Das Sachsenhausen Liederbuch'. Antifascism is widely acknowledged as having been one of the most important concepts for the legitimation of the GDR, and perhaps its most crucial 'founding myth'. On the forms that memory of communist resistance in the Nazi camps took in the GDR, particularly the ways in which the suffering of other camp victims (especially Jews) was downplayed, see e.g. Eve Rosenhaft, 'The Use of Remembrance: The Legacy of the Communist Resistance in the German Democratic Republic', in Francis R. Nicosia and Lawrence D. Stokes (eds.), *Germans against Nazism: Nonconformity, Opposition and Resistance in the Third Reich* (Oxford, 1990), 369–88; and Mary Fulbrook, *German National Identity after the Holocaust* (Cambridge, 1999), 28–35.

of daily life. In the case of music, the possibilities open to different groups were astonishingly divergent. What is more, German political prisoners were well placed to take advantage of the freedoms afforded them by the authorities, having already come to the camp with distinct advantages—not least among them a long-established conception of how music could be harnessed for group integration. Other groups found themselves in a comparatively powerless situation, and their experiences of the role music could play differed correspondingly.

In his diary, the Norwegian prisoner Nansen expressed some difficulty with the concept of entertainment as a necessary distraction in the camp. As a 'privileged' inmate, he was not only able to keep a journal but also to participate frequently in musical performances held in the camp's 'prominent' blocks. Although he derived much enjoyment from them, he insisted on juxtaposing in his diary the disparity between his experiences and those of other inmates:

8 May [1944]. There was an entertainment in twenty-five yesterday, and I took part. It was fun. But it's terrible to think that while we were doing that, in the mortuary of the *Revier* [infirmary] they were busy shovelling corpses on to a lorry. The bodies were so mutilated that they couldn't even count how many there were. Those were the remains of our 'comrades' who had gone out to work that very morning at the same time as we did. It's enough to drive one to complete despair when one pulls oneself together occasionally and looks things in the face as they really are. In fact, one mustn't do it, not like that; one couldn't go on. Therefore it's right to sing songs while others shovel away corpses.

12 February [1945]. The language is exhausted. I've exhausted it myself. There are no words left to describe the horrors I've seen with my own eyes ... It was in the isolation area between Blocks 13 and 14 ... Dante's inferno couldn't be worse. There were more than a thousand Jews, that is, they had once been Jews and human beings, now they were living skeletons, beast-like in their mad hunger. They flung themselves on the dustbins, or rather plunged into them, head and shoulders, several at a time ... But the worst was that the whole time, without a break, the blows from rubber truncheons were hailing down on them ... At night in the block there was concertina-playing, singing and high spirits. I sang, too, and made merry! Can it be possible?[91]

Nansen's observations restore perspective on several crucial factors. First, they remind us that for all its advantages, 'privilege' in the camp was nonetheless a relative concept. While some did what they could to assist fellow inmates, ultimately they did what was necessary to ensure their own survival. In the light of this idea, it must be emphasized that discussions about hierarchy and

---

[91] Nansen, *Day after Day*, 442, 478–9, 545–8.

'privilege' do not imply retrospective judgement, but are an important vantage point from which to consider how prisoners would have been able to engage with camp life and with one another. As Nansen's account indicates, even an awareness of the greater suffering of others in the camp could not eliminate one's own, nor did it negate the range of coping strategies one was able to use. Few prisoners could realistically bear to confront things 'as they really were'. There is clear evidence that music played a role in prisoners' struggles, even though it constituted only a minor element of camp life. Nansen reminds us, however, that its possible functions cannot be understood independent of the camp's complex social make-up.

Music is often one of the most important means through which displaced groups adapt to new conditions, both because it helps to restore something of the environment of their former lives, and because it is useful for strengthening, preserving, or restoring past group identities. This is certainly true of how it functioned in the camps, although the process varied depending on the groups in question. As has been suggested, some were naturally more cohesive than others: political prisoners, for example, had good reasons for communal identification, both in their shared political goals and in the simple fact that many knew each other from before the war. In the case of other inmates, however, a common national or religious identity did not always allow for the same kind of integration. People often came to the camps alone, without family or friends, and although small support groups were sometimes developed, these obviously did not substitute for larger networks.

The groups explored in this chapter all used music as a way of expressing a communal identity. This was not always a unified or consistent identity, but rather one that was informed by the experiences, traditions, fears, expectations, and internal dynamics of the community. Nonetheless, for each in different ways music also captured something characteristic of the larger group, encouraged feelings of belonging, and tried to incorporate new experiences into the continuity of tradition. The experiences of the German political prisoners serve as a final reminder, however, that even for those who were granted the freedom to engage in some independent activity, beyond a certain point all of their power and autonomy became irrelevant. While music was to some extent able to assist in building community and comforting prisoners in their struggles, ultimately the SS tolerated only what did not jeopardize the larger plan.

4

Fragments of Humanity: Music in Auschwitz

The Auschwitz Landscape

Auschwitz has undoubtedly become the most prominent and evocative symbol of the Nazi genocide. During its four and a half years of operation, between June 1940 and January 1945, approximately 1.1 million people died within its bounds, the majority of them Jewish.[1]

Auschwitz was not a single camp, but a vast complex—the largest in the Nazi camp system. It consisted of two principal centres and approximately fifty satellite camps, spread out (sometimes tens of kilometres apart) over the resource-rich south-western Katowice district of present-day Poland. Auschwitz I, which was to become the nucleus of the complex, was established in the spring of 1940 on the site of disused army barracks near the town of Oświęcim. At the height of its operations, it housed 30,000 prisoners, and occupied an area one kilometre long and 400 metres wide. Construction of Auschwitz II (Birkenau) three kilometres to the north-west began in October 1941, and the camp began to function in the spring of 1942. Made up of separate sectors enclosed by barbed wire, it was intended both to house slave labour and to function as a mass killing factory. In early 1942, two peasant cottages near Birkenau whose inhabitants had been evicted began functioning as provisional gas chambers, and the following year saw the initiation of four specially designed gas chambers and crematoria. These could 'process' over 4,000 victims in twenty-four hours. The first and largest of the satellite camps was Monowice (Monowitz), established in 1942 and located a few kilometres to the east of the main camp. This was the site of I. G. Farben's 'Buna Werke' factory for synthetic rubber. Most of the satellite camps were

---

[1] Franciszek Piper, 'The Number of Victims', in Yisrael Gutman and Michael Berenbaum (eds.), *Anatomy of the Auschwitz Death Camp* (Bloomington and Indianapolis, 1994), 61–76 at 71.

established close to industrial plants, mines, or foundries, and housed labourers ranging in number from dozens to several thousands.[2]

Auschwitz was one of the harshest establishments in the Nazi camp system, with a mortality rate far higher than that of other camps. When new transports arrived, SS officers conducted selections in order to determine who would be sent to the gas chambers and who would be selected for work. Almost a million victims transported from all over Nazi-occupied Europe were killed immediately upon arrival, without ever being registered. Of the over 400,000 prisoners of both sexes who were registered as labourers, as many as 200,000 are estimated to have died. Even those who left the camp alive in many cases did not see the liberation: some died in other camps, and many lost their lives in the last phase of the war.[3]

Those inmates selected for work lived under the ever-present threat of the gas chambers nearby, as selections were conducted on a regular basis. While the camp command continuously battled the tension between exploiting the available labour force and proceeding with the extermination of undesirable groups, this was to some extent reconciled through the policy of *Vernichtung durch Arbeit* (Destruction through work). The constant influx of new transports meant that labour was regularly renewable; as a result, inmates were worked to the limits of their strength and simply sent to the gas chambers when they had outlived their usefulness.[4]

The distinctive musical life that grew up in Auschwitz bore all the signs of this harsh environment. Its most visible feature was the specially constructed prisoner orchestras, which played at the camp gates each morning and evening as the labour contingents marched to and from work, and regularly accompanied executions. These orchestras played a valuable role in the extermination process, helping the operation to run smoothly and assisting in the maintenance of discipline and order. As in Sachsenhausen, the SS also imposed frequent forced singing sessions, and torture sessions in which music was used in inventive and sadistic ways.

Opportunities for voluntary activity among the labourer population were severely limited. First, the strict regimen of daily life left little space for self-

[2] Yisrael Gutman, 'Auschwitz—An Overview', in Gutman and Berenbaum (eds.), *Anatomy*, 16–17, 30.

[3] Ibid. 6–7; Piper, 'The Number of Victims', 71.

[4] Attitudes changed somewhat from 1942, with the increasing demands of war on the eastern front and corresponding shortages of manpower. Yisrael Gutman maintains that a tangible shift in policy was manifest particularly from 1943 onwards in modest improvements in prisoners' living conditions, and a subsequent lessening of the mortality rate. Although this policy saved the lives of some Jewish workers, it did not, however, substantially affect the progress of the genocide, which reached its apogee during this period. Gutman, 'Auschwitz', 9.

initiated activity. Prisoners were woken at 4.30 a.m., and after a mandatory roll-call set off to their places of work. Most forced labour was performed outdoors regardless of the season, and lasted for as long as twelve hours during the summer. Upon their return to the camp, prisoners attended another roll-call. If numbers did not tally with those taken in the morning, prisoners could be delayed for hours on the *Appellplatz*. The roll-call was often followed by individual or collective punishments. Only after these had been completed could prisoners return to their barracks, where they received their meagre food rations; a few hours later, they were confined to their blocks for the night. While camps such as Sachsenhausen, Dachau, and Buchenwald sometimes allowed for informal entertainment among certain groups, the hostile terrain of Auschwitz made this a near impossibility for the vast majority of inmates.

Apart from their demanding work duties, prisoners were constantly bombarded with orders from functionaries and the SS which demanded their immediate and accurate response. Their actions were closely monitored, and they could claim no privacy in their overcrowded barracks. In addition, endless hunger, lack of access to basic necessities, and the arbitrary punishments to which they were subjected meant that their attention was overwhelmingly focused on physical survival. Even on Sundays, when most were not required to work, mandatory cleaning, showering, and other activities kept them occupied.[5]

While the majority of Auschwitz prisoners only experienced music as it was imposed by the SS, for a small sector of 'prominent' prisoners, however, it was a popular and widely available commodity.

As elsewhere, the SS attempted to destabilize the masses by imposing unequal systems of division. A rigid prisoner hierarchy was in existence, governed by functionaries. The hierarchy was determined on the basis of various factors, primarily prisoner types, and national or religious origins. Jews and Gypsies were at the bottom of the racial ladder, outranked only marginally by Poles, Russians, and other Slavs.[6] German prisoners usually ranked highest, and at the outset assumed most functionary positions, although later this privilege was extended to Poles and Jews as well.

Once again, as elsewhere, the most powerful functionaries were the *Lager-älteste* (camp leader), *Blockälteste* (block leaders), and *Kapos* (in charge of

---

[5] Ibid. 20–1.

[6] Anna Pawełcyńska, *Values and Violence in Auschwitz: A Sociological Analysis* (Berkeley, Los Angeles, and London, 1979), 54.

work commandos). They enjoyed numerous advantages, including exemption from physical labour, extra food rations, a somewhat better supply of clothing, and better living conditions. Unlike Sachsenhausen, however, where political prisoners dominated the hierarchy for most of the camp's existence, in Auschwitz the most ruthless criminal prisoners were generally chosen, and given a considerable degree of power. *Kapos*, for example, were merely required to report the death of inmates under their supervision, but bore no responsibility for them.[7] Moreover, criminals were often actively recruited from other camps. The first Auschwitz serial numbers were assigned to thirty German criminals brought from Sachsenhausen in May 1940 in order to form the core of the prisoner leadership. Although some did not, many abused their authority by stealing food and clothes from prisoners, taking bribes, or arbitrarily singling out prisoners for punishment.[8] By investing certain prisoners with authority in this way, the SS aimed to encourage antagonism and hostilities, and to eliminate the possibility of group resistance. Political prisoners were only intermittently able to gain control in some parts of the camp complex.

Living under the command of criminal functionaries generally meant more terror, less rest, and severe restrictions on the already limited freedom of the prisoners. As Anna Pawełcyńska put it, a camp dominated by green triangles 'was a place where the law of the jungle ruled supreme'.[9] The effect, as far as music was concerned, was that inmates were unlikely to gain the support of functionaries, particularly their *Blockälteste*, for illegal activity. Since organized activities almost always relied on the assistance of higher-ranking prisoners, this meant that far fewer inmates were afforded the possibility of experiencing them than was the case in many other camps. In fact, organized communal events among 'ordinary' prisoners in Auschwitz were almost non-existent. The functionaries were sometimes as zealous as their SS overseers in punishing any signs of disobedience, and quashing undesirable behaviour; under such circumstances, initiating group activity became almost impossible.

In an attempt to destroy any potential cohesiveness, the SS also assigned living conditions in such a way as to separate national, political, or other homogeneous groupings. Although some inmates attempted to develop

---

[7] Danuta Czech, 'The Auschwitz Prisoner Administration', in Gutman and Berenbaum (eds.), *Anatomy*, 363.

[8] Pawełcyńska, *Values and Violence in Auschwitz*, 46.

[9] Ibid. 88.

informal support groups within their barracks, opportunities were limited: trust was not easily earned, and was usually reserved for relations and friends, people who had arrived on the same transport, or members of political or resistance groups. Attempts at forming groups were also repeatedly thwarted by alterations to block and work placements, and deaths of inmates. With its constant waves of transports and selections, the camp population was fluid and changeable. While informal groups that had been broken up sometimes maintained contact through the various channels of secret communication, these were severely restricted. Prisoners were thus generally unable to form groups large or secure enough to organize communal activities.[10]

SS tolerance for musical activities in ghettos and other camps derived, in part, from the realization that they assisted in maintaining order, calm, and compliance. They did so in a particularly convenient manner, as prisoners arranged their own activities; they were thus usually accepted if they were not perceived to pose a serious threat. The relative lack of such activities in Auschwitz suggests that the SS saw little reason to tolerate them. Tolerance for the mass of 'ordinary' prisoners did not extend far, most likely because there was no need to maintain a productive work force. In addition, it must be remembered that the possibility for voluntary musical activity to exist in the first place relied on several factors: a measure of free time, the stable physical condition of the prisoners, and the leniency of the SS and functionaries. Faced with constant brutality, hard labour, and fear of death, many of the Auschwitz inmates were so depleted as to be unable to engage in anything beyond the struggle for physical survival.

Songs for the Masses

The music-making that did occur amongst 'ordinary' prisoners can only be understood within the context of these severe restrictions. If they experienced self-initiated music at all, it was spontaneous, and happened on those rare occasions when they were relatively safe from the SS and hostile functionaries.

In almost all cases this music would be vocal, since few had access to musical instruments. Usually it took the form of individuals singing for one another, and less frequently of group singing. Only fragmentary evidence survives to indicate what form these sessions might have taken. The most

---

[10] Pawełcyńska, *Values and Violence in Auschwitz*, 33, 62, 66.

obvious reason for this is that many of the inmates who experienced them did not survive. In addition, since people feared denunciation and reserved their trust for few others, most private interactions remained the unrecorded knowledge of individuals or small groups. As such, even those who survived could bear witness only to the events that they experienced.[11]

Nonetheless, musical activity of this kind did occasionally occur, usually when small groups of friends sang among themselves, or when people approached members of their blocks or commandos asking them to sing for the group. A German-Jewish prisoner, Elisabeth Lichtenstein, who arrived at Auschwitz I in November 1943, recalled the scenario that followed the shaving and tattooing of her newly arrived group:

All the women were in a state of complete exhaustion and at the end of their nervous strength. Some were standing around apathetically, some were screaming and laughing hysterically, many squabbled and fought among themselves. There were also those that sang. A neighbour who had accompanied me from Szered and knew that I was a music-lover and that I had a good voice, said that I should sing something, so that we would not all go mad. I naturally did not have the courage to sing, but as the time dragged on and we had already been standing there waiting for hours, I began to sing the Ave Maria. I did not know the text, I sang only the melody. While I sang, it became quiet in the hall, those who were screaming fell silent, those who were fighting stopped.[12]

Other former inmates described similar musical episodes. They assigned them similar significance, claiming that they were a temporary distraction, and that they helped them to take their minds off reality and to calm them down. The prisoner-doctor Gisella Perl described how one of her young patients, ill with typhus, would sing for fellow inmates in the Birkenau hospital barracks. Perl maintained that the girl's offerings of classical arias and *lieder* were so eagerly received that it was almost as if the audience imagined itself in a beautiful concert hall, far from the camp world. The Jewish inmate Bracha Gilai, who was regularly asked to sing by the women in her barracks, claimed that her performances made her listeners feel better, and that they helped to create a more soothing and comforting atmosphere. As a result, she explained, they took particular care for her health and safety.[13]

As in Sachsenhausen, it was also not uncommon in Auschwitz for singers to give informal 'concerts' in different blocks, in exchange for food and other rewards. The Jewish prisoner Sam Goldberg recalled that in Birkenau he

[11] John Komski, USHMM, RG-50.042.16.
[12] Elisabeth Lichtenstein, WL, Eyewitness Testimony P.III.h. No. 1116.
[13] Gisella Perl, *I was a Doctor in Auschwitz* (New York, 1948), 136–7; Bracha Gilai, YV, 03/6665.

travelled from block to block telling jokes and singing songs from home; he maintained that people supported these sessions because they helped to keep them going and allowed them to forget the horrors around them. The Italian Emilio Jani, a singer in the Auschwitz I orchestra, frequently sang to fellow inmates, and even had a friend trying to organize him private engagements. Although his friend's advances were not always well received—the payments he demanded were sometimes excessive—Jani insisted that his singing was widely appreciated, and that, as with Gilai, people were concerned about his well being.[14]

Apart from these and other isolated examples, the most compelling evidence to suggest that singing took place comes in the form of short verses and couplets, newly composed or modified from pre-existing songs, that could only have circulated among the prisoner population through these kinds of haphazard, informal activities.[15] Although many songs have probably been lost, a substantial number were recovered after the war, mostly through oral accounts. Since in most cases they had never existed as written texts, there were sometimes several versions. In addition, details were often lacking: former inmates remembered only fragments of texts or melodies, could not recall exactly where or when they had heard a given song, or were unable to specify its authorship. Even at the time, people picked up verses in different circumstances without knowing their provenance, and passed them on to others in a similarly indiscriminate manner. The dearth of evidence makes it almost impossible to determine the context in which the songs were sung.

The very fact of their existence, however, reveals that even within the constraints of the camp the circulation of information did not cease. Auschwitz inmates were denied access to most of the basic channels of communication, not only with the outside world but also within the camp complex itself. As a result, the more informal communication channels through which knowledge and ideas could be transmitted—the unregulated and unrecorded words, gestures, and interactions that even in 'normal' society play an integral role in the production of meaning—assumed particular value in the camp, albeit in a radically modified form.

Songs, in the same way as stories, sometimes helped to reconnect individuals with their pre-war lives, or provided opportunities for imaginative escape into a world outside the camp. As Tadeusz Borowski wrote, '[e]verybody here tells stories—on the way to work, returning to the camp, working in the fields

---

[14] Sam Goldberg, USHMM, RG-50.042.12; Emilio Jani, *My Voice Saved Me: Auschwitz 180046* (Milan, 1961), 96.

[15] For listing of newly created songs from Auschwitz, see the Appendix, §VI.

and in the trucks, in the bunks at night, standing at roll-call'.[16] They not only functioned to strengthen past identities, but were also a valuable means of producing and communicating meaning about the camp world itself. Songs and stories circulated about various elements of camp life: prisoner functionaries, the state of the war, forced labour, food, the gas chambers, and so on. These did not have the sole purpose of spreading information, but also helped to connect inmates to a wider framework where the meaning of their experiences could be more communally negotiated and shared. This does not of course imply that their perceptions of their experiences were uniform, merely that ideas circulated and interacted beyond the level of individuals. Songs were also an effective means of communication with other camps.[17]

In this framework, songs functioned as a useful mnemonic device, recording experiences and responses in a way that could be easily remembered. For the most part, they were based on popular pre-existing melodies rather than on newly composed ones. Many songwriters took pains to portray camp life in explicit detail, in order to document the kinds of crimes being perpetrated: documentation served both as a means of contemporary news transmission, and as a way of bearing witness for the future. Songs in this category include 'Zwillingi' (Twins, 1944), which describes some of the medical experiments conducted by Dr Mengele; the Czech inmate Margit Bachner's 'Auschwitzlied' (Auschwitz song), which discusses everything from disease, heavy labour, and torture to the incessant longing for home and family; a song entitled 'Zug zum Krematorium' (Train to the crematorium) about the burning of victims in Birkenau in 1944; a harrowing song by Zbigniew Adamczyk called 'Znów śmierć zagląda mi w oczy' (Again death looks me in the eye, 1940) about the torturing of Auschwitz inmates; and the Greek-Jewish prisoner Ya'akov Levi's 'Saloniki' (1943), which documents some of the horrors of life in Auschwitz.[18]

Another example comes from the former inmate Adolf Gawalewicz, who recalled an anonymous verse called 'Gazownia' (Gas chamber; see Ex. 4.1) sung in 1942 to the tune of the pre-war tango 'Jest jedna jedyna' (There is only one):

[16] Tadeusz Borowski, *This Way for the Gas, Ladies and Gentlemen* (London, 1967), 124.

[17] A moving example is Jewish prisoner Aron Liebeskind's elegy 'A viglid far mayn yingele in krematoryum' (A lullaby for my little son in the crematorium), written in Treblinka and passed on to Kulisiewicz in Sachsenhausen by Liebeskind himself, before the latter's deportation to Auschwitz in 1943. See Linde (ed.), *KZ-Lieder*, 20–1.

[18] 'Zwillingi' and 'Zug zum Krematorium', cited in USHMM, RG-55.019.09 (Kulisiewicz Collection); 'Znów śmierć zagląda mi w oczy', cited in USHMM, RG-55.003.70 (research materials relating to Auschwitz, Kulisiewicz Collection); 'Auschwitzlied' and 'Saloniki', cited in Hoch, 'Ha'tarbut ha'muziqalit', 305–6, 308–15.

Ex. 4.1. 'Gazownia'. USHMM, RG-55.003.07

> Jest jedna gazownia,
> Gdzie się wszyscy poznamy,
> Gdzie się wszyscy spotkamy,
> Może jutro—kto wie?[19]
>
> There is one gas chamber,
> Where we will all get to know each other,
> Where we will all meet each other,
> Maybe tomorrow—who knows?

Former Auschwitz inmates remarked that the shock experienced by new arrivals quickly turned into a kind of numbed calmness, and that the constant violence was quietly assimilated into their consciousness. Like 'Gazownia', many of the verses reflected this attitude, revealing the astonishing equanimity with which inmates came to relate to the grim reality around them. A song written in 1944 by the Birkenau inmate Jadwiga Laszczyńska called 'Frauenlager' (Women's camp) was almost flippant in its approach to the camp world. Sung to the popular Russian melody 'Wolga, Wolga' (Volga, Volga), it was a collage of camp images and jargon, all in German. Laszczyńska used these common phrases to create an impression of the sights and sounds of the Birkenau women's sub-camp:

> 'Kaffee holen!' und 'Aufstehen!'—
> 'Appell, Appell!'—'Alle r-raus!'—
> 'Und zu Fünfen!'—'Achtung!'—'Ruhe!'
> 'Zählappell!'—'Es stimmt genau!'
>
> Revier, Grippe und Fleckfieber,
> Durchfall, Scheisse, Krätze, Laus!
> 'Kranke fertig!', Leichen, Kamin,
> Krematorium, Spritze, Gas![20]

---

[19] Research materials relating to Birkenau (Kulisiewicz Collection), USHMM, RG-55.003.07.
[20] *Przegląd Lekarski* articles in German translation (Kulisiewicz Collection), USHMM, RG-55.019.09.

'Get your coffee!' and 'Get up!'—
'Roll-call, roll-call!'—'Everyone out!'—
'And in fives!'—'Attention!'—'Quiet!'
'Head count!'—'It's exactly right!'

Sickbay, flu and typhus,
Diarrhoea, shit, scabies, lice!
'The sick are finished!', corpses, chimney,
Crematorium, injection, gas!

Laszczyńska's song has a certain black humour in its suggestion that the only German words the Polish prisoners acquired were these aggressive commands and descriptions of death and disease. The kinds of humour to which inmates tended seem to have become increasingly dark and vulgar the more their situation degenerated, and the more their existence was reduced to basic bodily functions. Kulisiewicz confirmed that prisoners particularly enjoyed singing songs that contained vulgar and graphic descriptions such as these. Acknowledging and recording their reality in this way might also have helped inmates to alleviate some of their sense of helplessness. Inmates such as the Pole Janina Mielczarek indeed claimed that they found some personal relief in the act of recording what they had witnessed, often in crude and explicit ways.[21]

The songs were also a way of making light of the camp. According to one of Kulisiewicz's informants, one of the most popular Polish songs was 'W Auschwitz-Lager gdy mieszkałem' (When I lived in the Auschwitz camp), a cheerful march that sarcastically described the 'paradise on earth' that was Auschwitz, where prisoners were infested with lice, subjected to daily violence and beatings, and above all made to suffer through endless roll-calls. Several new stanzas were added by inmates during the time of the camp's existence.[22]

From what we can gather, verses and songs such as these circulated informally and unpredictably, in most cases between individuals and small groups of friends. Occasionally, however, larger communal song sessions occurred spontaneously among groups of 'ordinary' prisoners. In most cases, these consisted of people of common national or religious origin singing pre-existing songs. Some Czech women interned in Birkenau, for example, recalled grouping together behind their blocks and singing a variety of Slovak and Czech folk melodies. The Auschwitz I prisoner Edmund Polak similarly remembered a day when the *Kapo* of his commando unexpectedly allowed them to sing traditional Polish songs, including patriotic offerings

---

[21] Ibid.
[22] Songs with notation from Auschwitz (Kulisiewicz Collection), USHMM, RG-55.004.14.

such as the 'Warszawianka'. The Birkenau inmate Lin Jaldati recalled an evening in her block shortly after her arrival in late 1944, when Dutch, Hungarian, French, Polish, and German inmates sang national anthems, folk songs, and nostalgic melodies from their respective homelands. Although the various languages posed some difficulties in communication, Jaldati claimed that the emotional session created a palpable sense of unity.[23]

Perhaps the most famous account of communal singing was former *Sonderkommando* member Filip Müller's description of Czech Jews from the family camp about to be gassed in Birkenau in July 1944:[24]

At last they had been told straight to their faces what awaited them ... Their voices grew subdued and tense, their movements forced, their eyes stared as though they had been hypnotized. The atmosphere in the room was one of immense gravity. Most of the people now began to undress, but some were still hesitating ... Suddenly a voice began to sing. Others joined in, and the sound swelled into a mighty choir. They sang first the Czechoslovak national anthem and then the Hebrew song 'Hatikvah'. And all this time the SS men never stopped their brutal beatings. It was as if they regarded the singing as a last kind of protest which they were determined to stifle if they could. To be allowed to die together was the only comfort left to these people. Singing their national anthem they were saying a last farewell to their brief but flourishing past, a past which had enabled them to live for twenty years in a democratic state, a respected minority enjoying equal rights. And when they sang 'Hatikvah', now the national anthem of the state of Israel, they were glancing into the future, but it was a future which they would not be allowed to see. To me the bearing of my countrymen seemed an exemplary gesture of national honour and national pride which stirred my soul.[25]

In a similar setting, Jarosław Warchoła witnessed the singing of 'La Marseillaise' by French Jews being led to their deaths in late 1943.[26] While communal nationalist sentiment did not disappear in the Auschwitz camps, it remained weak, as I have suggested, because of the deliberate dispersal of national

---

[23] Kuna, *Musik an der Grenze*, 97; *Przegląd Lekarski* articles in German translation (Kulisiewicz Collection), USHMM, RG-55.019.09; Lin Jaldati and Eberhard Rebling, *Es brennt, Brüder, es brennt: Jiddische Lieder* (Berlin, 1966), 409–10.

[24] The family camp was established in Sept. 1943 for Jewish prisoners who had been brought from Theresienstadt. They did not undergo selection on arrival; instead, they were placed in a separate camp, where they were allowed to keep their clothes, their hair was not cut, and men, women, and children were allowed to remain together. Their living conditions, however, were no different from those in other Birkenau sub-camps. The purpose of the camp, which was liquidated in July 1944, was apparently to refute reports of the mass murder of Jews at Auschwitz in the event of a visit by the International Red Cross. Nili Keren, 'The Family Camp', in Gutman and Berenbaum (eds.), *Anatomy*, 428–9.

[25] Filip Müller, *Auschwitz Inferno: The Testimony of a Sonderkommando* (London, 1979), 110–11.

[26] Testimony of and correspondence with Jarosław Warchoła (Kulisiewicz Collection), USHMM, RG-55.003.15.

groups. Although musical expression of a nationalist kind was correspondingly sporadic, these and other examples suggest that where it was possible, and particularly at moments of crisis, inmates found value in affirming a sense of group identity and belonging.

Although Jewish prisoners made up the vast majority of the Auschwitz population, only a handful of their songs have been recovered. In part, this is the result of the particularly high mortality rate among Jews, which meant that fewer survived to give evidence. We also know, however, that when they did have occasion to sing, Jewish inmates often drew on pre-existing music, such as Yiddish folk songs, or songs related to religious festivals. This was both because existing music helped to rekindle a sense of past communal identity, and a result of the simple fact that Auschwitz left Jews with little opportunity to create anything new. Even so, Kaczerginski and Leivick included in their collection three songs by Jewish inmates recalled by survivors. The inmate Yosef Wolf recalled a short verse entitled 'Kum tsu mir' (Come to me), which described a prisoner's longing for his beloved. The author was unknown, but he maintained that it began to circulate in Monowitz in 1943. 'Ikh vil zen mayn meydele' (I want to see my little girl) was credited to an unknown female inmate of Birkenau, who wanted the 'black locomotive' that had brought her to the camp to take her back home to see her daughter.[27] Kaczerginski and Leivick also included the Yiddish translation of a Polish song written by an unnamed Jewish girl who did not survive the camp. It was known as 'Der tango fun Oshvientshim' (The Auschwitz tango), and the former inmate Irke Yanovski recalled that it was sung to the melody of a pre-war tango (see Ex. 4.2). This song mourned the lack of music in the camp, but expressed the hope that song would once again uplift the prisoners:

> Mir hobn tangos, fokstrotn un melodiyes
> Gezungen un getantst nokh far dem krig.
> Di tsarte lider, tseklungene, farbenkte
> Hobn mit libe undz dem kop farvigt.
> Un itst milkhome, keyner shaft keyn lider
> Fun yene yunge yorn in der shtot.
> Zing-oyf, o meydl, an ander lidl
> Fun teg un nekht in lager hinter drot.
> > Undzer shklafn-tango—unter knut fun shleger,
> > O der shklafn-tango fun dem Oshvientshimer lager.
> > Shtolene shpizn fun di vekhter-khayes—
> > O, es ruft di frayhayt un di tsayt di fraye.

---

[27] Kaczerginski and Leivick, 219, 256.

Ex. 4.2. 'Der tango fun Oshvientshim'. Kaczerginski and Leivick, 410

Der neger nemt bald aher zayn mandoline
Un vet bald oyfdrimplen zayn lidl do,
Un der englender, frantsoyz zingen a nigun,—
Vet fun troyer vern a triyo.
Un oykh der polak a nem tut bald zayn fayfl
Un er vet gebn filn gor der velt,—
Vet dos gezang dan ontsindn di hertser,
Vos lekhtsn nokh der frayhayt vos zey felt.
Undzer shklafn-tango . . . [28]

---

[28] Kaczerginski and Leivick, 254, 410.

We danced tangos and foxtrots and sang melodies
Even before the war.
The gentle songs, resounding, yearning,
Rocked us to sleep with love.
And now war, no one writes songs
About those young years in the city.
Oh strike up a song, young girl, another song
About days and nights in the camp behind wire.
    Our slave-tango—under the whip of the oppressors,
    Oh the slave-tango of the Auschwitz camp.
    Steel spears of the guard-animals—
    Oh, freedom and free times are calling.

The Negro soon brings his mandolin
And will soon tinkle his song here,
And the Englishman, Frenchman sing a tune,—
From sorrow will come a trio.
And also the Polack soon takes up his little flute
And he will make the whole world feel—
Let song then rouse the hearts,
That yearn for the freedom they lack.
    Our slave-tango . . .

Interestingly, this song lacks the anger and ferocity of many of the Polish songs. The Yiddish songs that came out of Auschwitz, as elsewhere, were characterized by a tone of melancholy, nostalgia, and deep loss, but did not confront the horrors of the camp in the explicit manner of some of their counterparts. Tango was a popular song genre in the pre-war period, and, as we have seen, continued to be used by prisoners across the camp and ghetto spectrum as a basis for new lyrics. Particularly in the setting of the sad tango melody—one of those 'gentle songs' belonging to a time gone by—this song captured a poignant sense of longing for the past. It is striking to note, however, that unlike many of the Yiddish songs we have encountered thus far, those from Auschwitz were generally inwardly focused: none talked about the urge to document for posterity, and the only suggestion of the future was the vague reference to 'free times'. Songs of this kind made gestures towards the immediate landscape— 'days and nights in the camp behind wire'—rather than confronting it directly. Above all, they seem to have been an opportunity for temporary diversion, for dreaming of freedom and of harmonious music-making between nations— dreams that quickly dissolved in the face of harsh reality.

It is impossible to know how many more such songs were written by Jewish inmates. We do know, however, that some of the ghetto songs eventually found their way to the camps as well. In particular, Glik's partisan hymn 'Zog nit keynmol' had travelled to the far reaches of Nazi-occupied Europe by the time of the liberation.[29]

Life amongst 'Prominents'

All of these examples show that 'ordinary' inmates found occasion to engage with music, and that it assumed a certain value particularly as far as informal communication was concerned. However, it is important to recognize that for the mass of 'ordinary' prisoners, music of their own making was only a minuscule part of life, if it played a part at all. After mere weeks in the camp, people entered a state of being in which the first priority was physical survival. They pursued that end by whichever means necessary, often forced as a result to behave in ways that undermined the values of their pre-war existence. Even for those who were not completely subsumed by the deterioration of their bodies, the songs they sang filled only intermittent moments in a world of violence and hard labour. In an attempt to puncture exaggerated assumptions about the role cultural activities could play, the French inmate Charlotte Delbo insisted that the prerequisite was a level of physical welfare that most prisoners did not possess:

You may say that one can take away everything from a human being except the faculty of thinking and imagining. You have no idea. One can turn a human being into a skeleton gurgling with diarrhoea, without time or energy to think. Imagination is the first luxury of a body receiving sufficient nourishment, enjoying a margin of free time, possessing the rudiments from which dreams are fashioned. People did not dream in Auschwitz, they were in a state of delirium.[30]

For certain categories of inmates, however, life at Auschwitz was significantly more comfortable than it was for the masses. Aside from functionaries, the largest group of prisoners to whom this applied were those placed in 'prominent' work units such as Canada and the *Effektenkammer* (both located in Birkenau),[31] the administration office, the *Zimmerei* (carpenters' detach-

---

[29] The song became the official hymn of most of the east European partisan brigades, and was translated into a number of European languages. Rubin, *Voices of a People*, 453.

[30] Charlotte Delbo, *Auschwitz and After* (New Haven, 1995), 168.

[31] 'Canada' was the name by which the warehouse used to sort belongings from newly arrived transports came to be known. It was so called because it was viewed as a place of great wealth. The *Effektenkammer* (property registry office), housed in its own separate enclosure, was used to store the carefully inventoried possessions of people who had been sent to the camp by the Gestapo, and on whom personal dossiers were kept. A position in this commando constituted one of the highest in

ment), the kitchen, and the infirmaries. Inmates assigned to these commandos were considered 'privileged', as their positions afforded them several advantages: they worked indoors and were thus spared exposure to the cold, their tasks were less tiring, they had better living conditions, more opportunities to 'organize' food and clothing, and were not subject to the same kind of *Kapo* brutality as were those working outside the camp. They also had freedom of movement within the camp, and more autonomy than their fellow prisoners. Even more significant, however, was the stable, contained nature of the work groups, which helped to counteract isolation and anonymity. Small support groups could be formed and maintained over a period of time. In addition, working with the same functionaries and SS on a regular basis meant that relations were more personal, and that greater cooperation could develop. In some cases commandos were restricted to skilled people such as doctors, plumbers, or translators. In most cases, however, they were not, although assignment to one of them often depended on one's having connections with functionaries or prisoners with influence.[32]

The gap between 'ordinary' prisoners and the elite in Auschwitz was enormous. It must be emphasized that the latter group was made up not only of those who had knowingly joined the 'apparatus of terror', but also those who had acquired their positions through lucky chance and did what was subsequently necessary to preserve their 'privilege'.[33] Because of the power they wielded, they were often courted by inmates offering to perform diverse activities—ranging from domestic assistance to various forms of entertainment, including prostitution—in exchange for food, cigarettes, or shelter from hard labour. Status in Auschwitz was thus reflected not only in one's access to the basic necessities for physical survival, but perhaps even more so in the realm of leisure and amusement.

Music was popular and widely available, but was nonetheless a commodity that had to be 'organized'. As they had the means, 'privileged' prisoners could take advantage of this extravagance. According to Laks, the music-organizing 'industry' took on unprecedented proportions 'with the continually increasing influx of "gas meat" and the accompanying prosperity of the privileged classes of Auschwitz society [because of the valuable possessions the new arrivals invariably brought with them]'.[34] In the main camp, Birkenau, and

the camp hierarchy. According to Szymon Laks, 'except for freedom [these people] had everything one could wish'. Szymon Laks, *Music of Another World* (Evanston, Ill., 1989), 98; see also Krystyna Żywulska, *I Came Back* (London, 1951), 105–6.

[32] Pawełcyńska, *Values and Violence in Auschwitz*, 48, 70.

[33] Ibid. 80.

[34] Laks, *Music of Another World*, 94.

Monowitz, musicians were frequently recruited for their services. Usually they would be drawn from the ranks of orchestra members, but sometimes were discovered by chance by functionaries who overheard them singing for fellow inmates, or when musicians were actively sought. They would be invited to 'prominent' blocks or to functionaries' rooms to perform, and were rewarded for their work. The Norwegian Jew Herman Sachnowitz, for example, recalled how in December 1942, before he joined the Monowitz orchestra, he and four of his fellows were requested by their *Blockälteste* to sing at a Christmas concert for functionaries. They earned a pot of soup for their efforts, as well as an additional engagement in block 4, where most of the camp 'aristocracy' was housed. The Birkenau inmate Gilai was one of those regularly called on by her *Blockälteste* to sing songs in exchange for bread and soup. Gilai attributed her subsequent placement in the *Effekten-kammer* to her close relationship with this functionary.[35] In the main camp, the Jewish inmate Matetyahu Nissim sang regularly on Sundays for Polish *Kapos* who came specially to hear him:

I didn't agree to it until they offered me cigarettes. When the quantity of cigarettes offered was big enough I agreed to sing. Two or three groups would come, and they would hold a competition between them as to the quantity of cigarettes that they would give me. I took the cigarettes, went to the block with my brother and would sing for them. There was a guitar there. In Auschwitz, one could say that I didn't suffer... singing saved me. I am alive thanks to my singing.[36]

These kinds of arrangements were common practice, and as they were convenient to all parties involved were tolerated. For musicians who did not have the good fortune to play in the orchestras, the rewards they obtained through these informal activities were invaluable, and many, like Nissim, attributed their survival to their additional 'earnings'.

For members of the orchestras, performances for 'prominent' inmates were a regular feature of life. In the Birkenau women's camp, the music block was a veritable meeting house for the elite, who came to listen in on rehearsals or to solicit individuals for private concerts. Musicians were approached on a daily basis by people seeking informal performances for their own pleasure, or entertainment for occasions such as birthdays and holidays. Laks described a typical celebration in the Birkenau men's camp:

---

[35] Herman Sachnowitz, *Auschwitz: Ein norwegischer Jude überlebte* (Frankfurt/M., 1981), 46–9; Bracha Gilai, YV, 03/6665.
[36] Matetyahu Nissim, YV, 03/4273.

The musicians chosen, generally three or four, got up from their pallets earlier than the others so that they could awaken the celebrant before reveille with the sounds of a triumphant march or serenade. The hero of the festivities would pretend convincingly that this attention was a complete surprise to him and moved him deeply. He would quickly get up and hand the musician-alarm clocks various presents. This introductory ceremonial ended with a sentimental romantic tune and traditional greetings, which the musicians had learned in several languages, for sometimes there were non-German celebrants.

The second act of the holiday most often took place in the VIP's private room, after evening roll call and with the participation of a larger number of musicians. The guests would sit down to an amply set table, with plenty of food and drink. After the meal, the company, quite tipsy and moved to tears, would recall their remote, precamp days, all the while crooning melancholy songs or frivolous airs—German obviously. It sometimes happened that some esman [SS man] unexpectedly barged into this sanctuary of camp bliss, to get a bite to eat and to down a glass of schnapps. This in no way disturbed the prevailing atmosphere; the merrymaking continued and sometimes lasted late into the night.[37]

Because of the authority vested in them by the SS, the elite were also afforded far greater freedom than 'ordinary' prisoners to engage in musical activities such as performance and composition themselves. In the first place, they were more likely to have the space in which to write, and the ability to do so without fear of serious retribution. In addition, they had greater access to writing materials. For those who lived in the orchestra blocks, paper and pencils were freely available; for others, particularly those working in the administration, they were easy to come by.

Shortly after the establishment of the main camp, the orchestra member Franek Stryj wrote 'Pieśń Oświęcimska' (Auschwitz song), based on the melody of a prison song (see Ex. 4.3). Dedicated to a Polish family from the town of Kończyc, the song was a graphic description of what had befallen Stryj's family, framed by emotive references to the fate of Poland:

Ex. 4.3. 'Pieśń Oświęcimska'. USHMM, RG-55.004.14

---

[37] Laks, *Music of Another World*, 95.

Obóz śmierci Oświęcimia zatrzasł za mną bramę swą.
Przepojona jest tu ziemia potem, łzami, polską krwią.
Bo Ojczyznę ukochaną skuł w kajdany Czarny Ptak.
Nad jej krwią broczącą raną zatknął swój drapieżny znak.
Dom rodzinny wraz z kołyską oddał innym, obcym nam.
Świętych zniczów starł ognisko, nas do łagru zagnał bram.
Mojej mamie serce pękło, trup jej padł u kata stóp.
A kat—z twarzą krwią nabrzękłą kopnął ją w przydrożny grób.
Młodsza siostra przymuszona obcym panom ciągnąć pług.
Może gdzieś przy pracy skona jako jedna z biednych sług.
Mnie wraz z ojcem, wespół z bratem do Auschwitzu zagnał los.
Pod katowskim gniem się batem, w troskach nam pobielał włos.
Ojciec padł rażony kulą, brat na rękach skonał mi.
W nowym życiu się utulą, mnie zostały żal i łzy.
Jeśli serce mi nie pęknie, w pracy nie zabiją mnie,
Lub na śmierć się nie zatęsknię, za swe krzywdy pomszczę się!
Gdy i mnie los z ziemi zmaże, wzlecę w niebo jako dym.
Proch mój stanie się ołtarzem, stąd dam rozkaz braciom swym:
Zrzućcie z siebie twarde pęta! Zdepczcie wraże gniazdo żmij!
Niech powstanie Polska święta, Polsko moja, trzykroć żyj![38]

Death camp Auschwitz shut its gate behind me.
The soil in here is saturated with sweat, tears, and Polish blood,
Because our beloved homeland is imprisoned by the black bird.
Over her wound, gushing with blood, it imposed its predatory sign.
Our family home, together with the cradle, it gave to others alien to us.
The fire of holy light has been extinguished, we have been shut behind the Lager's gate.
My mother's heart broke, her corpse fell at the feet of the executioner,
And the executioner—with face swollen with blood, kicked her into the grave by the road.
My younger sister was forced to pull the plough of the foreign masters.
Maybe she will die one day at work, as one of the poor servants.
I, my father, and my brother were chased to Auschwitz by fate,
Under the whip of the executioner our hair became white.
My father fell hit by a bullet, my brother died in my arms.
In the new life they will hug each other, I am left with sorrow and tears.
If my heart won't break, they won't kill me at work,
Or I won't die of longing, I will avenge my loss!
When fate wipes me too from this earth, I will float to the sky as smoke.
My ash will become an altar, from where I will give orders to my brothers:
Drop the hard chains! Crush the viper's nest!
Let saint Poland be reborn, my Poland, live forever!

[38] Songs with notation from Auschwitz (Kulisiewicz Collection), USHMM, RG-55.004.14.

The sheer length of the song positions it in stark contrast to the brief verses sung by 'ordinary' prisoners. It clearly demonstrates the impulse to document the camp world, and distinguishes itself not only in the candidness of its descriptions but also in the openness of its nationalistic fervour. Stryj's membership of the orchestra probably meant that he was less afraid to write such a subversive text, or that its presence was less likely to be discovered. He was also able to arrange that it be performed at a communal evening organized by Poles in July 1941.

It is unclear how frequently these communal evenings occurred, but evidence from another source confirms that they often served as a forum for explicitly nationalistic sentiment, and for open condemnation of what was being perpetrated in the camp. The Polish prisoner Jarosław Warchoła, who worked in the Birkenau infirmary, recalled one of the song evenings that he attended, organized by the long-time prisoner and *Blockälteste* Józef Polak. The performance was tightly guarded by Soviet fellow prisoners, and consisted of 'forbidden songs from the streets of Warsaw': songs from the occupation, soldiers' songs, old Russian songs, and several provocative songs newly created in the camp. One of these was his own composition, entitled simply 'Birkenau' (see Ex. 4.4):

Drutami okołony skrawek świata,
Gdzie ludzie tylko numerami są.
Gdzie brat spodłony gnębi swego brata,
I śmierć kościstą dłoń wyciąga swą.
Tam tyle krwi—tyle łez już pociekło,
Tam co noc z krzykiem trwogi budzisz się ze snu,
A gdy cię ktoś zapyta: gdzie jest piekło?—
To śmiało odpowiedzieć możesz mu:
Birkenau, przeklęte Birkenau,
Oblane krwią i łzami,
Przez Boga zapomniane piekła dno.
Birkenau—cierniowa droga,
Milionów ofiar wspólny grób,
Królestwo zła, gdzie nie ma Boga—
To Birkenau!
Płomieniem rzyga komin krematorium,
Odorem ciał spalonych cuchnie w krąg,
Cierniowej ścieżki więźnia kres i znoju,
Wędrówki kres—i koniec ludzkich mąk.
Tu grobu mieć nie będziesz, przyjacielu,
Popiołów garść rozwieje polny wiatr,

Ex. 4.4. 'Birkenau'. USHMM, RG-55.003.15 and RG-55.003.16

Nieważne to—wszak jesteś jeden z wielu,
Z tych wielu, co zapomniał o nich świat.[39]

The piece of the world surrounded by barbed wire,
Where people are only numbers.
Where the vile brother oppresses his brother,
And death is stretching its bony hand.
There has been so much blood there—so many tears shed,
There every night you wake up from your dream with a scream of fear,
And when someone asks you: where is Hell?—
You can easily answer:
Birkenau, damned Birkenau,
Bathed in blood and tears,
Forgotten by God, the bottom of hell.
Birkenau—the most terrible ordeal,
The common grave of the millions of victims,

---

[39] Testimony of and correspondence with Jarosław Warchoła (Kulisiewicz Collection), USHMM, RG-55.003.15; research materials concerning Warchoła's song 'Birkenau' (Kulisiewicz Collection), USHMM, RG-55.003.16.

The kingdom of evil where there is no God—
That's Birkenau!
The crematorium chimney is vomiting flames,
Vomiting with the stench of burned bodies all around,
It is the end of the prisoner's terrible ordeal
The end of the road—and the end of human torture.
Here you won't have a grave, my friend;
The handful of ash will be scattered by the wind,
That's not important—as you are one of the many,
Many that have been forgotten by the world.

After the war, no fewer than eight musical versions of the song were collected, suggesting that it went through multiple stages of modification as it passed between groups. This indicates, in turn, that it made a significant impact on a fair number of inmates, although it is unlikely that it spread beyond those 'privileged' prisoners who were able to attend communal gatherings. Both Warchoła and Stryj's songs make it clear, however, that even these people were not safe in the world 'where the vile brother oppresses his brother'. Once again, it seems that the text, with its graphic descriptions of death, despairing religious allusions, and resigned hopelessness, served both as a vent for the inmates' emotions, expressed in a communal setting, and as an acknowledgement of their suffering.

Both of these songs could only have been written by inmates in 'privileged' positions. The first and most obvious factor was the context within which they were first performed: the kinds of organized events almost always restricted to 'privileged' prisoners and functionaries. In addition, only songs that could be written down could afford to be so long. Those that could rely only on oral transmission, as we have seen, were restricted to short verses that were easily remembered and conveyed. The candidness of the songs' imagery and their openly expressed anger suggests the authors had more time, freedom, and personal space within which to express their views (Stryj in the orchestra and Warchoła in the hospital), although they also had to contend to some degree with the fear of retribution. Lastly, both Stryj and Warchoła apparently managed to retain these documents throughout their time at the camp, and to keep them when they left.

Medley from the *Effektenkammer*

One of the most extraordinary creations to have emerged from Auschwitz was Krystyna Żywulska's 'Wiązanka z Effektenkammer' (Medley from the

Effektenkammer). When she arrived at Birkenau in 1943, 25-year-old
Żywulska had never written poetry. Soon after her arrival, however, she
began composing short verses in her head as a way of relieving the boredom
of endless roll-calls. As an 'ordinary' prisoner, she was unable to write them
down, but she remembered some snippets after the war, and recalled that her
companions enjoyed singing them when sitting on their bunks or in the
latrines. Through unknown channels, one of Żywulska's verses reached an
influential old prisoner named Wala, who was impressed enough to organize
for her a transfer to the *Effektenkammer*. There, in her newly 'privileged'
position, she was able to write down her poems, to circulate them among her
fellow workers, and even to send some by messenger to a friend in the men's
camp.[40]

The 'Wiązanka' seems to have been the only of Żywulska's writings set to
music. It was a work of considerable scope and substance, made up of fifty-
four interconnected sections, each consisting of between six and thirty-two
bars of music with accompanying text. Most of the music was drawn from
pre-existing Polish melodies, including some well-known film tunes. However, Żywulska probably also composed parts of the work herself, including
the instrumental links at sections 37 and 44. The work, which Żywulska typed
herself in the camp, was arranged into two separate booklets of equal length.

In correspondence with Kulisiewicz after the war, Żywulska emphasized
the unusual circumstances under which the 'Wiązanka' was written. First, she
urged that the context of the *Effektenkammer* be made clear, since an unin-
formed reader might get the impression that Birkenau was no worse than a
'boarding school for young women'. While her commando suffered comparatively little, chances of survival for 'ordinary' prisoners were minimal. In
addition, she explained that the 'Wiązanka' was written hurriedly in late 1944,
when the front was nearing and liberation was already imminent. As a result,
discipline was more lax and the inmates had more freedom to entertain
themselves, and more cause to be optimistic. The sentimental, occasionally
frivolous rhymes were apparently what the women wanted to hear at this
time, although Żywulska once again emphasized that the 'Wiązanka' would
sound tasteless and insufferable if considered independently of its context.[41]

On first reading, the text is quite disjointed and fragmentary. Taken
together with Żywulska's post-war account, however—published in English
translation as *I Came Back*—it is clear that the 'Wiązanka' was intended as a

---

[40] Żywulska, *I Came Back*, 60, 105, 174.
[41] Żywulska, cited in USHMM, RG-55.019.09 (Kulisiewicz Collection).

collage of life in the *Effektenkammer*, and that all the cryptic, seemingly disconnected allusions would have been understood by her audience. Unlike many of the Polish camp songs, it contained only a few allusions to the bleaker aspects of camp life, the most explicit of which was this verse (see Ex. 4.5):

> (25) Już bucha, już dyszy, już każdy ją słyszy
> Walizek wciąż w górę tajemniczy dziwny dym.
> Szef nadchodzi, nic nie szkodzi, ważny jest wikt,
> Z nami jeszcze nie poradził nikt.[42]

> (25) [The train] is huffing and puffing, everyone can hear it,
> There is a pile of suitcases, and a mysterious, weird smoke,
> The boss is coming, but it doesn't matter, what's important is the diet,
> Because no one has dealt with us yet.

This verse is typical of Żywulska's idiosyncratic style. She did not clarify who 'the boss' was, nor what it meant to be 'dealt with', although in the context of Auschwitz it is possible to guess. The reference to 'us' was an expression of identity: Żywulska was not alone in her experiences, but part of a group of women who performed their daily tasks with a sense of security (albeit temporary) from the 'mysterious' smoke in the distance. However, it is clear that *Effektenkammer* workers were deeply affected by what was happening around them, particularly in the light of their own 'privileged' status. The lost possessions of murdered families—represented here in a 'pile of suitcases'— affected Żywulska particularly. On several occasions both in the 'Wiązanka' and in her book, she alluded to her distress at finding piles of photographs in Canada (see Exx. 4.6 and 4.7):[43]

Ex. 4.5. 'Wiązanka z Effektenkammer', Verse 25. USHMM,
RG-55.004.02 (all examples)

---

[42] Songs with notation from Birkenau (Kulisiewicz Collection), USHMM, RG-55.004.02 (the source of this and subsequent verses quoted from the 'Wiązanka').

[43] Żywulska, *I Came Back*, 160, 201–2.

Ex. 4.6. 'Wiązanka z Effektenkammer', Verse 22

Ex. 4.7. 'Wiązanka z Effektenkammer', Verse 23

(22) W personalnym wre,
Akta piętrzą się, miłych rozmów gwar,
A z pamiątek rodzinnych tchnie czar...

(22) In the personnel department it is frenetic,
The files are piling, you can hear the hum of nice conversations,
And the family souvenirs exude charm...

(23) Patrzę na twoją fotografię, którą dziś wyjęłam z akt,
I wypowiedzieć nie potrafię, jak mnie boli taki fakt.

(23) I look at your photograph, which I took out from the file today,
And I can't express how this fact hurts me.

Apart from these and a few fleeting examples, however, the 'Wiązanka' was based entirely in the world of the *Effektenkammer*, which Żywulska characterized as 'a beautiful oasis' in a country 'where everything is evil'. Many of the verses reveal the kinds of 'privileges' the *Effektenkammer* workers enjoyed: lenient functionaries, access to alcohol and luxury food items, musical entertainment, and—particularly when discipline became more lax—the chance for contact with inmates of the opposite sex. Several of the personalities mentioned in Żywulska's book also made brief appearances, including a typist from the *Schreibstube* named Mrs Ziutka, a Russian inmate from the *Effektenkammer* named Tania, and the block *Kapo* Maria. Although at times cryptic and surreal, the fragments create a colourful and compelling picture of this unusual space in the camp (see Ex. 4.8–4.12):

Pę - dem do ba - ra - ków mknie kapo Ma - ri - a,

ka - żdy za - raz znaj - dzie błąd kapo Ma - ri - a,

wszy - stko wi - dzi wszy - stko wie kapo Ma - ri - a,

le - ci nie wia - do - mo skąd kapo Ma - ri - a.

Ta na - sza ko - cha - na Ma - ry - ja co bez niej zro - bił - by szef?

Ex. 4.8. 'Wiązanka z Effektenkammer', Verse 28

Ba - rwny ich strój, ba - rwny strój, ta - kie śli - cznie skro - jo - ne pa -

sia - ki! O, Bo - że mój, Bo - że mój, jak to mi - ło jak o - bok chło-

pa - ki! Wo - rki aż drżą, wor - ki drżą, jak się

czu - le przy - bli - żam do nie - go, Prze - mi - li

są ci pa - no - wie z 'E - fek - tu' mę - ski - e - go.

Ex. 4.9. 'Wiązanka z Effektenkammer', Verse 30

(28) Pędem do baraków mknie—kapo Maria,
Każdy zaraz znajdzie błąd—kapo Maria,
Wszystko widzi wszystko wie—kapo Maria,
Leci nie wiadomo skąd—kapo Maria.
Ta nasza kochana Maryja . . . co bez niej zrobiłby szef?

(28) She is running to the barracks—Kapo Maria,
She will find every mistake—Kapo Maria,

Ex. 4.10. 'Wiązanka z Effektenkammer', Verse 32

Ex. 4.11. 'Wiązanka z Effektenkammer', Verse 39

Ex. 4.12. 'Wiązanka z Effektenkammer', Verse 49

She knows everything, sees everything—Kapo Maria,
You don't know where she comes from—Kapo Maria.
This is our beloved Maria . . . what would our boss do without her?

(30) Barwny ich strój, takie ślicznie skrojone pasiaki!
O, Boże mój, jak to miło jak obok chłopaki!
Worki aż drżą, jak się czule przybliżam do niego,
Przemili są ci panowie z 'Efektu' męskiego.

(30) Their clothes are colourful, such beautifully cut striped uniforms!
Oh my God, how nice when there are boys near us!
The sacks are trembling when I approach him,[44]
Charming are these men from the male 'Effekt'.

(32) Piłam... Kto mówi, że nie piłam?
Butelkę wytrąbiłam i jeszcze dwie butelki.
Kapo tak bardzo wódzię lubi, o to się nie poczubi,
Wypiję z nami też...
Pić—to jest jedyny życia sens i zagryźć tortu kęs,
Uśmiechnąć się spod rzęs.
Pić—to jest największy życia dar,
Żyć w świecie złudnych mar, mieć w sobie czar...

(32) I have been drinking... who says I haven't?
I drank a bottle, and then another two.
Kapo likes vodka so much, he won't be angry about this,
He'll drink with us...
To drink—is the only meaning of life, and to have a bite of cake,
To smile flirtatiously.
To drink—is the biggest gift in life,
To live in the world of false illusions, to have charm...

(39) To Bolek na harmonii
Gra i dusza łka, i serce łka...
A każdą chwilę szczęścia ma,
Bo ślicznie gra, tak rzewnie gra...

(39) Bolek on the harmonica
He plays and my soul is crying, and my heart is crying,
While each moment is filled with happiness,
Because he plays so beautifully, he plays so sadly.

(49) Flaszkę wina weź, troszkę konserw masz,
Ja cię nie wydam i ty mnie nie
Worek leży tam, wpakuj w worek ten,
Zniknij już za drzwiami jak ten złoty sen...

(49) Take a bottle of wine, you have some tinned meat,
I won't betray you and you won't betray me

---

[44] Żywulska explained that as contact between male and female workers was officially prohibited, they would meet secretly in the storehouses between the sacks of clothing. Cited in USHMM, RG-55.019.09 (Kulisiewicz Collection).

The sack lies there, let's pack it,
Disappear behind the door like a golden dream . . .

Although it is not mentioned in Żywulska's book, it is almost certain that the 'Wiązanka' was performed as a cabaret in the *Effektenkammer* during the final months of the camp's existence. Kulisiewicz had information to suggest that this was the case, and Żywulska's frequent observations that the women needed light-hearted entertainment indicate that this type of performance would not have been out of place.[45] The text of the 'Wiązanka' conformed with many traditional aspects of cabaret both in style and content, as did its musical accompaniment. The melodies were often quite sophisticated, and were clearly not intended for group singing. Żywulska also included hand-written performance directions on her score, suggesting that the context of performance was more formal than the communal song evenings. Lastly, several of the verses were explicitly directed at a live camp audience. There was an acknowledgement of their difficulties, but ultimately a light-hearted note of consolation and encouragement prevailed (see Ex. 4.13—4.16):

Ex. 4.13. 'Wiązanka z Effektenkammer', Verse 1

Ex. 4.14. 'Wiązanka z Effektenkammer', Verse 51

[45] Żywulska, *I Came Back*, 147–8, 229–30; biographies of contributing authors to Kulisiewicz's planned anthology (Kulisiewicz Collection), USHMM, RG-55.006.11.

Ex. 4.15. 'Wiązanka z Effektenkammer', Verse 53

Ex. 4.16. 'Wiązanka z Effektenkammer', Verse 54

(1) Już nie zapomnisz nas, przypomni Ci o nas piosenka
I zawsze nas będziesz pamiętać przez wiele lat.
I chociaż przejdzie czas, nie jedna zostanie ci scenka,
pojedzie ta nasza piosenka za Tobą w świat...

(1) You won't forget us, this song will remind you about us,
And you will always remember us, for many years.
And even though the time will come, you will be left with many images.
Our song will go with you into the world...

(51) Dwanaście godzin, to samo codzień, co noc to samo,
Ten sam los zły.
Lecz śmiej się zawsze, bądź dzielna zawsze,
Przyjdą łaskawsze dla ciebie dni.

(51) Twelve hours, the same every day and every night,
The same cruel fate.
But laugh always, be brave always,
Better days will come for you.

(53) Choć nas rozdzieli czas,
Przyjdą inne zmartwienia,
Drogie będą wspomnienia,
Drogi przebyty czas.

(53) Even though time will part us,
Other worries will come,
The memories will be precious,
And the time spent will be precious.

(54) I jak ktoś zanuci w Twojej wiejskiej ciszy,
W Twoim cichym domku piosnkę naszą znów usłyszysz...
Wyda Ci się dziwna, tak Ci będzie miło,
Że się już skończyło i że masz Swój dom...

(54) And when someone starts singing in the silence of your village,
In your quiet house you'll hear our song again...
It'll seem strange, but you'll feel nice,
That it's all over and you have your own house...

The songs of Żywulska, Warchoła, and Stryj serve to remind us that even 'privilege' in Auschwitz had vastly different categories. For these inmates, 'privilege' did not mean power over others as it did for those in positions of authority, like *Blockälteste* and *Kapos*. Rather, their 'privilege' derived from the closed, comparatively protected environments within which they worked. Moreover, their writings reveal in a powerful way that even those with the kinds of 'privilege' they enjoyed were not spared the brutality of the regime. While all had had the good fortune to be placed in work units with better status and chances for survival, they had also experienced profound individual and communal loss. Stryj's song was not so much an assertion of a Polish nationalistic spirit as an angry and agonizing chronicle of his family's destruction. Warchoła's was a harrowing lament that revealed its author firmly rooted in the isolated, hostile daily reality of Birkenau, where brothers destroy brothers. Żywulska, although milder in her descriptions, made clear that the camp was a place from which everybody, including her, wanted to get out.

At the same time, their world was obviously a far cry from that of most 'ordinary' prisoners, and their writings remind us even more powerfully of all that was not open to tens of thousands of others. 'Privileged' prisoners could use song as a medium for the expression not only of individual but also of national fate. They could organize gatherings where these kinds of songs would be performed for them, where they could vent their anger, their pain, and their hope to return home once again. Although these were not life-saving advantages as such, they allowed people to feel less isolated and helpless. They also gave people the opportunity to process their experiences in the context of a larger group. Moreover, they offered people the opportunity to record what they had experienced, sometimes with the hope that it would be preserved for future generations.

Forced Singing, the Orchestras, and the Nazi Authorities

As we have seen, both Auschwitz and Birkenau were stratified societies in which different classes of inmates had access to vastly different things. Szymon Laks, the former conductor of the Birkenau men's orchestra, confirmed that

[VIPs] had—except for freedom—everything their souls could want, and for them music was entertainment and an additional luxury for which they paid generously... For the class of paupers, however, if music had any effect at all, it had a disheartening one and deepened still further their chronic state of physical and mental prostration.[46]

Until now, this chapter has dealt with music as a voluntary activity across the spectrum of the inmate community. Laks's observation, however, reveals perhaps the most potent way in which the disparity between the powerful and the powerless was made manifest. The phenomenon of forced music-making was not unique to Auschwitz, but there it assumed a particularly visible role. Unlike other camps, the only music that the majority of prisoners were likely to experience was that designed by the SS to fulfil a variety of sadistic purposes.

As was the case in Sachsenhausen, forced singing sessions were a common element of life. Usually these would take place on the *Appellplatz* or as the commandos marched to and from work, and unsatisfactory performances would be duly punished. The repertoire consisted almost invariably of well-known German folk songs, or pre-existing songs whose lyrics had been modified, such as 'Im Auschwitz-Lager bin ich zwar' (I am in the Auschwitz camp), a modification of the Esterwegen song.[47] The Czech inmate Alžběta Hellerová recalled that *Kapos* forced her commando to sing a mocking version of the song 'Hamburg ist ein schönes Städtchen' (Hamburg is a beautiful little town), with the modified title 'Auschwitz ist ein schönes

[46] Laks, *Music of Another World*, 118.
[47] *Przegląd Lekarski* articles in German translation (Kulisiewicz Collection), USHMM, RG-55.019.09; Henryk Król, Auschwitz-Birkenau State Museum Archive (hereafter ABSM), 1710/159301.

Städtchen'.[48] Many Polish inmates similarly described how the SS forced them to sing sentimental songs as a way of torturing them. One of the favourites was 'Góralu czy ci nie żal' (Man of the mountains, is it not sad for you), a nostalgic nineteenth-century song about a man who had left his home in the mountains and yearned terribly to return.[49]

Music was also used as accompaniment for executions. According to the former Auschwitz I inmate Hinda Tennebaum, the killing of prisoners at the infamous execution wall adjacent to Block 10, the medical experimentation block, often took place to the sounds of music. Another prisoner in the main camp, one of the many twins subject to the experiments of Dr Mengele, described how he was forced to watch as people were tortured to death to the accompaniment of the orchestra. In Monowitz, the orchestra performed at special ceremonies conducted to celebrate the retrieval of escapees. The musician Herman Sachnowitz recounted how the captured man would be forced to shout the words 'Hurra, hurra, ich bin wieder da!' (Hurrah, hurrah, I am back again!) while marching through the ranks of prisoners and banging on a drum. He would subsequently be hanged while the orchestra played parade music. Members of the orchestras insisted, however, that they did not play while people were marched to the gas chambers (one of the rumours which grew in the post-war years).[50]

As we have seen, by 1940 many of the larger concentration camps already had their own orchestras. At Auschwitz, however, the camp orchestra took on new and elevated importance. Between 1940 and 1943 no fewer than five orchestras of varying sizes were set up by the SS in the main camp and Birkenau alone; several additional ensembles were set up in Monowitz and other satellite camps, and they became a prominent feature of daily life. Auschwitz I inmate Jerzy Brandhuber gave this description:

The orchestra. Yes, the orchestra is a permanent, daily component of life here. It plays when you go out to work or when you come back. It plays—sometimes when the wagon carrying the dead is already driving through the gate. Sometimes it plays during work, or when a commission comes, it plays concerts in the camp on Sundays

---

[48] Cited in Gabriele Knapp, *Das Frauenorchester in Auschwitz: Musikalische Zwangsarbeit und ihre Bewältigung* (Hamburg: von Bockel, 1996), 36.

[49] Jan Wawrosz, an inmate in Auschwitz I, recounted how in Mar. 1943 eight Poles were forced to sing patriotic Polish songs in order to cover up the sounds of people undergoing interrogation. Małgorzata Chrobok similarly described how in July 1944 the Birkenau women's camp commander Mandl forced a group of women to sing the English waltz 'What is as beautiful as your love?' Cited in USHMM, RG-55.019.09 (Kulisiewicz Collection); Hoch, 'Ha'tarbut ha'muziqalit', 184.

[50] Hinda Tennenbaum, WL, P.III.h. No.1135; Shlomo Malek, YV, 03/9647; Sara Rat (Manschfreund), YV, 03/6927; Joseph Spira, YV, 03/6527; John Fink, YV, 069/116; Sachnowitz, *Auschwitz*, 98; Laks, *Music of Another World*, 58.

and in front of its gates. And when suddenly it is no longer there—then it is strangely empty. Its absence is as depressing as the absence of something that is absolutely essential to life. Like a deep, enduring grief—the orchestra is nowhere to be heard. How different, the day begins cheerfully, when a march rings out again in the morning.[51]

The orchestras were made up of both amateur and professional musicians drawn from all sectors of the prisoner population. As soon as an order was received for the establishment of an ensemble, functionaries were sent out to recruit suitable inmates. Some had, upon their arrival, specified that they were professional musicians; they were thus easy to locate. Most of the time, however, they had to be found by word of mouth. Announcements that musicians were being sought were made by *Blockälteste*, *Kapos*, and workers in the infirmary. Some obliged willingly; some were volunteered by friends. Others, who did not know why they were being recruited, were too afraid to come forward. Later, when orchestras were in need of additional players, musicians were sought out from the newly arrived transports. Often the recruitment process was haphazard, and many were discovered only through chance conversations with SS officers or functionaries.[52]

For some inmates, the first encounter with the camp involved one of these orchestras. From 1944, when new transports were delivered directly onto the infamous ramp at Birkenau, an orchestra would be positioned to greet the new arrivals. This was part of an elaborate design to deceive them about what was being perpetrated in the camp. Aware of the fact that newcomers would be on the lookout for revealing information about this unknown place, the SS ensured that they encountered reassuring signs: neatly groomed gardens, signposts indicating baths and changing rooms, and music. The selections that were subsequently staged on the ramp took place against the background of musical accompaniment.[53] The orchestras would generally play popular pre-war songs, sentimental ballads, and dance melodies. The Gypsy inmate Alexander Ramati recalled that on his arrival in March 1944 the orchestra was

[51] Jerzy Brandhuber, 'Vergessene Erde', *Hefte von Auschwitz*, 5 (1962), 83–95 at 91.

[52] Szymon Laks, for example, was discovered while playing bridge with some prisoner functionaries: Laks, *Music of Another World*, 32. Shortly after his arrival at the camp, Emilio Jani was approached by some SS officers, whom he told that he was a professional opera singer; one of the men took him over to a group of men who had been selected for forced labour, thus saving him from the gas chambers: Jani, *My Voice Saved Me*, 72–3. Anita Lasker-Wallfisch described her discovery as follows: 'I will never know what prompted me to tell [the girl that processed me on arrival] that I played the cello. It might have seemed a superfluous piece of information under the circumstances, but I did tell her, and her reaction was quite unexpected. "That is fantastic," she said, and grabbed me. "Stand aside. You will be saved".' Anita Lasker-Wallfisch, *Inherit the Truth 1939–1945* (London, 1996), 72.

[53] See e.g. Rachel Bar-Neu (Folk), YV, 03/6925; Esther Reichmann, YV, 03/9206.

playing Strauss waltzes; others remembered excerpts from Lehár's *Die lustige Witwe* and the 'Barcarolle' from Offenbach's *Les Contes d'Hoffmann*. Numerous former inmates recalled that the presence of the orchestras had indeed restored a sense of calm, and led them to think that 'things could not be so bad'.[54] The orchestras thus functioned to divert the newcomers from what was really happening to them and to mitigate their shock, making it easier to gain their cooperation.

Although the musicians were aware of the role they were playing in this scenario of deception, they were castigated for showing any signs of emotion. Rachel Olewski-Zalmanowitz described how one of her fellow musicians in the Birkenau women's orchestra, a Greek double bass player named Yvette Assael, often cried when she witnessed the arrival of the new transports. On one occasion, an SS officer angrily reminded her that it was forbidden to cry, and threatened to dispose of anyone who behaved in this manner.[55]

The first orchestra was established in Auschwitz I in December 1940. Under the leadership of the Polish inmate Franz Nierychło (also *Kapo* of the prisoners' kitchen), an initial group of six musicians was assembled, playing violin, percussion, double bass, accordion, trumpet, and saxophone. A rehearsal space was designated for them in block 24. Some musicians were given permission to write home for their instruments; additional instruments were taken from musicians living in the area of the camp. In 1942 Nierychło was replaced as conductor by the well-respected Warsaw musician Adam Kopyciński, who retained this position until the orchestra's dissolution in 1945. With the constant influx of new inmates, the orchestra grew steadily in size. By 1942 it had approximately 100 players, and by 1944 over 120, making it the largest orchestra in any of the Nazi camps. The men were primarily of Polish, German, and Russian origin, and many were professional musicians. Jews were not allowed to join, although several were admitted after a change of policy in late 1944.[56]

---

[54] These sentiments are expressed in a number of testimonies: Jennie Alpert, USHMM, RG-50.091.002; Estelle Beder, USHMM, RG-50.091.004; Alice Ben-Hurin, USHMM, RG-50.091.008; Violette Fintz, YV, 069/253; Sheva Ganz (Fisher), YV, 03/5423; Esther Greenberg, YV, 069/366; Moshe Hella, YV, 03/9442; Regina Mendel, YV, 03/8089; Henry Meyer, YV, 03/6273; Jay Nubenhaus, YV, 069/346; Henia Razmowitz, YV, 03/5296. See also Seweryna Szmaglewska, 'Rauch über Birkenau', in Gerhard Schoenberner (ed.), *Wir haben es gesehen: Augenzeugenberichte über die Judenverfolgung im Dritten Reich* (Hamburg, 1962), 242–7.

[55] Rachel Olewski-Zalmanowitz, YV, 03/4444. See also Hélène Scheps, cited in Richard Newman and Karen Kirtley, *Alma Rosé: Vienna to Auschwitz* (London, 2000), 272.

[56] Hermann Langbein, *Menschen in Auschwitz* (Vienna, 1972), 150; Henryk Król, ABSM, 1710/159301; Herman Boasson, YV, 01/168. The former orchestra member Boasson claimed that in Sept. 1944, with the approach of the Red Army imminent, the SS transported groups of 'favoured' prisoners out of the camp, including many musicians from the orchestra. The resulting spaces were then filled by Jews. He added, however, that the new ensemble was inferior to its predecessor.

Birkenau boasted four orchestral ensembles during the course of its existence: one each in the men's and women's sub-camps, in the Gypsy camp, and,
for a short time, in the Czech family camp. The men's orchestra was
established in July 1942, shortly after the building of Birkenau had been
completed. At the order of the sub-camp commander Johann Schwarzhuber,
sixteen musicians from the main camp orchestra were brought over to form
the core of the new ensemble. The number of musicians increased gradually,
taking in new arrivals from Holland, Greece, Poland, France, and Germany,
and when the orchestra was disbanded in October 1944 it had approximately
forty members, Jews and non-Jews. The women's orchestra was set up in April
1943 under the leadership of the Polish prisoner Sofia Tchaikovska, and at its
peak had approximately forty-five members, most of whom were amateur
musicians. The family camp orchestra was a small ensemble, made up of
between six and twelve musicians, who were exempt from hard labour. They
were frequently forced to perform for the SS, as well as to accompany the
torture sessions inflicted on prisoners who had committed minor offences.[57]
Little information exists regarding the Gypsy camp, although numerous
references have been made in the testimonial literature to an orchestra and
to several smaller ensembles.[58]

The last substantial ensemble was set up in September 1943 in Monowitz.
It consisted of between forty and fifty players of various nationalities, and
permitted Jews to be members. Many of the players were accomplished
professional musicians, including several famous jazz instrumentalists from
Holland.[59]

All of the orchestral musicians fell into the category of 'privileged'
prisoners. Nonetheless, the conditions they experienced were not uniform.
In Monowitz, orchestra members received additional food rations and
warmer clothing, including special uniforms. Most were placed in easier
work commandos than their fellow inmates, and they regularly received
cigarettes after private concerts performed for the SS.[60] In the main camp,

[57] Laks, *Music of Another World*, 90–1; Elias, *Triumph of Hope*, 119–20.

[58] See Alexander Ramati, *And the Violins Stopped Playing: A Story of the Gypsy Holocaust* (London,
1985), 193–4; Lucie Adelsberger, *Auschwitz: A Doctor's Story* (London, 1995), 41–2; Coco Schumann,
Der Ghetto-Swinger: Eine Jazzlegende erzählt (Munich, 1997), 81–2; Esther Bejerano, cited in Susann
Heenen-Wolff, m Haus des Henkers: Gespräche in Deutschland (Frankfurt/M., 1992), 278–300; Max
Benjamin, WL, P.III.h. No. 817; and Rudolf Höss, *Commandant of Auschwitz* (London, 1959), 52.

[59] Jack Louis, Fortunoff Video Archive, T-1604; 'Ha'khatsotsra sh'hitsila: Shney y'hudim
sh'nignu b'tizmoret Auschwitz nifgeshu b'yisrael' (Saul Ben-Khaim), YV, 03/3533; John Fink, YV,
069/116; Czesław Sowul, ABSM, 1590/157979; Ignacy Stopka, ABSM, 951/108176; Sachnowitz,
Auschwitz, 46–9, 97.

[60] Moshe Angel, YV, 03/3533.

however, while the musicians enjoyed distinct advantages, they were in some respects not given preferential treatment. They lived together in the same barracks, but their housing was the same as that of other inmates. The food they were given was also the same, although they had many more opportunities to earn or 'organize' additional income, and were also occasionally given cigarettes. They were still expected to do forced labour during the day, and then to attend rehearsals in the evenings, but were often assigned to 'easier' commandos such as laundry or potato peeling. In addition to the standard prisoner garb, they were provided with special uniforms for their activities. They were, however, still subject to regular selections; as a result, the make-up of the group was constantly changing. Former inmates maintained that literally hundreds of prisoners passed through the orchestra's ranks, and described the ways in which countless musicians suddenly 'disappeared' or committed suicide.[61]

The initial situation in the Birkenau men's orchestra was much the same. Under the leadership of its first conductor, Jan Zaborski, until October 1942, and subsequently under Franz Kopka, musicians were subject to the same living conditions and (apart from a select few) to the same heavy labour as the rest of the prisoners. They also underwent periodic selections, although the constant influx of new transports meant that the size of the orchestra remained relatively stable. From mid-1943, however, when informal leadership was assumed by Laks (a Jewish prisoner who until then had worked in the orchestra as violinist and copyist), and even more so when his position became official later that year, many changes were instituted. The orchestra was transferred to block 5, where the *Zimmerei* was also housed. Here, it was given a separate music room where rehearsals could take place, and where the *Notenschreiber* (music copyists) could work. The men were assigned to safer and less tiring work placements, received additional food rations, and experienced some improvement in their living conditions. Throughout its existence, the orchestra enjoyed much support, both formal and informal, from the SS, and Schwarzhuber himself often arranged for the provision of scores and instruments.[62]

Members of the women's orchestra in Birkenau were better off than any of their male counterparts. Under their first conductor, Sofia Tchaikovska, their living and working conditions were no different from those of other camp

---

[61] Herman Boasson, YV, 01/168; Theodor Liese, YV, 03/4170; Tadeusz Pawlak, USHMM, RG-55.003.18; Adam Kopyciński, ABSM, 1397/154898.

[62] Laks, *Music of Another World*, 57, 66; Albert Menasche, *Birkenau (Auschwitz II): (Memoirs of an Eye-Witness). How 72,000 Greek Jews Perished* (New York, 1947), 29.

inmates. In August 1943, however, Tchaikovska's replacement by the Viennese musician Alma Rosé brought about marked improvements. When Rosé arrived at the camp in July 1943, she was already something of a legend. She had established a reputation for herself as an accomplished violinist in pre-war Europe, and also had impressive familial credentials: her father, Arnold Rosé, was the founder and first violinist of the esteemed Rosé quartet in Vienna, her husband was the well-known Czech violinist Váša Příhoda, and her uncle was the composer Gustav Mahler. In addition to these factors, it was presumably also Rosé's dedication to her new job that led her superiors to support her activities in Birkenau to the extent that they did. Many former inmates emphasized the unprecedented relationship that she enjoyed with the SS, and the high esteem in which they held her. She ensured that the women in her orchestra also benefited from the power she wielded, and to a large extent, the players had her to thank not only for their exceptional status, but also for their subsequent survival.

Thanks to the intervention of the camp commander Josef Kramer and SS officers Franz Hössler and Maria Mandl, all of whom demonstrated continued support for Rosé, a separate block was designated for the musicians. It included separate lodgings for Rosé and the *Blockälteste*, as well as a rehearsal room (replete with conductor's podium and a table for the copyists). Each of the women had her own bed, a luxury, considering that 'ordinary' prisoners slept several to a bunk, with little or no bedding. Housed together with them were other 'prominent' prisoners such as *Appellplatz* workers, translators, runners, and workers from the administration office. Their living conditions were more hygienic than elsewhere, and they were allowed to use the showers on a regular basis, and separate latrines.[63] Apart from their musical activities, the women were not expected to perform any forced labour, and they attended roll-call inside their blocks. In addition, they were provided with special uniforms. Under the pretext of needing to keep the musical instruments in good condition, Rosé managed to acquire an oven, which helped to keep the musicians warm during the winter months. She also convinced the

---

[63] Fania Fénelon, *Playing for Time* (Syracuse, NY, 1977), 43; Newman and Kirtley, *Alma Rosé*, 250. Fénelon's account—the earliest published about the women's orchestra—is a controversial one. Many of the musicians have objected to her distorted portrayal of their behaviour in the camp, and in particular to her embellished depiction of her own role versus that of Rosé in 'saving' the orchestra (she only arrived at the camp in Jan. 1944). The book is written in a novelistic style, and fictitious names were given to those former members whom Fénelon believed were still alive at the time of publication. It is nonetheless a detailed and useful source for many of the orchestra's activities. Most of the women address the issue of Fénelon's book in their testimonies; see also Knapp, *Das Frauenorchester*, 286–90.

SS that the musicians should not be required to play at the gates when the weather was particularly bad. On the point of food rations, former inmates diverged, with several insisting that the women ate the same as their fellow prisoners. Even if they were not given substantially bigger rations, however, they certainly earned additional food from the SS and functionaries for whom they gave private performances.[64]

Rosé had unquestioned control over who was accepted to play in the orchestra. In the first weeks after taking up her position, she caused controversy by dismissing many of Tchaikovska's Polish musicians and replacing them primarily with Jewish women. Although some condemned her perceived preference for Jews, most believed that she was more concerned about recruiting qualified musicians for her ensemble. They also agreed that she attempted to save as many lives as possible by involving them in her commando: the ousted musicians were kept on as assistants and copyists, and several women who later failed their auditions for the orchestra were assigned secondary tasks in the block.[65] At the outset, under Tchaikovska, the women were subject to regular selections. Under Rosé, this practice was discontinued on the basis that it was making it difficult to maintain the standard of the ensemble.[66]

For the Auschwitz I, Birkenau men's, and Birkenau women's ensembles, and the Monowitz band, the primary task was to play at the camp gates each morning and evening as the commandos marched to and from their places of work. The morning sessions began shortly after the morning roll-call and generally lasted for 45 minutes. In Birkenau, both the male and female orchestras would also be expected to play while marching from their block to their designated position at the gates, and to provide interim entertainment for functionaries while they waited for the work detachments to be formed. Once the last commando had left, the women would return to their barracks for day-long rehearsals, while the men prepared for their own work assignments. They would return from the day's labour a little earlier in the evening in order once again to welcome in the marching commandos.[67]

[64] Rivka (Regina) Bezia, YV, 03/6707; Shulamit Khalef, YV, 03/6810; Rachel Olewski-Zalmano-witz, YV, 03/4444; Margrita Schwalbová, YV, M38/273; Anita Lasker-Wallfish, WL, P.III.h. No. 707.

[65] The cellist Anita Lasker-Wallfisch confirmed that 'Any excuse was good enough to attempt to rescue as many people as possible and bring them into this relative haven. Some people who could not really play at all were taken in': Lasker-Wallfisch, *Inherit the Truth*, 76. See also Rivka (Regina) Bezia, YV, 03/6707; Margrita Schwalbová, YV, M38/273; Rachel Olewski-Zalmanowitz, YV, 03/4444; Knapp, *Das Frauenorchester*, 73–4; and Kuna, *Musik an der Grenze*, 99.

[66] Shulamit Khalef, YV, 03/6810.

[67] Numerous prisoners described these daily marching sessions in their post-war accounts. See e.g. Susan Beer, USHMM, RG-50.091.006; Adita Moskowitz, YV, 03/10064; Ava-Chava Yakowo-

The repertoire at these sessions consisted primarily of German march tunes, which would be played over and over again. Some of the more popular items were well-known tunes such as 'Alte Kameraden' (Old comrades), 'Liebling, ich bin traurig' (Darling, I am sad), 'Florentiner Marsch' (Florentine march), and 'Parade-Marsch' (Parade march). The main camp orchestra also performed original compositions by orchestra members, including the violinist Henryk Król's 'Arbeitslager-Marsch' (Labour camp march) and the conductor Nierychło's 'Arbeit macht frei!' (Work makes free).[68] The women's orchestra occasionally performed more sophisticated repertoire, including excerpts from operas and operettas, and dance melodies. Common selections included 'Rosamunde', Schubert's 'Marche militaire', and various marches by Sousa and Strauss.[69]

Some musical manuscripts were retrieved from the belongings of newly arrived prisoners for use by the orchestras (Birkenau was, ironically, a place of great wealth, as people often took their most valuable possessions with them when they were deported). Apart from these manuscripts, and some provided by the SS, the orchestras had limited access to scores. At the outset, musicians in Auschwitz I themselves assumed the costs of having scores sent to them, and the other ensembles later made use of their collection. In Rosé's case, the SS sometimes imported music from outside the camp, but these were usually piano scores that needed to be arranged. Both Birkenau orchestras and the main camp ensemble were forced to recruit several copyists to orchestrate music and transcribe parts for each group's combination of instruments. The copyists' role was particularly challenging when membership of the orchestras was in flux: the sudden 'holes' in the musical texture caused by the disappearance of certain instruments made it necessary for them to use a special kind of orchestration, which made provisions for pieces to be played by any combination of musicians.[70] Most of the time, the copyists arranged music from piano scores or from memory, but they would also often be required to harmonize and arrange melodies chosen by SS officers. During Laks's time as

witz (Spitzer), YV, 03/7232; Rachel Herzl-Rosenberg, YV, 03/6228; Brandhuber, 'Vergessene Erde', 89; Elie Wiesel, *Night* (London, 1972), 60; Margareta Glas-Larsson, *I Want to Speak: The Tragedy and Banality of Survival in Terezin and Auschwitz* (Riverside, Calif., 1991), 58; Żywulska, *I Came Back*, 40; Menasche, *Birkenau*, 31; Laks, *Music of Another World*, 37–8.

[68] Henryk Król, ABSM, 1710/159301; Henryk Król: 'Arbeitslager Marsch', USHMM, RG-24.014.01.

[69] *Przegląd Lekarski* articles in German translation (Kulisiewicz Collection), USHMM, RG-55.019.09; Czeslaw Sowul, ABSM, 1590/157979; Franek Stryj, ABSM, 2271/166318; Laks, *Music of Another World*, 38, 53; Knapp, *Das Frauenorchester*, 69; Lasker-Wallfisch, *Inherit the Truth*, 79; Bracha Gilai, YV, 03/6665.

[70] Laks, *Music of Another World*, 48.

conductor, commissions came to the Birkenau men's orchestra for arrangements of the marches 'Deutsche Eichen' (German oaks), 'Argonner Wald'
(Argonne forest), and 'Gruss an Obersalzberg' (Greetings to Obersalzberg).[71]

The daily march sessions were the most frequent point of contact between
the orchestra and the prisoner masses. Almost without exception, inmates
construed their purpose as being to facilitate discipline. Marching in time, in
neat rows of five, the prisoners were easier to count; the operation of moving
out of the camp could thus be conducted in an orderly and efficient manner.
For many, the playing of cheerful music against such a gruesome background
was macabre, and served to exacerbate their suffering even further.[72] In a rare
post-war account, SS officer Pery Broad gave this description:

At the camp gate a prisoners' band played a jolly German marching tune, to the
accompaniment of which work squads marched to their afternoon work. It was not
easy for them to keep in step in their clumsy wooden shoes, and with blistered feet. If
one of the prisoners failed to do this, he was mercilessly kicked or beaten in the face.[73]

Musicians and marchers alike emphasized how harrowing the scenes were,
particularly in the evenings: many of the prisoners could only limp in time to
the music, while others struggled to carry the seriously ill, or those who had
died during the day. The former Birkenau inmate Mali Fritz was struck by the
bizarreness of this daily ritual:

The return march into the death camp is arduous, we can lift our legs only with
difficulty and are too tired to say anything. Always this sense that I am carrying on
my shoulders layers of mud and dust and above all, the ashes of those who are no
longer marching...As we march into the camp, this madhouse music really tries to
play in time, but why?...Our ghostly column must look as if it has come crawling
out from the bowels of the earth. And left, and left, and left, two, three...damned
rhythm of fear.[74]

Primo Levi believed that these 'monstrous' activities had been planned with
'meditated reason' in order to kill the individual will of the prisoners, and to
set them 'marching like automatons':

The tunes are few, a dozen, the same ones every day, morning and evening: marches
and popular songs dear to every German. They lie engraven on our minds and will be
the last thing in Lager that we shall forget: they are the voice of the Lager, the

---

[71] Laks, *Music of Another World*, 70–1.
[72] See e.g. Maria Zumanska, WL, P.III.h. No. 867; Theodor Liese, YV, 03/4170; Romana
Duraczowa, cited in USHMM, RG-55.019.09 (Kulisiewicz Collection).
[73] Rudolf Höss, Pery Broad, and Johann Paul Kremer, *KL Auschwitz Seen by the SS* (Oświęcim,
1997), 112.
[74] Mali Fritz, *Essig gegen den Durst: 565 Tage in Auschwitz-Birkenau* (Vienna, 1986), 22.

perceptible expression of its geometrical madness, of the resolution of others to annihilate us first as men in order to kill us more slowly afterwards.[75]

It is difficult, particularly in hindsight, to consider any positive effects these marches might have had for the prisoners, and only very few expressed contrasting sentiments.[76]

For their part, the musicians also experienced these activities as painful and distressing. To begin with, they were forced to observe the suffering of their fellow inmates and the random cruelty inflicted on them by the SS with the knowledge that they could do nothing to help. They were loath to jeopardize their own chances of survival through rebellious behaviour, and attempts at protest would in any event have been of little use. In addition to these emotional challenges, many musicians also experienced physical difficulties from playing on a regular basis, often in sub-zero temperatures.[77]

There is the compelling likelihood, however, that music of this kind also served important functions for the SS that went beyond the tormenting functions identified by their victims. Several recent studies have explored similar ideas in relation to other features of camp life. Inge Clendinnen, for example, examines what she calls the 'consciously theatrical' activities initi-ated by the Auschwitz SS, ranging from their immaculate physical presenta-tion to the process of prisoner initiation into the camp, obsessive roll-calls, neatly orchestrated gassings (replete with carefully signed changing rooms), and Sunday 'sport'. For some inmates, such as Fritz and Levi cited above, 'insane' activities such as these were expressions of 'absurd German precision', and the desire for an 'orderly, properly labelled world'. Clendinnen suggests, however, that perhaps even more than this, they were 'rituals' whose enact-ment held significant personal meaning and value for the SS. Unlike their comrades who were fighting 'real enemies' at the front, the SS in Auschwitz experienced daily life as unrewarding and 'dreary'. 'Theatre' of this kind allowed them to enact their superiority in substantial and practical ways, helping them to recover a sense of 'high purpose and invincibility', sustain their morale and self-image, and 'maintain the glamour still attaching to their

---

[75] Primo Levi, *If This Is a Man / The Truce* (London, 1979), 57.

[76] One of these was Kazimierz Gwidzka: 'When exhausted in KL Auschwitz by a full day's work the prisoners came staggering in marching columns and from afar heard the orchestra playing by the gate—this put them back on their feet. It gave them the courage and the additional strength to survive…we could clearly hear how our colleague musicians spoke to us in masterly fashion on their instruments, each of them in his own musical native language. They sent improvised greetings in colorful sound…"Don't give up, brothers! Not all of us will perish!" ' Cited in Laks, *Music of Another World*, 115.

[77] Henryk Król, ABSM, 1710/159301; Menasche, *Birkenau*, 31–2; Lasker-Wallfisch, *Inherit the Truth*, 76; Shulamit Khalef, YV, 03/6810.

gruesome calling'. In addition, the tasks with which they were confronted were trying both physically and emotionally, and they had 'some need of solace'. Clendinnen notes in this regard that the development of 'less personal' killing methods such as gassing were partially motivated by concern for the psychological health of the killers.[78]

On a related point, Michael Burleigh has argued that there was concern that the killers 'should not stray too far from the path of human decency':

> They were not to walk on the wild side. The object was to engineer selective moral disengagement, rather than to unleash demi-human predators... Expected to do abnormal things, these men were nonetheless required to remain normal. Hence Himmler's repeated attempts to couple hardness with decency and his insistence that killings should be followed by abstemious 'comradely get-togethers' over dinner to discuss 'the sublimities of German intellectual and emotional life'.[79]

Also addressing the construct of 'decency', Karin Orth has argued that this was an essential component of the SS men's self-perception, primarily as a way of legitimizing their acts both to themselves and before the public. Part of what facilitated this construction related to the personal sphere: families were an essential part of the SS community in the camps, and social and cultural events were encouraged because, as Burleigh suggests, they helped 'to couple hardness with decency'. Orth confirms, moreover, that 'decent' behaviour in certain areas of camp life was not at odds with murderous deeds, but that the two were 'inseparably interrelated'.[80]

Considered in the context of these discussions, music can to be seen to have formed an integral part of the 'theatre' staged by the camp SS. The first and most obvious instances were the meticulously organized daily marching sessions, which lent an orderly, even military air to what was otherwise a pathetic procession of weakened, emaciated prisoners. The brash, nationalistic tone of the march music was also an effective way of asserting German dominance and superiority over the multinational, multilingual camp community; forced singing of German songs played a similar role. The performances on the ramp were a different kind of stage (akin to the neat gardens and showers), deflecting from the messiness and sheer brutality of the killing process. One of the musicians themselves also suggested that this music helped to make the difficult work of selection more bearable for the SS.[81]

---

[78] Inga Clendinnen, *Reading the Holocaust* (Cambridge, 1999), 134–55.

[79] Michael Burleigh, *The Third Reich: A New History* (London, 2001), 614.

[80] Karin Orth, 'The Concentration Camp SS as a Functional Elite', in Ulrich Herbert (ed.), *National Socialist Extermination Policies: Contemporary German Perspectives and Controversies* (Oxford, 2000), 306–36 at 322–3.

[81] Shulamit Khalef, YV, 03/6810.

Even more important with regard to this discussion, however, were the many occasions when the SS solicited performances by inmate musicians for their own entertainment, both in the public and private realms. These performances presented opportunities for the SS to deal with their own emotional needs, both in terms of diverting themselves from their actions, and—perhaps more importantly—in terms of constructing their behaviour within a refined, 'civilized' paradigm. As we have seen, the Auschwitz SS provided considerable support and encouragement to their ensembles, even more so than was the case in other camps. While it might be tempting to view their appreciation for music and their brutal actions as irreconcilably contradictory, it seems in fact that music was an uncontested part of the camp's perverse logic. Above all, it provided a framework within which the SS could maintain a self-image of refined German culture and personal 'decency', not apart from but precisely in the context of the activities in which they were involved.

In addition to their duties at the gates, the orchestras were commissioned by the SS to play regular concerts. In the main camp, these were held on Sundays near the villa of camp commander Rudolf Höss. Johann Paul Kremer, a medical doctor who was assigned on SS duty to Auschwitz in the last few months of 1942, made reference to one of the concerts in his diary entry for 20 September: 'This Sunday afternoon from 3 p.m. till 6 p.m. I listened to a concert of the prisoners' orchestra in glorious sunshine; the Kappelmeister was a conductor of the Warsaw State Opera. 80 musicians. Roast pork for dinner, baked tench for supper.'[82] The repertoire presented at the concerts was somewhat more sophisticated than the music played at the marching sessions. In addition to some 'light' items, programmes included excerpts from operas and operettas, and substantial symphonic works. Several inmates recalled performances of Schubert's 'Unfinished' Symphony, and one remembered singing arias from Leoncavallo's *Pagliacci* and Puccini's *Tosca*.[83] The Birkenau men's orchestra performed at similar Sunday events, and in addition to the usual classical items also played special commissions from the SS. These included a potpourri based on Schubert songs entitled 'Erinnerungen an Schubert' (Memories of Schubert), and another called 'Schwarze Augen' (Dark eyes), based on Russian themes.[84] At their Sunday concerts the Monowitz orchestra played dance melodies, excerpts from operettas, and salon music.[85]

---

[82] Höss, Broad, and Kremer, *KL Auschwitz*, 165.

[83] Boleslaw Majcherczyk, ABSM, 1610/158157; Herman Boasson, YV, 01/168; Theodor Liese, YV, 03/4170; Jani, *My Voice Saved Me*, 75.

[84] Laks, *Music of Another World*, 74.

[85] Sachnowitz, *Auschwitz*, 138.

In the women's camp, concerts were held in front of the delousing block or 'Sauna', which was situated between the men's and women's sub-camps. When the weather was particularly bad, they would be held inside the building. This orchestra boasted a larger and more impressive repertoire than its counterparts, primarily as a result of the dedicated effort Rosé put into raising the quality of the ensemble. Former musicians characterized her as a strict and demanding conductor, who worked with almost absurd fervour and energy to produce quality music from the group. The level of playing improved within a matter of weeks after she took over, and the repertoire soon moved beyond Tchaikovska's initial offerings of German marches and Polish soldiers' songs to include a wide array of German hit songs, arias, excerpts from symphonies and other large-scale orchestral works, and solo works for violin and piano. Some of the compositions performed at the concerts included Schumann's *Träumerei*, excerpts from operettas by Lehár and von Suppé, arias from operas by Verdi, Puccini, and Rossini, and orchestral music by Brahms, Mozart, Schubert, Dvořák, and Johann Strauss.[86]

In all the camps, these concerts were presented before SS officers as well as inmates. The musicians often maintained that for the prisoners, the concerts were a kind of escape or 'asylum' from the horrors of Auschwitz. They described the audience members listening to the music with tears in their eyes, and guessed that at those moments they were imagining themselves in another world, perhaps at home with their families. The musicians also emphasized, however, that most inmates were not given the opportunity to attend these performances. This privilege was reserved for 'prominent' prisoners and functionaries, or those who had been interned in the camp for many years. Only occasionally could 'ordinary' prisoners attend, and in these cases they stood at the back of the hall, at attention. The SS forbade applause.[87]

The relationship between the orchestras and the SS extended beyond these official functions. Groups of individual musicians were frequently called on to perform informally, both in their rehearsal room and at private functions such as dinner parties, birthdays, and other special occasions. At these events, they would sometimes be asked to play 'forbidden' repertoire, particularly

---

[86] Lasker-Wallfisch, *Inherit the Truth*, 79; Fénelon, *Playing for Time*, 103. For a fuller listing of the repertoire performed by the women's orchestra see Knapp, *Das Frauenorchester*, 78–82.

[87] Shulamit Khalef, YV, 03/6810; Theodor Liese, YV, 03/4170; Adam Kopyciński, ABSM, 1397/154898; Tadeusz Pawlak, USHMM, RG-55.003.18; Kitty Hart, *I Am Alive* (London, 1961), 74–5; Fénelon, *Playing for Time*, 104, 131.

jazz.[88] The use of this kind of repertoire once again confirms that, in certain cases, issues of official policy could easily be subsumed by the simple desire for certain kinds of musical entertainment amongst the SS. Certain SS personalities also often visited the music blocks in the main camp, Birkenau, and Monowitz in order to listen to rehearsals, hear renditions of their favourite pieces, or simply to chat about music. Musicians would be expected to drop all their activities and perform whatever was requested. In the women's block, regular informal visitors included Hössler, Kramer, and the infamous Dr Mengele. In the main camp, they included Rapportführer Balz and several unnamed guards, and in the men's camp, Rapportführer Joachim Wolff and Rottenführer[89] Pery Broad, who sometimes joined in himself with the playing. For these activities the musicians would be rewarded lavishly with food and cigarettes.[90]

Many musicians were disturbed by the fact that SS officers came to their block for light relief after selections or other murderous activities. In this context they experienced them in a more human light, and several observed with distress that the SS became unexpectedly 'humanized' during the time they spent with the musicians. The violinist Theodor Liese, for example, recalled a Hauptsturmführer in the main camp whose job consisted of selecting new arrivals for the gas chambers. After the day's work, he often came to talk with the musicians and to play chamber music with them. Liese characterized him as a charming, pleasant, and highly cultured man. Several musicians recalled that it was not unusual for SS visitors to cry when they listened to music. From the ways in which they describe these visits, it is apparent that the musicians found it difficult to reconcile that the same people who were behaving with such brutality in the camp could at the same time show the appreciation they did for art. It was clearly also

---

[88] This was reported by Henry Meyer, a violinist in the Birkenau men's orchestra, and Herman Sachnowitz, a trumpeter in the Monowitz ensemble. Henry Meyer, 'Musste da auch Musik sein? Der Weg eines Geigers von Dresden über Auschwitz nach Amerika', in Hanns-Werner Heister, C. Maurer Zenck, and P. Petersen (eds.), *Musik im Exil: Folgen des Nazismus für die internationale Musikkultur* (Frankfurt am Main, 1993), 29–40 at 36; Sachnowitz, *Auschwitz*, 106. According to Sachnowitz, the SS often requested the jazz musicians to play American melodies such as 'Alexander's ragtime band', 'Dinah', 'Sweet Sue', and 'I can't give you anything but love'. Laks observed that the Birkenau orchestra also contained virtuoso jazz musicians, most of them Dutch, whose playing was appreciated by certain of the SS. Laks, *Music of Another World*, 81.

[89] Corporal. For other SS ranks, see Yerger, *Riding East*, 217. A Rapportführer was an SS non-commissioned officer in a concentration camp, responsible for taking roll-call and for general administrative duties. Helmut Krausnick and Martin Broszat, *Anatomy of the SS State* (London, 1968), 281.

[90] Informal visits of the SS are described in numerous accounts: Rachel Olewski-Zalmanowitz, YV, 03/4444; Shulamit Khalef, YV, 03/6810; Theodor Liese, YV, 03/4170; Laks, *Music of Another World*, 79–81; Fénelon, *Playing for Time*, 98–9, 155; Sachnowitz, *Auschwitz*, 140.

psychologically trying for them to observe the SS revealing their own emotional struggles regarding the activities in which they were involved.[91]

Accounts suggest that these informal musical sessions were held frequently, even on a daily basis. It is clear that for the SS, they were also an effective source of diversion; this is further confirmed by the fact that they were often accompanied by heavy drinking.[92] Orchestral musicians were not the only ones to offer such services: numerous inmates performed private concerts in order to earn food and, in some cases, temporary reprieve. The means through which they were recruited were various and unsystematic. One woman remembered an isolated incident, shortly after her arrival, when an SS guard overheard her singing for her fellow inmates, and ordered her back to her private quarters to perform a selection of songs. The guard never called on her again, but after this incident assigned her to a different block where she had a greater chance of survival. Another inmate in the main camp actively solicited work, and on several occasions successfully persuaded the SS to allow him to sing for them. Through his activities he earned new clothes, food, and plenty of cigarettes. In autumn 1944 two well-known Czech musicians who had recently arrived from Theresienstadt, the violinist Otto Sattler and the pianist Kurt Meyer, were actively sought out by the SS. They were accommodated in separate living quarters, and were given comfortable clothing, extra rations, and cigarettes. In exchange for these privileges, they performed regularly for the SS, who increasingly needed to drown the sorrows of imminent defeat in music and alcohol.[93]

The only occasions at which the orchestras played for 'ordinary' prisoners in an official capacity was in the hospital blocks. That they were assigned to this task in the first place is disturbing, since the hospitals hardly constituted places of healing—a fact openly acknowledged by both inmates and the SS. Selections were regularly carried out there, and most prisoners considered being sent to the infirmary as a certain death warrant. Nonetheless, the orchestras in the main camp and in Birkenau were commanded to play there on an occasional basis. Liese maintained that, as the SS were often afraid to enter these blocks, the concerts actually offered the players unprecedented freedom in their choice of repertoire. He remembered playing

---

[91] Lasker-Wallfisch, *Inherit the Truth*, 77–9; Theodor Liese, YV, 03/4170; Sachnowitz, *Auschwitz*, 96–7; Fénelon, *Playing for Time*, 98–9; former inmates cited in Knapp, *Das Frauenorchester*, 130.

[92] Knapp, *Das Frauenorchester*, 131; Fénelon, *Playing for time*, 67; Kuna, *Musik an der Grenze*, 299.

[93] Elisabeth Lichtenstein, WL, P.III.h. No. 1116; Matetyahu Nissim, YV, 03/4273; Kuna, *Musik an der Grenze*, 298–9. Related incidents are described in Adita Moskowitz, YV, 03/10064 and Ramati, *And the Violins Stopped Playing*, 197.

Polish music, and on one occasion even including sections of the Polish national anthem.[94] However, the extent to which this freedom could be used to positive ends was negligible. Some prisoner doctors and nurses enjoyed listening to the music, but most of the patients either reacted badly to it or paid it no attention at all.[95] Laks recalled being sent to the women's hospital at Christmas 1943, on the command of Schwarzhuber, to console the sick with some carols. He described their distressed response—and his own:

I would rather not describe the sight that spread out before our eyes or the stink that blew on us when we crossed the threshold. It was unbelievable that this was a hospital whose calling was the treatment and care of weak, emaciated women who were near death. I chased away gloomy thoughts. We had come here to play, not to lament over the fate of others. So we played, hardly able to breathe. We started with the traditional German carol 'Silent Night, Holy Night'... which the audience listened to attentively. In our repertoire we still had 'Sleep, Little Jesus', 'He Lies in the Cradle', 'They Came Running to Bethlehem', and 'God is Born'. We began with the first. After a few bars quiet weeping began to be heard from all sides, which became louder and louder as we played and finally burst out in general uncontrolled sobbing that completely drowned out the celestial chords of the carol. I didn't know what to do; the musicians looked at me in embarrassment. To play on? Louder? Fortunately, the audience itself came to my rescue. From all sides spasmodic cries, ever more numerous, ever shriller—in Polish, which I alone understood—began to roll in on me: 'Enough of this! Stop! Begone! Clear out! Let us croak in peace!' I got the impression that if these creatures had not been so weakened, they would have flung themselves on us and pummelled us with their fists. What could we do? We cleared out. I did not know that a carol could give so much pain.[96]

Unsurprisingly, we have few reports from patients to counter descriptions such as this one. What we know of the dire conditions experienced by Auschwitz inmates makes it fairly obvious that, for most, music no longer had the capacity to move and inspire. Time and again, prisoners explained in their post-war accounts how after weeks or even days in the camp, they lost all sensitivity to what was happening, and developed a kind of numbness. If most succumbed to desensitization as an instinctive coping strategy, it is reasonable to assume that their ability to engage with music, both in positive and negative ways, was limited. Laks saw music as just another facet of camp life that 'stupefied the newcomer...and to which he gradually became

[94] Theodor Liese, YV, 03/4170.
[95] Margrita Schwalbová, YV, M38/273; Knapp, *Das Frauenorchester*, 116–71; Fénelon, *Playing for Time*, 132–5; Adam Kopyciński, ABSM, 1397/154898; Menasche, *Birkenau*; Jacques Stroumsa, *Violinist in Auschwitz: From Salonika to Jerusalem 1913–1967* (Konstanz, 1996), 48; Theodor Liese, YV, 03/4170.
[96] Laks, *Music of Another World*, 98–9.

"habituated" in time—up to the moment of complete acclimatization and callousness'.[97] Occasionally, prisoners could come to the music blocks to hear the orchestra in rehearsal, or could go to the 'secret spaces' where individual members played classical pieces or particular national offerings for their fellow inmates.[98] But these occasions were few and far between. As a rule, the benefits of music in Auschwitz were limited to those who voluntarily consumed it.

The musicians, however, were in some measure able to recruit music for positive ends. Their duties were for the most part difficult and traumatic, and on occasion they themselves were the targets of malicious treatment by the SS.[99] Nonetheless, in addition to the life-sustaining material advantages as well as the individual identity their jobs afforded them, some derived emotional relief and support from their activities. Members of the women's orchestra believed that in attempting to fulfil Rosé's ceaseless demands for high quality, and thus engrossing themselves thoroughly in the music, they were in fact able to forget temporarily the reality around them. Tadeusz Pawlak and Kopyciński from the main camp claimed that despite being starving and exhausted, musicians rushed to rehearsals after a day of hard labour in order to 'lose themselves' in the music. Liese similarly insisted that music was a means of escape, and a 'sort of psychological tearing away from this tragic reality'. During free time, the musicians could also make music among themselves, which they found to be meaningful and enjoyable.[100]

Music and the Death Camp Universe

In addition to Auschwitz, five camps in the Nazi system were specifically designated as death camps (places where the genocidal process was actively carried out in facilities like gas chambers and crematoria). These were Bełżec, Sobibór, Treblinka, Chełmno, and Majdanek. While the first four operated almost exclusively for the purpose of efficient mass murder, Auschwitz and

---

[97] Laks, *Music of Another World*, 117.

[98] Langbein, *Menschen in Auschwitz*, 151; Brandhuber, 'Vergessene Erde', 91–2; Adam Kopyciński, ABSM, 1397/154898.

[99] Members of the Birkenau men's orchestra described how they were occasionally made to play concerts for the SS inside the crematoria. On one occasion, the SS amused themselves by throwing pebbles at the musicians. Meyer, 'Musste da auch Musik sein?', 35; Henry Meyer, YV, 03/6273; Gregor Rosenblum, cited in Knapp, *Das Frauenorchester*, 60–2.

[100] Tadeusz Pawlak, USHMM, RG-55.003.18; Adam Kopyciński, ABSM, 1397/154898; Theodor Liese, YV, 03/4170; Herman Boasson, YV, 01/168; Sachnowitz, *Auschwitz*, 139.

Majdanek also accommodated slave labour for the surrounding factories and mines, and thus had substantial resident populations.[101]

In these camps, music also featured as an element of daily life. In Treblinka, new arrivals were greeted with a perfectly designed scenario of deception: a train station replete with signposts, train timetables, and waiting areas, and a ten-piece uniformed orchestra conducted by the Jewish inmate Artur Gold playing jazz and Jewish folk tunes. The camp also possessed a violin, clarinet, and harmonica trio, which fulfilled various musical duties for the SS and the small resident prisoner population:[102] playing at morning roll-calls, accompanying the singing of the prisoners, performing at the frequent request of the SS and functionaries, and most importantly playing outside the gas chambers during their daily operations.[103] As in Auschwitz, prisoners were forced to sing during the roll-call and while marching to and from work; the repertoire consisted of German soldiers' songs and sentimental songs, and a specially composed hymn nicknamed 'The anthem of Treblinka'.[104]

In Bełżec and Sobibór, small orchestras were set up in order to greet newly arrived transports, and to entertain the SS staff. In Bełżec, the band played in the area between the gas chambers and the burial pits, where it often served as accompaniment to the work of the *Sonderkommando*. The orchestras were also occasionally used to greet visiting dignitaries, and to accompany torture sessions and forced singing.[105] Majdanek similarly housed a small orchestra between January and November 1943. Prisoners were subject to regular

---

[101] On the complex history of Nazi attitudes towards forced labour and the relationship between its conflicting ideological and economic factors, see Ulrich Herbert, 'Labour and Extermination: Economic Interest and the Primacy of *Weltanschauung* in National Socialism', *Past and Present*, 138 (1993), 44–195; and Browning, *Nazi Policy, Jewish Workers, German Killers*.

[102] Treblinka was divided into an 'upper camp' and a 'lower camp', the former consisting of the *Totenlager* (death camp), and the latter of *Wohnlager* (living area) and *Auffanglager* (reception area). One cordoned-off section of the lower camp contained barracks housing Jewish prisoners, who were employed in workshops as tailors, shoemakers, and carpenters. Prisoners were recruited from the incoming transports, put to work for a few days or weeks, and subsequently killed and replaced by new arrivals. They performed various additional tasks in the camp: manual labour, including work related to the killing process; construction work, which proceeded even while the killings were in operation; and attending to the personal needs of the camp staff. Gutman (ed.), *Encyclopedia*, 1481–4; Yitzhak Arad, *Belzec, Sobibór, Treblinka: The Operation Reinhard Extermination Camps* (Bloomington and Indiananapolis, 1987), 37–43.

[103] Oscar Strawczinski and Jerzy Rajgrodzki, cited ibid. 232–5; Krzepicki, cited in Hoch, 'Ha'tar-but ha'muziqalit', 168.

[104] Jean Francois Steiner and Wassili Grossman, cited in USHMM, RG-55.019.09 (Kulisiewicz Collection); Arad, *Belzec, Sobibór, Treblinka*, 233.

[105] Rudolf Reder, Tovia Blatt, and Philip Bialowicz, cited in Arad, *Belzec, Sobibór, Treblinka*, 228–31; Reder, cited in USHMM, RG-55.019.09 (Kulisiewicz Collection).

singing sessions, where one of the favourite items was a derisive song entitled
'Judenlied des KGL Lublin' (Jew song of the Lublin POW camp).[106]

The only death camp in which no musical activity was recorded was
Chełmno. The existence of music in all the other camps confirms, however,
that its use in Auschwitz was not merely the result of local initiative, but
evidence of a general policy on the part of the SS to employ music in the
process of extermination.

As we have seen, music could aid in this process in several ways. When
people came off the transports, shocked and disoriented, the orchestras
helped to pacify them by creating a comforting atmosphere. At other times,
music used at executions and torture sessions assisted directly in demoralizing
the prisoners—an important element of Nazi strategy. The German marches
and popular tunes played at the daily marching sessions facilitated the
counting of the prisoners, and encouraged them to march in an orderly
manner.

At the same time, SS officers consumed orchestral music for their own
purposes, both at the Sunday concerts and at private sessions. They did so in
order to relax and find temporary distraction from their work, often in
combination with heavy drinking. We know that they generally took great
pleasure and pride in their orchestras, and that they often went beyond the
call of duty in backing their activities. Some inmates argued that officials saw
their orchestras as status symbols, and that they established ensembles primarily for this reason. The occasional 'exchange concerts' performed by
orchestras in different sub-camps bear out this suggestion. The Birkenau
men's and women's orchestras, for example, occasionally performed Sunday
concerts at their parallel sub-camps. On a few occasions both the men's
orchestra and the main camp orchestra were sent to perform at the women's
camp, and on several occasions, the men's orchestra was brought by Schwarzhuber to perform in the Czech family camp.[107]

We must also take into consideration the quality of these ensembles,
however, which by the accounts of former members was often mediocre to
poor.[108] If orchestras were intended to hold such levels of importance, one
might assume that the authorities would have endeavoured to spare more
musicians from selections, if only to avoid the unpredictable quality created

---

[106] Materials relating to Polish camp songs compiled by Kulisiewicz, AdK, 31; *Przegląd Lekarski*
articles in German translation (Kulisiewicz Collection), USHMM, RG-55.019.09.

[107] Laks, *Music of Another World*, 98–101; Jani, *My Voice Saved Me*, 99–100; Kuna, *Musik an der
Grenze*, 246–7.

[108] Meyer, 'Musste da auch Musik sein?', 36; Laks, *Music of Another World*, 38, 116.

by constant changes to the groups' make-up. These factors suggest that while possession of an orchestra was something that was valued, its quality was not of crucial importance per se. It is equally possible that although the level of performance did not satisfy musicians accustomed to higher musical standards, the SS found it perfectly adequate for their needs. Guido Fackler confirms that on the whole, camp officials wanted the quality of their ensembles to be good, as they functioned as symbols of power and prestige.[109]

Attempting to explain the passion displayed by the SS for their orchestras, Laks quoted the following anecdote:

A certain foreign tourist, while crossing the main square of a German town, sees a rather sizeable brass band playing before the balcony of the town hall. The tourist turns to one of the bystanders and asks, 'In whose honour is the band playing?' 'What do you mean, in whose honour? In honour of our mayor! Today is his birthday!' 'I understand. But why doesn't the celebrant show himself on the balcony?' 'Because he can't. He's playing in the band himself.'[110]

Part of the orchestras' value obviously lay in the daily tasks they fulfilled. The case of Rosé's orchestra in particular, however, suggests that music was valuable to the SS at another level. More than any of the other groups, the women's orchestra under Rosé was enjoyed and protected by the sub-camp and higher-ranking SS authorities. It is no coincidence that this was also by far the superior ensemble, and that its conductor—a cultivated, elegant Viennese woman—had long been established as an exceptional talent. As Laks suggested in his anecdote, many considered the existence of music in Auschwitz as a logical extension of the national German passion for music. Notwithstanding the light-heartedness of his observations, there is the unmistakable sense that, apart from all their practical functions, the orchestras enjoyed the prominent existence they did because the SS valued a sense of 'civilized' culture, and valued the self-image they were able to promote (if only internally) through engagement with it. Music was not seen as incongruous with what was happening in the camp; in fact, its pervasive presence in daily life went largely unremarked and unquestioned. This suggests, contrary to our post-war assumptions, that music was not considered to be unusual at all, but rather a vital and thoroughly appropriate part of the camp enterprise.

[109] Fackler, *'Des Lagers Stimme'*, 346.
[110] Laks, *Music of Another World*, 69.

Epilogue

Music is not only itself a subject of historical memory, but also a vehicle for the transmission of memory. Since the immediate post-war years, it has played an important part in commemoration ceremonies, both those organized by survivors and those instituted later by second- and third-generation communities. Growing up in South Africa, I remember attending the annual Holocaust remembrance ritual held at West Park cemetery in Johannesburg. At the conclusion of the gathering we always sang 'Zog nit keynmol az du geyst dem letstn veg' (Never say that you are walking the final road), bearing out in the most literal sense the Vilna songwriter Hirsh Glik's prediction that the song would pass 'like a watchword ... from generation to generation'. At ceremonies I have attended over the years, this song has almost always featured; other favourites are the 'Varshever geto-lid fun frumer yidn' (Song of religious Jews in the Warsaw ghetto), Mordekhai Gebirtig's 'Es brent', and partisan songs from the ghettos. The tendencies revealed in these choices are not only manifest in the realm of commemoration: in recordings and writings about the subject as well, the emphasis on heroism and resistance is unambiguous.

We have seen that, at the time of their creation, songs such as these were indeed intended to be encouraging and morale-building. Particularly when conditions in ghettos and camps worsened, inmates sought words of solace and reassurance in their struggle to grapple with what was happening. Describing music as a manifestation of spiritual resistance thus has a certain validity. However, this explanation only goes part of the way towards explaining its possible roles.

Encouragement in the ghettos and camps was not always a simple or straightforward sentiment. For the most part, it bore little relation to the spirit of defiant optimism found amongst German political prisoners or Jewish partisans. It was usually accompanied by an acknowledgement of hardship, and an intuited sense that much would still be lost before liberation was gained. In songs, victims did not assert an uncomplicated hope, but rather the instinctive, uncertain, and often desperate hope that they would live to see the end of these experiences.

For survivors in the post-war years, the songs fulfilled functions that were closely related to those they had fulfilled during the war: affirming a feeling of togetherness in suffering, and restoring a sense of dignity and moral victory to those who did not survive. It was when songs were appropriated by communities that had not experienced the events, however, that a shift occurred. Independent now from the complicated psychological needs of the victims, the songs were nonetheless used to retain the emphasis on resistance. Although this was only one element among many that characterized people's thinking at the time, it came to dominate public perception of who the people were that were being remembered.

To some extent, simplification is an inevitable part of commemoration, particularly as it concerns the survivors. However, it is not only in commemoration ceremonies that the kinds of mythicized portrayals to which I have referred have emerged: as we have seen, historical studies have also supported redemptive conceptions of how people counteracted the dehumanizing effects of internment. Taking from the songs this straightforward narrative of heroism, post-war communities have in effect failed to recognize the complexity of experience that they represented. What is more, they overlook the simple fact that many songs from both ghettos and camps did not follow this model at all.

This book has proposed that we extend our view beyond narratives of optimism and reassurance, and probe music for the wider range of human experience that it both expressed and enacted. Songs tackled a wide range of issues relating to camp and ghetto life: shock, massacres witnessed, children left orphaned, religious crises, corruption in the communities, the profound desire to have suffering acknowledged. They also expressed a diversity of attitudes to the events, from the feisty optimism of the ghetto children to the morbid sarcasm and black humour of Polish camp inmates. Since the bulk of what we know about victims' experiences has come from the accounts of those who survived, these contemporary sources are a precious glimpse into how people—both as individuals and groups—felt, thought, and confronted life at the time. Though the access they offer is inevitably partial, taken alongside other contemporary sources and post-war testimonies they help to deepen our understanding of the experience of victimhood, offering insight into what were complex, changing, uncertain, often contradictory, and ultimately human responses to harsh realities.

Particularly in the camps, where ordinary channels of communication broke down or were prohibited from functioning, music became an informal place where experiences could be shared and negotiated. Songs were a way of spreading information related to the immediate landscape: about the gas chambers or the *Effektenkammer*, social issues like begging, smuggling, and delinquent children, or what was happening in Treblinka and Ponar. They also allowed for social and political commentary, often regarding power structures within the inmate communities themselves, but occasionally also regarding the German authorities, as we saw particularly in the Polish anti-Nazi songs created in Sachsenhausen.

On a deeper level, the songs created a space where responses could be formulated and engaged with on a more communal level. This applies not only to large-scale events such as sing-songs, but equally to interaction between individuals and small groups. In an isolated and alienating environment, songs became a storehouse for shared interpretations of what was happening. They acknowledged wishes, fears, and uncertainties in the public realm; as they circulated, people identified with them, modified them, added to them, or rejected them; sometimes they did not engage with them at all. This process was informal and unregulated, and it would be impossible to extract from the songs an essential collective narrative. Nonetheless, patterns of popularity show how, in active but not always conscious ways, communities articulated the ideas and perspectives with which they identified most strongly at the time.

Songs were also a way of connecting with the outside world, or, perhaps more precisely, with the future that many feared they might not live to see. The idea of bearing witness was one of the most frequently returned to both in contemporary writings and post-war testimonial literature. Cut off from the world both emotionally and literally, victims felt it crucial that something or someone survive to attest to what had happened: that their song 'from the depths of hell' be heard, and that their 'brothers from over the sea' mourn their loss. Particularly since they could be orally transmitted, songs were an obvious medium; indeed, the lyrics themselves often explicitly articulated this intention.

Amidst the different musical developments that we have explored, there emerged another common trend: using music to establish continuity with pre-war existence. In their songs, camp and ghetto inmates often drew from their past—past musical traditions, past identities, or past frameworks of understanding—to construct a frame within which the new experiences would be more assimilable. For ghetto Jews, this often meant documenting the new events in terms of archetypal concepts of sacrifice and martyrdom. Even assimilated German Jews, driven to unprecedented despair, sought solace by defining their place along the continuum of Jewish suffering. Those groups who drew on political connections, particularly German communists, were able to construct their responses to the camps within the framework of a long-standing tradition. In the case of the Poles, appeals to group identity came out both in recurring religious motifs, and in a fierce nationalistic sentiment. Even for the German authorities, the position that music was afforded in the camps accorded appropriately with pre-existing notions of how 'civilized' societies should be constructed.

It is thus clear that music was an important means of connection: to the past, to the outside world, and within communities. Above all, it was used in order to construct a narrative of experience, emphasizing meaningful aspects of identity and promoting particular interpretations and responses. It is important to remember, however, that it did not fulfil these functions in straightforward or unmediated ways. As we have seen, victims' narratives of self-understanding—in the songs as elsewhere—almost invariably carried the imprint of surrounding social and political forces.

Writing about events that are still in living memory, particularly extreme events of this kind, is not a straightforward task. In my case, living memory refers specifically to Jewish memory, both on a collective level and a personal one (my maternal grandparents survived the war). Most of what I have heard and read about the general subject over the years, in the popular realm but also in an academic context, bears at least some marks of emotion: the unsurprisingly passionate responses of those who survived the events, and, perhaps less defensibly, their echo in the words of present-day writers. In my own writing, I had to make a conscious effort to avoid the emotive vocabulary of 'martyrs', 'barbarous Nazis', and 'incomprehensible events' that I so often encountered elsewhere.

Contending with the impact of this living memory involves more than just modification of language, however. On the one hand, I share the profound sense of loss caused by the genocide, not only for the members of my extended family that were lost, but also for the destruction of Jewish life and culture in eastern Europe. On the other hand, I remain unconvinced that the forms that memory of these events has taken have always been productive. The boundary between emotion and sober historical explanation is a difficult one to tread, particularly considering the sensitive atmosphere of moral vigilance surrounding issues of anti-Semitism and Holocaust denial that still permeates Jewish communities.

As we have seen, the discourse that surrounds my subject frequently returns to the consoling idea that, however barbaric and merciless the treatment they received, inmates of Nazi ghettos and camps could ultimately not be robbed of their basic human dignity. Music is seen as one of the most meaningful media through which this was preserved. Apart from the countless testimonies, memoirs, and contemporary writings that suggest otherwise, the song texts themselves confirm that this could not always be the case. For some, music helped to restore and strengthen a positive sense of identity, or to allow victims to bond together in their suffering. As we have seen, however, this was seldom uncomplicatedly heroic. In addition, the invasive climate of the ghettos and camps made it almost impossible for individuals to remain unaffected by the forces surrounding them. The misleading assumption, in other words, is that people had the power to choose whether or not to be robbed of their dignity in the first place.

My scepticism with regards to discourses of heroism and resistance does not mean that I have less respect for the victims, or that their deaths were any less meaningful. Rather, it is my belief, and has been my intention in this book to demonstrate, that acknowledging the richness of their lives—replete with hope, optimism, and strength as well as fears, antagonisms, inconsistencies, and contradictions—is in fact a more truthful way of honouring their memory.

For reasons that we have explored, music has often seemed an appropriate subject for sentimental, mythicized portrayals of camp or ghetto life. Ironically, however, perhaps the most important perspective that it restores is the *human* face of the experience, in all its complex dimensions. To some extent, music initiated by the SS in the camps provides insight into the kinds of meanings with which perpetrators invested their actions; the stories recounted by orchestral musicians who had personal contact with them in particular restore a human face to their behaviour. Above all, however, it is the songs that open our ears to voices from within the maelstrom. They reveal to us the kinds of things that people thought about their fellow inmates or those who held power over them, the macabre things they thought about singing to their children, how they tried to distract themselves with memories of home or dreams of freedom, how they tried to make sense of or play down what they were experiencing through humour or denial, how they wanted to remember what their lives had been, and how they imagined they would be remembered. Considered in the context within which it operated, the music itself—both as object and activity—thus actively refutes the very stereotype that it has been used to create. It helps us to think about victims as people unsure of what was happening to them, full of intersecting and conflicting wishes, hopes, fears, and predictions. Perhaps most importantly, it allows us to remember them in the context of the rich and diverse experiences they represented, and not only the mechanized process of their destruction.

APPENDIX

Repertoire Listings

The following repertoire listings have been compiled from a wide range of sources, including published and unpublished songbooks, testimonies, interviews, and various other archival materials. Principal sources for the ghetto listings are Shmerke Kaczerginski and H. Leivick, *Lider fun di getos un lagern*; Shmerke Kaczerginski (ed.), *Dos gezang fun Vilner ghetto* (Paris, 1947); Eleanor Mlotek and Malke Gottlieb (eds.), *We Are Here*; and Philip Friedman, *Martyrs and Fighters: The Epic of the Warsaw Ghetto* (London, 1954). For Sachsenhausen, the principal sources for the German political prisoners' repertoire are the sixteen surviving songbooks (see the detailed discussion in Ch. 3); for Polish prisoners, USHMM files RG-55.004.18, RG-55.006.05, and RG-55.006.16; and for the orchestral repertoire, concert programmes in GMSD, III 418, III 419, III 626, and III 627. The principal sources for Auschwitz are USHMM RG-55.006.05, RG-55.019.09, and RG-55.006.16; Moshe Hoch, 'Ha'tarbut ha'muziqalit'; Kaczerginski and Leivick, *Lider fun di getos un lagern*; Ruta Pups and Bernard Mark, *Dos lid fun geto*. While the lists of songs from Warsaw, Vilna, Sachsenhausen (Polish songs), and Auschwitz represent, as far as I am aware, the majority of newly created songs that were preserved, they cannot claim to be comprehensive listings. 'Newly created' refers to songs in which either music or lyrics were new, but not necessarily both. These lists do not include pre-existing repertoire that was performed.

I. WARSAW: NEWLY CREATED SONGS

A yid
Der hoyfzinger fun Varshever geto
Der kleyner shmugler
Di bone
Di broyt farkoyferin
Di tefile fun khaper
Hot's mitlayd, hot's rakhmones
Hot's rakhmones, yidishe hertser
In Joint kumt tsu geyn a yid
Kh'shem zikh
Kulis
Moes, moes

Motele fun Varshever geto
Oyb nit keyn emune
Shlof, mayn kind
Treblinka
Varshever geto-lid fun frumer yidn

II. Vilna: Newly Created Songs

Aroys iz in Vilne a nayer bafel
Az a libe shpiln
Bay undz iz shtendik fintster
Bombes
Der rayter
Di nakht
Dos elnte kind
Dos transport-yingl
Dremlen feygl oyf di tsvaygn
Du geto mayn
Efsher vet geshen a nes
Es benkt zikh, es benkt zikh
Es iz geven a zumertog
Es shlogt di sho
Es vet zikh fun tsvaygl tsebliyen a boym
Farvos iz der himl
Friling
Froyen
Fun Kolkhoz bin ikh
Geto
Gro un fintster iz in geto
Hot zikh mir di shikh tserissen
Ikh benk aheym
Ikh bin shoyn lang do nit geven
Ikh vart af dir
In lager
Itzik Vitnberg
Kh'vil tsaytn andere
Korene yorn un vey tsu di teg
Lid fun umbakantn partisan
Mariko
Mir lebn eybik
Mir shpannen tsum bessern morgn
Mir zaynen oykh fun fleysh un blut

Moyshe halt zikh
Neger-lid
Pak zikh ayn
Partizaner-marsh
Peshe fun Reshe
Rose
Rozinkes mit mandlen
Shlof in der ruikayt
Shotns
Shtil, di nakht iz oysgeshternt
Shtiler, shtiler
Tsi darf es azoy zayn?
Tsu eyns, tsvey, dray
Unter dayne vayse shtern
Varshe
Yid, du partizaner
Yisrolik
Yugnt himn
Zog nit keynmol az du geyst dem letstn veg

III. SACHSENHAUSEN: GERMAN POLITICAL PRISONERS' SONGBOOKS

Abendlied
Ade, zur guten Nacht
Alle Birken grünen
Am Brunnen vor dem Tore
Am Golf von Byskaja
An der Saale hellem Strande
Asien bebe
Auerhahn
Auf der Lüneburger Heide
Auf der Reeperbahn
Auf, Jungens, auf!
Auf Wandershaft
Aus der Jugendzeit
Beim Kronenwirt
Bin ein fahrender Gesell
Bin ich auch den ganzen Tag allein
Bodensee
Bohnenpott
Börgermoor

Brommelbeerlied
Brüder, zur Sonne, zur Freiheit
Buchenwalder Lagerlied
Buerdeern un Schipper
Caracas
Chinesisches Soldatenlied
Das Edelweiss
Das frivole Lied
Das Glöckchen
Das Kalbfell klingt
Das Käuzlein
Das Lauenburger Land
Das Lieben bringt gross Freud
Das Wandern ist des Müllers Lust
Das war ein kreuzfideles Haus
Dat du min Leevsten büst
De Buer, de wull to Acker gahn
De Groffsmit
De Seiler
Den Spaten geschultert
Denn alles geht vorüber
Der blaue Heinrich
Der brave Peter
Der Freiheit eine Gasse
Der Mai ist gekommen
Der Männerschreck
Der Mond
Der rote Sarafan
Der Steirabur
Der Störtebecker ist unser Herr
Der Tod von Flandern
Der Trommler schlägt Parade
Der Trommlerknabe
Der Wind weht über Felder...
Der Winter ist vergangen
Die Bauern wollten frei sein
Die blauen Dragoner
Die Dorfsglocken
Die Feder aus Sturmhut
Die Fiedel an die Seit' getan
Die Gedanken sind frei
Die Glocken stürmten vom Bernwardsturm
Die Islandfischer

Die Jugendfahr
Die Landstrasse
Die Lindenwirtin
Die Mühle im Schwarzwald
Die Müllerin
Die Prager Musikanten
Die schwarze Reiterei
Die Steppe zittert
Die ungarischen Husaren
Die Zither lockt, die Geige klingt
Dir hing der Himmel voller Geigen
Dorfglocken
Dörflein
Dort oben auf dem Berge
Dort unten in der Mühle
Dort wo der Rhein
Drei Lilien
Drei Zigeuner
Drum singt mir ein Lied
Drunten im Unterland
Du liebes teures Mutterherz
Durchs Turmhaus zum Tor hinaus
Ein Heller und ein Batzen
Ein Schiff fährt nach Schanghai
Ein Sohn des Volkes
Einsam tönet das Glöcklein von Ferne
Elternhaus
Es blies ein Jäger wohl in sein Horn
Es dunkelt schon in der Heide
Es klappert der Huf am Stege
Es leben die Soldaten
Es schlägt ein fremder Fink
Es stehen drei Birken
Es war ein Knabe gezogen
Es zog ein Regiment
Es zogen im sonnigen Segen
Esterwegen
Fahrende Gesellen
Fährjunge
Fiaker-Lied
Fichtemarsch
Flamme empor
Fliesst Wasser fliesst

Frei ledig
Freiheit, die ich meine
Geusenlied
Gewandert sind wir
Gold und Silber
Graue Kolonnen
Grossstadtbild
Grün ach grün wie lieb' ich dich
Grüne Heide
Grüne Kolonnen
Grüsst mir das blonde Kind
Guralo
Hab' mein Wagen vollgeladen
Haberstroh
Hamborger Jungs
Hänschen klein
Heia Safari!
Heiss ist die Liebe
Herrlicher Baikal
Heute geht es an Bord
Heute noch sind wir hier zu Haus
Heute wollen wir das Ränzlein schnüren
Hoch auf dem gelben Wagen
Holder Jüngling
Horch, Kind, horch
Horch, was kommt von draussen rein
Ich atme mit Wohlbehagen
Ich hab' ein kleines Hüttchen
Ich habe Lust, im weiten Feld
Ich schiess' den Hirsch
Ich schreit' auf grünen Wegen
Ich sing mir ein Lied
Ich trag' in meinem Ranzen
Ich weiss einen Lindenbaum
Ich weiss nicht, was soll es bedeuten
Ich ziehe meine Strasse
Ick wull wi weern noch kleen
Ihr Wandervögel in der Luft
Ihren Schäfer zu erwarten
Im Feldquartier
Im Frühtau zu Berge wir ziehn
Im grünen Wald
Im Krug zum grünen Kranze

Im schönsten Wiesengrunde
Im Walde von Sachsenhausen
In der Kneipe von Moor
In der Lüneberger Heide
In einem kühlen Grunde
Jan Hinnek
Je höher der Kirchturm
Jenseits des Tales
Jetzt gang i ans Brünnle
Jetzt kommt der Sommer in das Land
Jetzt wollen wir uns wenden
Kamerad nun lass dir sagen
Kameraden der Berge
Kameraden lasst uns singen
Kameraden wann sehen wir uns wieder
Kaukasische Weise
Kaukasisches Wiegenlied
Kehr ich in der Heimat wieder
Köln am Rhein
Komm mein Mädchen
Kommt a Vogerl geflogn
Konzentrationäre
La Cucaracha
Lagerwache
Le temps des cérises
Leise zieht durch mein Gemüt
Lichtenburger Lagerlied
Liebeslied
Lied an die Elbe
Lied der Landstrasse
Lied der Legion
Lied der Prager Studenten
Lied der Wikinger
Lola
Lore
Lustig ist das Zigeunerleben
Lustig, lustig
Matrosenlied
Mein Mädel hat einen Rosenmund
Mein Riesengebirge
Mein Schatz ist eine Alpnerin
Moorsoldatenlied
Morgen müssen wir verreisen

Müde kehrt ein Wandersmann zurück
Mütterchen, Mutter
Nach meiner Heimat zieht's mich wieder
Nach Süden nun sich lenken
Neuengammer Lagerlied
Nordseewellen
Nun ade du mein lieb' Heimatland
Nun leb wohl, du kleine Gasse
Nun singt mir ein Lied
Petsamo
Pfarfherr du Kühler
Rose Marie
Rosenstock Holderblüt
Rote Husaren
Sachsenhausenlied
Sah' ein Knab' ein Röslein steh'n
Sang der Alten
Sängergruss
Sauerland
Schlaf mein Kind
Schlesierland
Schmiede der Zukunft
Schon wieder blühet die Linde
Schwarzbraun ist die Haselnuss
Seeräuberlied
Sonne und Regen
Steht ein Häuslein mitten im Walde
Stenka Rasin
Tiroler Land
Törg von Frundsberg
Trina, kumm mal vör de Dör
Trumm, trumm, terum, trumm, trumm
Über die Heide
Übern Ural, übern Fluss
Und der Hans schleicht umher
Und keiner ist da, der feige verzagt
Und rings die Heide blüht
Und unser lieben Frauen
Und wenn wi wedder no Hamborg komt
Und wenn wir marschieren
Unromantische Romanze
Unser die Sonne, unser die Erde
Verklungen sind die alten Weisen

Vom Barette schwankt die Feder
Waldeslust
Wanderlied
Wandern meine Lust
Wann wir schreiten Seit an Seit
Warum bist du denn so traurig
Wein im Becher, froher Zecher
Weit ist der Weg
Weit lasst die Fahnen wehen
Wenn alle Brünnlein fliessen
Wenn am Sonntagmorgen früh
Wenn am Walde die Heckenrosen
Wenn der Frühling kommt
Wenn die Arbeitszeit zu Ende
Wenn die bunten Fahnen wehen
Wenn die Landsknecht' trinken
Wenn ich des Morgens früh aufsteh'
Wer geht mit juchhe über die See
Westen und Osten
Westfalenland
Wiegenlied aus dem dreissigjährigen Krieg
Wiegenlied aus Estland
Wie hat es Gott so schön gemacht
Wie lang es auch noch dauern mag
Wie schön blüht uns der Maien
Wilde Gesellen
Wildgänse rauschen durch die Nacht
Winkelried
Wir kühlen nicht mehr im Moore
Wir sassen in Jonnys Spelunke
Wir schreiten fest im gleichen Schritt
Wir Seeleute haben's wirklich fein
Wir sind des Geyers schwarze Haufen
Wir sind jung
Wir sind Moorsoldaten
Wir traben in die Weite
Wir wollen zu Land ausfahren
Wir ziehen über die Strassen!
Wir ziehen über taufrische Höhn
Wir zogen in das Feld
Wo das Lager steht
Wo den Himmel
Wohlan, die Zeit ist kommen

Wohlan, jetzt geht's auf Wanderschaft
Wohlauf, die Luft geht frisch und rein
Wohlauf, Kameraden aufs Pferd!
Wohlauf zum Wandern
Wuppertal
Zu Rüdesheim

IV. SACHSENHAUSEN: NEWLY CREATED POLISH SONGS

A Gdy Häftlingi!
A Kiej Bydzie Dym sie Dzwigał
Była Moja Panieneczka
Była u Mnie Matka Boska
Chorał z Piekła Dna
Czarny Böhm
Czterdziestu Czterech
Dicke Luft!
Dumka
Egzekucja
Erika
Gdy Wrócisz
Germania
Heil Sachsenhausen!
Hej, pod Berlinem!
Hymn
Kolęda 1944
Kolęda Wieżniarska
Kołysanka
Koncentrak
Kostuś Moja!
Krakowiaczek 1940
Krzyczą Serca Dna!
Krzyk Ostateczny
Le Crucifié
aminsynek w Koncentraku
Mister 'C'
Młyny
Moja Brama
Muzulman-Kippensammler
Nie Płacz o Mnie
Nienawiść
Notturno 1941

Oj, Lublinie!
Oj, Mania, Mania
Olza
Pięciu z Sachsenhausen
Pieśń o Wandzie z Ravensbrücku
Pieśń Wieczorna
Piosenka Niezapomniana
Pod Berlinem Płynie Woda
Pożegnanie Adolfa ze Swiatem
Powrót
Repeta!
Sen Miałem Dzisiaj
Sen o Míru
Sen o Poloju
Spalona Matka
Szymon Ohm
Tańcuj, Tańcuj, Połamańcze!
Tango 'Truponoszów'
Tęskotna
Travička Zelená
Tu, w Sachsenhausen
Ty Jesteś Moim Słonkiem
Ukrzyżowany 1944
Wielka wygrana!
Więzniarko Czy Ci Nie Żal?
Za Siódmą Górą
Zawieźli do Lagru
Zimno Panie!
Żywe Kamienie

V. Sachsenhausen: Repertoire of Orchestra

Adolphe Adam	Overture from *La Poupée de Nuremberg*
Beethoven	March (opus number not specified)
	String Quartet in F (opus number not specified)
	Egmont Overture
Bizet	Fantasy from *Carmen*
Blankenburg	'Deutschland Waffenehre' (march)
Brahms	Hungarian Dance No. 6
Buchholtz	'Soldatenklänge' (march)
Chopin	Nocturne, arranged for violin and orchestra

Collin	'Olympia-Marsch'
Dvořák	Lento from String Quartet (opus number not specified)
Grieg	*Peer Gynt*
Josef Gung'l	*Die Hydropathen*, Op. 149 (Waltzes)
Haydn	selected works
	Symphony No. 6
Kott	solo works for trumpet
Král	'Brucker Lager-Marsch'
Eduard Künneke	Melodies from *Der Tenor der Herzogin*
Léhar	*Gold und Silber* (waltzes)
	Mädchenträume (waltzes)
Leoncavallo	Fantasy from *Pagliacci*
Paul Lincke	Overture from *Nakiris Hochzeit*
	Overture from *Frau Luna*
Lohmann	'Bayrische Polka' (trombone solo)
Monti	'Czardas' (saxophone solo)
Mozart	*Eine kleine Nachtmusik*
Perl	'Liebeslied' (cello solo)
Pressel	'An der Weser'
Reindel	*Ungarische Rhapsodie*
Rhode	'Schön ist die Jugend' (medley)
	'Dornröschens Brautfahrt' (character piece)
Rimsky-Korsakov	Hindu chant from *Sadko*
Rivelli	'Serenata Napolitana'
Rixner	Bagatelle
	arranged medley of works by Peter Kreuder
Sarasate	*Sérénade andalouse*, Op. 28
Schreiner	Fantasy on themes from Bizet's *Carmen*
Schroder	'Pro Patria' (March)
Schubert	Allegro from String Quartet in D (opus number not specified)
Johann Strauss	*Morgenblätter*, Op. 279 (waltzes)
	An der schönen, blauen Donau, Op. 314 (waltzes)
	melodies from *Die Fledermaus*
Franz von Suppé	Overture from *Leichte Kavallerie*
Tchaikovsky	First movement from Symphony No. 6
Carl Teike	'In Treue fest' (march)
Ambroise Thomas	Overture from *Mignon*
Urbach	Fantasy on themes from works by Wagner
	'Per aspera ad astra' (march)
Verdi	selected works
	Overture from *Nabucco*
Wagner	Overture from *Rienzi*

Henryk Wieniawski   'Obertas' (violin solo)
Wigge   'Auf Wiederhören' (march)
    'In alter Frische' (march)

VI. Auschwitz Camp Complex: Newly Created Songs

Ach, Gdybyś Była Tu!
Auschwitzlied
Benkshaft nakh Saloniki
Birkenau
Boże, Coś Polsce
Czardasz 'Birkenau'
Czekam Cie
Das Bienchen
Der tango fun Oshvientshim
Dosyć
Frauenlager
Fun Oshvientshim
Gazownia
Ikh vil zen mayn meydele
Kolęda Obozowa
Kołysanka Oświęcimska
Krankenstand
Kum tsu mir
Maleńka, Czekaj Mnie
Marsz Pasiaków
My Młodzi
Niewolnicze Tango
Obóz Smierci Oswięcimia
Pieśń Oświęcimska
Pisz Do Mnie Częsciej!
Przyjazd do Obozu
Rezygnacja
Saloniki
Taka Piosnka
Tam od Krakowa
Tęsknota do Wolnosci
Ukochana W Transporcie
Untitled (Zofia Bator)
W Auschwitz-Lager Gdy Mieszkałem
Wejście
Wiązanka z Effektenkammer

Wokoło Lasy
Zamkneli Nas Pomiędzy Druty
Znów Śmierć Zagląda Mi w Oczy
Zug zum Krematorium
Zwillingi

Glossary

Aktion Operation (military)
Appellplatz Roll-call square
Betar Revisionist Zionist youth organization
Blockälteste Block leader
Canada Warehouse in Birkenau used to sort belongings from newly arrived transports
Effektenkammer Property registry office (Auschwitz)
Einsatzgruppen Mobile killing units
Gazeta Żydowska Official newspaper of ghettos in the Generalgouvernement
Generalgouvernement General government; name given to parts of Poland not incorporated into the Reich
Ha'no'ar ha'tsiyoni Zionist Youth
Ha'shomer ha'tsa'ir The Young Guard; Zionist Youth Organization
Hitlerjugend Hitler Youth
Judenrat Jewish Council
Kapo Leader of work commandos
Lagerälteste Camp leader
Notenschreiber Music copyists
Schallerabend Communal sing-song
Scheine Official work-permits issued in the ghettos
Schreibstube Administration office
Schutzstaffel (SS) Protection squad
Sonderkommando Special commando (death camps)
Sonderlager Special camp for Jewish prisoners (Sachsenhausen)
Stubenälteste Room leader
Warthegau Territorial administrative unit established in the Polish territories annexed to the Reich
Zimmerei Carpenters' detachment

BIBLIOGRAPHY

A. ARCHIVES

Akademie der Künste, Berlin, Arbeitlerliedarchiv (AdK)
Auschwitz-Birkenau State Museum Archive (ABSM)
Fortunoff Video Archive for Holocaust Testimonies, Yale University
Gedenkstätte und Museum Sachsenhausen, Archiv (GMSA)
Gedenkstätte und Museum Sachsenhausen, Depot (GMSD)
Imperial War Museum Sound Archive
United States Holocaust Memorial Museum Archive (USHMM)
United States Holocaust Memorial Museum, Photo Archive
Wiener Library, London (WL)
Yad Vashem Archive (YV)

B. LITERATURE

ACKERMANN, EMIL, and SZEPANSKY, WOLFGANG (eds.), ... *denn in uns zieht die Hoffnung mit: Lieder, gesungen im Konzentrationslager Sachsenhausen* (Berlin: Sachsenhausenkomitee Westberlin, n.d.).

ADELSBERGER, LUCIE, *Auschwitz: A Doctor's Story*, trans. Susan Ray (London: Robson Books, 1995).

ADLER, HANS GÜNTHER, LANGBEIN, HERMANN, and LINGENS-REINER, ELLA (eds.), *Auschwitz: Zeugnisse und Berichte* (Frankfurt am Main: Europäische Verlagsanstalt, 1979).

ADLER, STANISLAW, *In the Warsaw Ghetto 1940–1943: An Account of a Witness*, trans. Sara Philip (Jerusalem: Yad Vashem, 1982).

ALPERSON, PHILIP (ed.), *What is Music?* (University Park, Pa.: Pennsylvania State University Press, 1994).

ANDERT, PETER, 'Rosebery d'Arguto: Versuche zur Erneuerung des proletarischen Chorgesangs', in Klaus Kändler, Helga Karolewski, and Ilse Siebert (eds.), *Berliner Begegnungen: Ausländische Künstler in Berlin 1918 bis 1933* (Berlin: Dietz, 1987), 340–5.

ARAD, YITZHAK, *Belzec, Sobibór, Treblinka: The Operation Reinhard Extermination Camps* (Bloomington and Indianapolis: Indiana University Press, 1987).

—— *Ghetto in Flames: The Struggle and Destruction of the Jews in Vilna in the Holocaust* (New York: Holocaust Library, 1982).

ARAD, YITZHAK, GUTMAN, YISRAEL, and MARGALIOT, ABRAHAM (eds.), *Documents on the Holocaust: Selected Sources on the Destruction of the Jews of Germany and Austria, Poland, and the Soviet Union* (Jerusalem: Yad Vashem, 1981).

AUERBACH, RACHEL, *Varshever tsavoes: bagegenishn, aktivitetn, goyroles 1933–1943* (Tel Aviv: Yisroel-Bukh, 1974).

BALFOUR, MICHAEL (ed.), *Theatre and War 1933–1945: Performance in Extremis* (Oxford: Berghahn Books, 2001).

BARTOSZEWSKI, WLADYSLAW, 'The Martyrdom and Struggle of the Jews in Warsaw under German Occupation 1939–43', in Bartoszewski and Polonsky (eds.), *The Jews in Warsaw*, 312–48.

—— *The Warsaw Ghetto: A Christian's Testimony*, trans. Stephen G. Cappellari (London: Lamp Press, 1989).

—— and POLONSKY, ANTONY (eds.), *The Jews in Warsaw: A History* (Oxford: Blackwell, 1991).

BARTOV, OMER, *Murder in our Midst: The Holocaust, Industrial Killing, and Representation* (Oxford: Oxford University Press, 1996).

BAUER, YEHUDA, *They Chose Life: Jewish Resistance in the Holocaust* (Jerusalem: The Institute of Contemporary Jewry, 1973).

BAUMAN, JANINA, *Winter in the Morning: A Young Girl's Life in the Warsaw Ghetto and Beyond, 1939–1945* (Bath: Chivers, 1986).

BAUMAN, ZYGMUNT, *Modernity and the Holocaust* (Cambridge: Polity, 1989).

BEINFELD, SOLON, 'The Cultural Life of the Vilna Ghetto', in Joshua Sobol, *Ghetto* (London: Nick Hern, 1989), pp. xxii–xxviii.

BERNSTEIN, MICHAEL ANDRÉ, *Foregone Conclusions: Against Apocalyptic History* (London: University of California Press, 1994).

BERNSTEIN, YITZHAK, *Ghetto: Berichte aus dem Warschauer Ghetto 1939–1945* (Berlin: Union, 1966).

BODEK, RICHARD HAROLD, 'We Are the Red Megaphone!: Political Music, Agitprop Theater, Everyday Life and Communist Politics in Berlin during the Weimar Republic' (Ph.D. diss., University of Michigan, 1990).

BOR, JOSEF, *Terezin Requiem*, trans. Edith Pargeter (London: Heinemann, 1963).

BOROWSKI, TADEUSZ, *This Way for the Gas, Ladies and Gentlemen*, trans. Barbara Vedder (London: Penguin, 1967).

BRANDHUBER, JERZY, 'Vergessene Erde', *Hefte von Auschwitz*, 5 (1962), 83–95.

BRAUN, JOACHIM, *Jews and Jewish Elements in Soviet Music* (Tel Aviv: Israeli Music Publications, 1978).

BROWNING, CHRISTOPHER R., *Nazi Policy, Jewish Workers, German Killers* (Cambridge: Cambridge University Press, 2000).

BURGER, ADOLF, *Des Teufels Werkstatt: Im Fälscherkommando des KZ Sachsenhausen* (Berlin: Verlag Neues Leben, 1983).

BURLEIGH, MICHAEL, *The Third Reich: A New History* (London: Pan, 2001).

CARUTH, CATHY (ed.), *Trauma: Explorations in Memory* (London: Johns Hopkins University Press, 1995).

CLENDINNEN, INGA, *Reading the Holocaust* (Cambridge: Cambridge University Press, 1999).

CORRSIN, STEPHEN D., 'Aspects of Population Change and of Acculturation in Jewish Warsaw at the End of the Nineteenth Century: The Censuses of 1882 and 1897', in Bartoszewski and Polonsky (eds.), *The Jews in Warsaw*, 212–31.

CUMMINS, PAUL, *Dachau Song: The Twentieth-Century Odyssey of Herbert Zipper* (New York: Peter Lang, 1992).

CZECH, DANUTA, 'The Auschwitz Prisoner Administration', in Gutman and Berenbaum (eds.), *Anatomy of the Auschwitz Death Camp*, 363–78.

DAUER, HANNELORE, 'Kunst im täglichen Schatten des Todes: Künstlerischer Widerstand in Konzentrationslagern und Ghettos', *Tribüne*, 90 (1984), 116–24.

—— 'Was kann Kunst? Der kulturelle Widerstand der Juden in Ghettos und Lagern', *Tribüne*, 89 (1984), 120–30.

DAWIDOWICZ, LUCY S., *The War against the Jews, 1933–1945* (London: Penguin, 1975).

DELBO, CHARLOTTE, *Auschwitz and After*, trans. Rosette C. Lamont (New Haven: Yale University Press, 1995).

DOBROSZYCKI, LUCJAN (ed.), *The Chronicle of the Łódź Ghetto, 1941–1944* (New Haven: Yale University Press, 1984).

DROBISCH, KLAUS, and WIELAND, GÜNTHER, *System der NS-Konzentrationslager 1933–1939* (Berlin: Akademie Verlag, 1993).

DUNIN-WĄSOWICZ, KRZYSZTOF, *Resistance in the Nazi Concentration Camps 1933–1945*, trans. Halina Dzierżanowska, Maria Paczyńska, and Maria Kasza (Warsaw: Polish Scientific Publishers, 1982).

DUTLINGER, ANNE D., and MILTON, SYBIL, *Art, Music and Education as Strategies for Survival: Theresienstadt 1941–1945* (London: Herodias, 2000).

DWORZECKI, MARK, 'The Day-to-Day Stand of the Jews', in Yisrael Gutman and Livia Rothkirchen (eds.), *The Catastrophe of European Jewry: Antecedents—History—Reflections* (Jerusalem: Yad Vashem, 1976), 367–99.

—— *Yerushalayim de-Lita in kamf un umkum* (Paris: L'Union Populaire Juive en France, 1948).

ELIAS, RUTH, *Triumph of Hope: From Theresienstadt and Auschwitz to Israel* (New York: John Wiley, 1998).

FACKLER, GUIDO, *'Des Lagers Stimme'—Music im KZ: Alltag und Häftlingskultur in den Konzentrationslagern 1933 bis 1936* (Bremen: Temmen, 2000).

—— 'Musik im Konzentrationslager', *Informationen*, 41 (1995), 25–33.

FASS, MOSHE, 'Theatrical Activities in the Polish Ghettos during the Years 1939–1942', *Jewish Social Studies*, 38 (1976), 54–72.

FATER, YISASKHAR, *Yidishe muzik in Poyln tsvishn beyde velt-milkhomes* (Tel Aviv: World Federation of Polish Jews, 1970).

FEDER, ZAMI, *Zamlung fun katset un geto lider* (Bergen-Belsen: Central Jewish Committee in Bergen-Belsen, 1946).

FELMAN, SHOSHANA, and LAUB, DORI, *Testimony: Crises of Witnessing in Literature, Psychoanalysis and History* (London: Routledge, 1992).

FÉNELON, FANIA, 'Ensemble der Hölle: Das Mädchenorchester in Auschwitz. Ein Gespräch mit der Sängerin Fania Fénelon', in Annette Kuhn and Valentine Rothe (eds.), *Frauen im Deutschen Faschismus*, ii (Düsseldorf: Schwann, 1982), 200–4.

—— (with Marcelle Routier), *Playing for Time*, trans. Judith Landry (London: Sphere, 1977).

FLAM, GILA, *Singing for Survival: Songs of the Lodz Ghetto* (Urbana: University of Illinois Press, 1992).

FRIEDLÄNDER, SAUL, 'Trauma, Memory, and Transference' in Geoffrey H. Hartman (ed.), *Holocaust Remembrance: The Shapes of Memory* (Oxford: Blackwell, 1994), 252–63.

—— (ed.), *Probing the Limits of Representation: Nazism and the 'Final Solution'* (Cambridge, Mass., and London: Harvard University Press, 1992).

FRIEDMAN, PHILIP (ed.), *Martyrs and Fighters: The Epic of the Warsaw Ghetto* (London: Routledge & Kegan Paul, 1954).

FRITZ, MALI, *Essig gegen den Durst: 565 Tage in Auschwitz-Birkenau* (Vienna: Verlag für Gesellschaftskritik, 1986).

FULBROOK, MARY, *German National Identity after the Holocaust* (Cambridge: Polity, 1999).

FÜRSTENBERG, DORIS (ed.), *Jeden Moment war dieser Tod: Interviews mit jüdischen Frauen, die Auschwitz überlebten* (Düsseldorf: Schwann, 1986).

GILBERT, SHIRLI, 'Music in the Nazi Ghettos and Camps (1939–1945)' (D.Phil. thesis, University of Oxford, 2002).

GLAS-LARSSON, MARGARETA, *I Want to Speak: The Tragedy and Banality of Survival in Terezin and Auschwitz*, trans. Lowell A. Bangerter (Riverside, Calif.: Ariadne Press, 1991).

GOLDSTEIN, BERNARD, *Finf yor in Varshever geto* (New York: Undzer Zeit, 1947).

GUTMAN, YISRAEL, 'Auschwitz—An Overview', in Gutman and Berenbaum (eds.), *Anatomy of the Auschwitz Death Camp*, 5–33.

—— *The Jews of Warsaw, 1939–1943: Ghetto, Underground, Revolt*, trans. Ina Friedman (Brighton: The Harvester Press, 1982).

—— (ed.), *Encyclopedia of the Holocaust*, 4 vols. (London: Macmillan, 1990).

—— and MICHAEL BERENBAUM (eds.), *Anatomy of the Auschwitz Death Camp* (Bloomington and Indianapolis: Indiana University Press, 1994).

HANHEIDE, STEFAN, 'Lieder im Angesicht des Volkermords: Zu den Funktionen der Musik im Ghetto von Wilna', *Krieg und Literatur*, 6/11–12 (1994), 69–85.

HART, KITTY, *I Am Alive* (London: Corgi, 1961).

HEENEN-WOLFF, SUSANN, *Im Haus des Henkers: Gespräche in Deutschland* (Frankfurt am Main: Dvorah Verlag, 1992).

HELLER, CELIA S., *On the Edge of Destruction: Jews of Poland between the Two World Wars* (New York: Columbia University Press, 1977).

HERBERT, ULRICH, 'Labour and Extermination: Economic Interest and the Primacy of *Weltanschauung* in National Socialism', *Past and Present*, 138 (1993), 144–95.

HERBERT, ULRICH, ORTH, KARIN, and DIECKMANN, CHRISTOPH, 'Die nationalso-zialistischen Konzentrationslager: Geschichte, Erinnerung, Forschung', in Ulrich Herbert, Karin Orth, and Christoph Dieckmann (eds.), *Die nationalsozialistischen Konzentrationslager: Entwicklung und Struktur*, i (Göttingen: Wallstein, 1998), 17–40.

HILBERG, RAUL, STARON, STANISLAW, and KERMISZ, JOSEF (eds.), *The Warsaw Diary of Adam Czerniakow* (Chicago: Ivan R. Dee, 1999).

HIRSCH, DAVID D., 'Camp Music and Camp Songs: Szymon Laks and Aleksander Kulisiewicz', in G. Jan Colijn and Marcia Sachs Littell (eds.), *Confronting the Holocaust: A Mandate for the 21st Century*, xix (Lanham, Md.: University Press of America, 1997), 157–68.

HOCH, MOSHE, 'Ha'tarbut ha'muziqalit b'kerev ha'y'hudim tachat ha'shilton ha'natsi b'polin 1939–1945' (Ph.D. diss., Bar-Ilan University, 1992).

HOROWITZ, SARA, 'Voices from the Killing Ground', in Geoffrey H. Hartman (ed.), *Holocaust Remembrance: The Shapes of Memory* (Oxford: Blackwell, 1994), 42–58.

HÖSS, RUDOLF, *Commandant of Auschwitz*, trans. Constantine Fitzgibbon (London: Weidenfeld and Nicolson, 1959).

—— BROAD, PERY, and KREMER, JOHANN PAUL, *KL Auschwitz Seen by the SS*, trans. Constantine FitzGibbon and Krystyna Michalik (Osawiecim: The Auschwitz-Birkenau State Museum, 1997).

HOYM, CARL (ed.), *Proletarier singe! Ein neuzeitlich Liederbuch für jung und alt* (Hamburg: Willaschek, 1919).

HRDLICKA, MANUELA R., *Alltag im KZ: Sachsenhausen bei Berlin* (Leske and Budrich: Opladen, 1992).

JACOBSON, JOSHUA R., 'Music in the Holocaust', *Choral Journal*, 36/5 (1995), 9–21.

JALDATI, LIN, and REBLING, EBERHARD (eds.), *Es brennt, Brüder, es brennt: Jiddische Lieder* (Berlin: Rütten and Loening, 1966).

JANDA, ELSBETH, and SPRECHER, MAX M. (eds.), *Lieder aus dem Ghetto: Fünfzig Lieder jiddisch und deutsch mit Noten* (Munich: Ehrenwirth, 1962).

JANI, EMILIO, *My Voice Saved Me: Auschwitz 180046*, trans. Timothy Paterson (Milan: Centauro Editrice, 1961).

JELAVICH, PETER, *Berlin Cabaret* (Cambridge, Mass.: Harvard University Press, 1993).

JOHN, ECKHARD, 'Musik und Konzentrationslager: Eine Annäherung', *Archiv für Musikwissenschaft*, 48 (1991), 1–36.

KACZERGINSKI, SHMERKE, *Khurbn Vilne* (New York: Tsiko, 1947).

—— (ed.), *Dos gezang fun Vilner ghetto* (Paris: Committee of Jews of Vilna in France, 1947).

—— and LEIVICK, H. (eds.), *Lider fun di getos un lagern* (New York: Altveltlekher Yidisher Kultur-Kongres: Tsiko, 1948).

KALISCH, SHOSHANA, and MEISTER, BARBARA, *Yes, We Sang! Songs of the Ghettos and Concentration Camps* (New York: Harper and Row, 1985).

KALMANOVITCH, ZELIG, 'A Diary of the Nazi Ghetto in Vilna', *YIVO Annual of Jewish Social Science*, 8 (1953), 9–81.

KAPLAN, CHAIM A., *Scroll of Agony: The Warsaw Diary of Chaim A. Kaplan*, trans. and ed. Abraham I. Katsh (London: Macmillan, 1965).

KARAS, JOŽA, *Music in Terezín 1941–1945* (New York: Beaufort, 1985).

KATER, MICHAEL H., *The Twisted Muse: Musicians and their Music in the Third Reich* (Oxford: Oxford University Press, 1997).

KEREN, NILI, 'The Family Camp', in Gutman and Berenbaum (eds.), *Anatomy of the Auschwitz Death Camp*, 428–40.

KLEIN, KATJA, *Kazett-Lyrik: Untersuchungen zu Gedichten und Liedern aus dem Konzentrationslager Sachsenhausen* (Würzburg: Könighausen and Neumann, 1995).

KNAPP, GABRIELE, *Das Frauenorchester in Auschwitz: Musikalische Zwangsarbeit und ihre Bewältigung* (Hamburg: von Bockel, 1996).

Komitee der Antifaschistischen Widerstandskämpfer der Deutschen Demokratischen Republik, *Sachsenhausen: Dokumente, Aussagen, Forschungsergebnisse und Erlebnisberichte über das ehemalige Konzentrationslager Sachsenhausen* (Frankfurt am Main: Röderberg, 1982).

KON, HENECH (ed.), *Thirty Songs of the Ghetto* (New York: Congress for Jewish Culture, 1960).

—— *Twenty Songs of the Ghettos* (New York: Congress for Jewish Culture, 1963).

KORCZAK, JANUZ, *Ghetto Diary*, trans. Aaron Zeitlin (New York: Holocaust Library, 1978).

KOWALSKI, ISAAC (ed.), *Vilner almanakh* (New York: Moriah Offset Co., 1992).

KRAUSNICK, HELMUT, and BROSZAT, MARTIN, *Anatomy of the SS State*, trans. Dorothy Lang and Marian Jackson (London: Paladin, 1968).

KREUZHECK, HANS-LUDGER, ' "Unsere Kuhle": Musik im KZ Neuengamme und in anderen Lagern', in Peter Peterson (ed.), *Zündende Lieder, verbrannte Musik: Folgen des Nationalsozialismus für Hamburger Musiker und Musikerinnen* (Hamburg: VSA-Verlag, 1988), 55–68.

KRUK, HERMAN, 'Diary of the Vilna Ghetto', *YIVO Annual of Jewish Social Science*, 13 (1965), 9–78.

—— *Togbukh fun Vilner geto* (New York: YIVO, 1961).

KULISIEWICZ, ALEKSANDER, *Adresse: Sachsenhausen. Literarische Momentaufnahmen aus dem KZ*, ed. Claudia Westermann, trans. Bettina Eberspächer (Gerlingen: Bleicher Verlag, 1997).

KUNA, MILAN, *Musik an der Grenze des Lebens: Musikerinnen und Musiker aus böhmischen Ländern in nationalsozialistischen Konzentrationslagern und Gefängnissen*, trans. Eliška Nováková (Frankfurt am Main: Zweitausendeins, 1993).

LACAPRA, DOMINICK, *History and Memory after Auschwitz* (Ithaca: Cornell University Press, 1998).

Das Lagerliederbuch: Lieder, gesungen, gesammelt und geschrieben im Konzentrationslager Sachsenhausen bei Berlin 1942 (Dortmund: Pläne, 1983).

LAKS, SZYMON, *Music of Another World*, trans. Chester A. Kisiel (Evanston, Ill.: Northwestern University Press, 1989).

LAMMEL, INGE, 'Lieder im faschistischen Konzentrationslager', *Musik und Gesellschaft*, 33 (1983), 16–20.

—— 'Das Sachsenhausen-Liederbuch', in Günter Morsch (ed.), *Sachsenhausen-Liederbuch: Originalwiedergabe eines illegalen Häftlingsliederbuches aus dem Konzentrationslager Sachsenhausen* (Berlin: Hentrich, 1995), 14–31.

—— 'Zur etischen Funktion des Deutschen KZ-Liedes', *Musik und Gesellschaft*, 16 (1966), 148–53.

—— and HOFMEYER, GÜNTER (eds.), *Lieder aus den faschistischen Konzentrationslagern* (Leipzig: Friedrich Hofmeister, 1962).

—— —— *Kopf hoch, Kamerad!: Künstlerische Dokumente aus faschistischen Konzentrationslagern* (Berlin: Henschelverlag, 1965).

LANGBEIN, HERMANN, *Menschen in Auschwitz* (Vienna: Europaverl, 1972).

LANGER, LAWRENCE L., *Admitting the Holocaust: Collected Essays* (Oxford: Oxford University Press, 1995).

—— *Holocaust Testimonies: The Ruins of Memory* (Nw Haven and London: Yale University Press, 1991).

—— *Preempting the Holocaust* (New Haven and London: Yale University Press, 1998).

LASKER-WALLFISCH, ANITA, *Inherit the Truth 1939–1945* (London: Giles de la Mare, 1996).

LAU, ELLINOR, and PAMPUCH, SUSANNE (eds.), *Draußen steht eine bange Nacht: Lieder und Gedichte aus deutschen Konzentrationslagern* (Frankfurt am Main: Fischer, 1994).

LENGYEL, OLGA, *Five Chimneys*, trans. Clifford Coch and Paul P. Weiss (London: Hamilton, 1959).

LETTOW, FRITZ, *Arzt in den Höllen: Erinnerungen an vier Konzentrationslager* (Berlin: edition ost, 1997).

LE VERNOY, ALEC, *No Drums, no Trumpets*, trans. Christine Pieters Le Vernoy and Joyce Bailey (London: Penguin, 1988).

LEVI, ERIK, *Music in the Third Reich* (London: Macmillan, 1994).

LEVI, PRIMO, *The Drowned and the Saved*, trans. Raymond Rosenthal (London: Abacus, 1988).

—— *If This Is a Man / The Truce*, trans. Stuart Woolf (London: Abacus, 1979).

LEWIN, ABRAHAM, *A Cup of Tears: A Diary of the Warsaw Ghetto*, trans. Christopher Hutton (London: Fontana, 1988).

LIDTKE, VERNON L., 'Songs and Nazis: Political Music and Social Change in Twentieth-Century Germany', in Gary D. Stark and Bede Karl Lackner (eds.), *Essays on Culture and Society in Modern Germany* (Arlington: Texas A and M University Press, 1982), 167–200.

LINDE, CARSTEN (ed.), *KZ-Lieder: Eine Auswahl aus dem Repertoire des polnischen Sängers Alex Kulisiewicz* (Sievershütten: Wendepunkt, 1972).

LINDENBERG, ERNST, 'Rosebery d'Arguto—Vorkämpfer der Arbeiterchorbewegung', *Musik und Gesellschaft*, 4 (1971), 231–40.

LUSTIGER, ARNO (ed.), *Sog nit kejnmol … Lieder des jüdischen Widerstandes: Jüdische Arbeiter- und Partisanen-Lieder* (Frankfurt am Main: no publisher, 1990).

MENASCHE, ALBERT, *Birkenau (Auschwitz II): (Memoirs of an Eye-witness). How 72,000 Greek Jews Perished*, trans. Isaac Saltiel (New York: Albert Martin, 1947).

MEYER, HENRY, 'Musste da auch Musik sein? Der Weg eines Geigers von Dresden über Auschwitz nach Amerika', in Hanns-Werner Heister, C. Maurer Zenck, and P. Petersen (eds.), *Musik im Exil: Folgen des Nazismus für die internationale Musikkultur* (Frankfurt am Main: Fischer, 1993), 29–40.

MICHEL, HENRI, *Oranienburg-Sachsenhausen: KZ-Erinnerungen und Hungermarsch in die Freiheit eines politischen Gefangenen* (Eupen: Grenz-Echo-Verlag, 1985).

MLOTEK, ELEANOR GORDON (ed.), *Mir trogn a gezang: Favourite Yiddish Songs of our Generation* (New York: The Workmen's Circle, 2000).

—— and GOTTLIEB, MALKE (eds.), *We Are Here: Songs of the Holocaust* (New York: The Education Department of the Workmen's Circle, 1983).

—— and MLOTEK, JOSEPH (eds.), *Pearls of Yiddish Song: Favourite Folk, Art and Theatre Songs* (New York: The Education Department of the Workmen's Circle, 1988).

MORSCH, GÜNTER (ed.), *Sachsenhausen-Liederbuch: Originalwiedergabe eines illegalen Häftlingsliederbuches aus dem Konzentrationslager Sachsenhausen* (Berlin: Hentrich, 1995).

MÜLLER, FILIP, *Auschwitz Inferno: The Testimony of a Sonderkommando*, trans. Susanne Flatauer (London: Routledge, 1979).

MUTH, WOLFGANG, 'Musik hinter Stacheldraht: Swing in Ghetto und KZ', in Bernd Polster (ed.), *Swing Heil: Jazz im Nationalsozialismus* (Berlin: Transit, 1989), 211–20.

NANSEN, ODD, *Day After Day*, trans. Katherine John (London: Putnam and Co., 1949).

NAUJOKS, HARRY, *Mein Leben im KZ Sachsenhausen 1936–1942: Erinnerungen des ehemaligen Lagerältesten* (Cologne: Röderberg im Pahl-Rugenstein Verlag, 1987).

NEUSTADT, MEILEKH, *Khurbn un oyfshtand fun di yidn in Varshe: eydes-bletter un azkores* (Tel Aviv: Executive Committee of the General Federation of Jewish Labour in Palestine, 1948).

NEWMAN, RICHARD, and KIRTLEY, KAREN, *Alma Rosé: Vienna to Auschwitz* (London: Amadeus Press, 2000).

NOVICK, PETER, *The Holocaust in American Life* (New York: Houghton Mifflin, 1999).

ORTH, KARIN, 'The Concentration Camp SS as a Functional Elite', in Ulrich Herbert (ed.), *National Socialist Extermination Policies: Contemporary German Perspectives and Controversies* (Oxford: Berghahn, 2000), 306–36.

—— *Das System der nationalsozialistischen Konzentrationslager: Eine politische Orga-nisationsgeschichte* (Hamburg: Hamburger Edition, 1999).

ORTMEYER, BENJAMIN (ed.), *Jiddische Lieder gegen die Nazis: Kommentierte Lieder-texte mit Noten* (Witterschlick and Bonn: Wehle, 1996).

PALLMANN, GERHARD (ed.), *Wohlauf Kameraden! Ein Liederbuch der jungen Man-nschaft von Soldaten, Bauern, Arbeitern und Studenten* (Kassel: Bärenreiter, 1934).

PATTERSON, MICHAEL, 'The Final Chapter: Theatre in the Concentration Camps of Nazi Germany', in Glen W. Gadberry (ed.), *Theatre in the Third Reich, the Prewar*

Years: Essays on Theatre in Nazi Germany (Westport, Conn., and London: Greenwood Press, 1995), 157–65.

PAWEŁCZYŃSKA, ANNA, *Values and Violence in Auschwitz: A Sociological Analysis*, trans. Catherine S. Leach (Berkeley, Los Angeles, and London: University of California Press, 1979).

PERL, GISELLA, *I Was a Doctor in Auschwitz* (New York: International Universitas Press, 1948).

PIPER, FRANCISZEK, 'The Number of Victims', in Gutman and Berenbaum (eds.), *Anatomy of the Auschwitz Death Camp*, 61–76.

POSMYSZ, ZOFIA, 'Die "Sängerin" ', *Hefte von Auschwitz*, 8 (1964), 15–32.

POTTER, PAMELA, *Most German of the Arts: Musicology and Society from the Weimar Republic to the end of Hitler's Reich* (New Haven: Yale University Press, 1998).

POWITZ, STEPHEN J., 'Musical Life in the Warsaw Ghetto', *Journal of Jewish Music and Liturgy*, 4 (1981–2), 2–9.

PROBST-EFFAH, GISELA, 'Das Lied im NS-Widerstand: Ein Beitrag zur Rolle der Musik in den nationalsozialistischen Konzentrationslagern', *Musikpädagogische Forschung*, 9 (1989), 79–89.

Projektgruppe Musik in Konzentrationslagern, *Musik in Konzentrationslagern* (Freiburg: Systemdruck and Verlags GmbH, 1992).

PUPS, RUTA, and MARK, BERNARD, *Dos lid fun geto: zomlung* (Warsaw: Yiddish-Bukh, 1962).

RAHE, THOMAS, 'Kultur im KZ: Musik, Literatur und Kunst in Bergen-Belsen', in Claus Füllberg-Stolberg et al. (eds.), *Frauen in Konzentrationslagern: Bergen-Belsen Ravensbrück* (Bremen: Edition Temmen, 1994), 193–206.

RAMATI, ALEXANDER, *And the Violins Stopped Playing: A Story of the Gypsy Holocaust* (London: Hodder and Stoughton, 1985).

RAN, LEYZER, *Vilna, Jerusalem of Lithuania*, trans. Marcus Moseley (Oxford: Oxford Centre for Postgraduate Hebrew Studies, 1987).

REICHMANN, HANS, *Deutscher Bürger und verfolgter Jude: Novemberpogrom und KZ Sachsenhausen 1937 bis 1939* (Munich: Oldenbourg, 1998).

REICH-RANICKI, MARCEL, *Mein Leben: Autobiographie* (Stuttgart: DVA, 1999).

REICHSJUGENDFÜHRUNG (ed.), *Unser Liederbuch: Lieder der Hitler-Jugend* (Munich: Zentralverlag der NSDAP, 1939).

RINGELBLUM, EMMANUEL, *Ksovim fun geto* (Warsaw: Yiddish-Bukh, 1961–3).

—— *Notes from the Warsaw Ghetto: The Journal of Emmanuel Ringelblum*, trans. and ed. Jacob Sloan (New York: Schocken Books, 1974).

—— *Notitsen fun Varshever geto* (Warsaw: Yiddish-Bukh, 1952).

ROLAND, CHARLES G., *Courage under Siege: Starvation, Disease and Death in the Warsaw Ghetto* (Oxford: Oxford University Press, 1992).

ROSENHAFT, EVE, 'The Use of Remembrance: The Legacy of the Communist Resistance in the German Democratic Republic', in Francis R. Nicosia and Lawrence D. Stokes (eds.), *Germans against Nazism: Nonconformity, Opposition and Resistance in the Third Reich* (Oxford: Berg, 1990), 369–88.

ROSKIES, DAVID, *Against the Apocalypse: Responses to Catastrophe in Modern Jewish Culture* (Cambridge, Mass., and London: Harvard University Press, 1984).

—— (ed.), *The Literature of Destruction* (New York: The Jewish Publication Society, 1989).

ROVIT, REBECCA, and GOLDFARB, ALVIN, *Theatrical Performance during the Holocaust: Texts, Documents, Memoirs* (Baltimore and London: The Johns Hopkins University Press, 1999).

RUBIN, RUTH, *Voices of a People: The Story of Yiddish Folksong* (Philadelphia: Jewish Publication Society of America, 1979).

RUDASHEVSKI, YITZKHOK, *The Diary of the Vilna Ghetto, June 1941–April 1943*, trans. Percy Matenko (Tel Aviv: Ghetto Fighters' House, 1973).

RUDAVSKY, JOSEPH, *To Live with Hope, to Die with Dignity: Spiritual Resistance in the Ghettos and Camps* (Lanham, Md., and London: University Press of America, 1997).

RUTTNER, FRANZ, 'Die jiddischen Lieder aus dem Wilnaer Getto', in Florian Freund, Franz Ruttner, and Hans Safrian (eds.), *Ess firt kejn weg zurik: Geschichte und Lieder des Ghettos von Wilna, 1941–1943* (Vienna: Picus, 1992), 123–9.

SACHNOWITZ, HERMAN, *Auschwitz: Ein norwegischer Jude überlebte* (Frankfurt am Main: Büchergilde Gutenberg, 1981).

SCHELLER, THILO (ed.), *Singend wollen wir marschieren: Liederbuch des Reichsarbeitsdienstes* (Potsdam: Voggenreiter, n.d.).

SCHMIDT, HUGO W. (ed.), *Uns geht die Sonne nicht unter: Lieder der Hitler-Jugend* (Cologne: Musikverlag Tonger, 1934).

SCHNEIDER, WOLFGANG, *Kunst hinter Stacheldraht: Ein Beitrag zur Geschichte des faschistischen Widerstandes* (Leipzig: Seemann, 1976).

SCHRIRE, GWYNNE (ed.), *In Sacred Memory: Recollections of the Holocaust by Survivors Living in Cape Town* (Cape Town: Cape Town Holocaust Memorial Council, 1995).

SCHUMANN, COCO, *Der Ghetto-Swinger: Eine Jazzlegende erzählt* (Munich: Deutscher Taschenbuch Verlag, 1997).

SCHWARZ-REIFLINGEN, ERWIN (ed.), *HJ singt: Die schönsten Lieder der Hitler-Jugend* (Leipzig: Schott, n.d.).

SEIDEL, SONJA, 'Kultur und Kunst im antifaschistischen Widerstandskampf im Konzentrationslager Buchenwald', *Buchenwaldheft*, 18 (1983), 1–84.

SEIDMAN, HILLEL, *Togbukh fun Varshever geto* (Buenos Aires: CFPJ, 1947).

SHMERUK, CHONE, 'Aspects of the History of Warsaw as a Yiddish Literary Centre', in Bartoszewski and Polonsky (eds.), *The Jews in Warsaw*, 232–45.

SKURKOVITZ, SIMA, *Sima's Songs: Light in Nazi Darkness*, trans. unknown (Jerusalem: Christian Friends of Israel, 1993).

SOFSKY, WOLFGANG, *The Order of Terror: The Concentration Camp*, trans. William Templer (Princeton: Princeton University Press, 1997).

STAAR, SONJA, 'Kunst, Widerstand und Lagerkultur: Eine Dokumentation', *Buchenwaldheft*, 27 (1987), 5–79.

STROUMSA, JACQUES, *Violinist in Auschwitz: From Salonika to Jerusalem 1913–1967*, ed. Erhard Roy Wiehn, trans. James Stewart Brice (Konstanz: Hartung-Gorre Verlag, 1996).

STUMME, WOLFGANG (ed.), *Liederblatt der Hitlerjugend: 1. Jahresband* (Berlin: Georg Kallmeyer, 1936).

—— *Liederblatt der Hitlerjugend: 2. Jahresband* (Berlin: Georg Kallmeyer, 1938).

SUTZKEVER, AVRAHAM, *Fun Vilner geto* (Moscow: Der Emes, 1946).

SVERRISSON, G., *Wohnt hier ein Isländer? Erinnerungen von Leifur Muller*, trans. Franz Gíslason and Wolfgang Schiffer (Bremerhaven: NW, 1997).

SZALET, LEON, *Experiment 'E': A Report from an Extermination Laboratory*, trans. Catharine Bland Williams (New York: Didier, 1945).

SZMAGLEWSKA, SEWERYNA, 'Rauch über Birkenau', in Gerhard Schoenberner (ed.), *Wir haben es gesehen: Augenzeugenberichte über die Judenverfolgung im Dritten Reich* (Hamburg: Rütten und Loening, 1962), 242–7.

SZPILMAN, WŁADYSŁAW, *The Pianist: The Extraordinary Story of One Man's Survival in Warsaw, 1939–45*, trans. Anthea Bell (London: Victor Gollancz, 1999).

THWAITE, EMILY, 'The Power of Music: Music in the Nazi Concentration Camps' (Master's thesis, University of Southampton, 1998).

TOERIEN, WILLEM ANDRÉ, 'The Role of Music, Performing Artists and Composers in German-Controlled Concentration Camps and Ghettos during World War II' (Master's thesis, University of Pretoria, 1993).

TRUNK, ISAIAH, *Judenrat: The Jewish Councils in Eastern Europe under Nazi Occupation* (New York: Macmillan, 1972).

TUCHEL, JOHANNES, *Die Inspektion der Konzentrationslager 1938–1945: Das System des Terrors* (Berlin: Hentrich, 1994).

TURKOW, JONAS, *Azoy iz es geven* (Buenos Aires: CFPJ, 1948).

—— *Hayo hayta varsha ha'y'hudit* (Tel Aviv: Tarbut v'khinukh, 1969).

WALDA, DICK, *Trompettist in Auschwitz: Herinneringen van Lex van Weren* (Amsterdam: De Boekerij, 1980).

WEISS, AHARON, 'Categories of Camps: Their Character and Role in the Execution of the "Final Solution of the Jewish Question"', in Yisrael Gutman and Avital Saf (eds.), *The Nazi Concentration Camps: Structure and Aims. The Image of the Prisoner. The Jews in the Camps* (Proceedings of the fourth Yad Vashem international historical conference, Jerusalem, January 1980; Jerusalem: Yad Vashem, 1984), 115–32.

WEISS-RÜTHEL, ARNOLD, *Nacht und Nebel: Aufzeichnungen aus fünf Jahren Schutzhaft* (Munich: Verlag Herbert Kluger, 1946).

WIESEL, ELIE, *Night*, trans. Stella Rodway (London: Fontana, 1972).

WIEVIORKA, ANNETTE, 'On Testimony', in Geoffrey H. Hartman (ed.), *Holocaust Remembrance: The Shapes of Memory* (Oxford: Blackwell, 1994), 23–32.

WOLFF, GEORG, *Kalendarium der Geschichte des KZ Sachsenhausen: Strafverfolgung* (Oranienburg: Nationalen Mahn- und Gedenkstätte Sachsenhausen, 1987).

YAHIL, LENI, *The Holocaust: The Fate of European Jewry*, trans. Ina Friedman and Haya Galai (Oxford: Oxford University Press, 1990).

YERGER, MARK C., *Riding East: The SS Cavalry Brigade in Poland and Russia 1939–1942* (Atglen, Pa.: Schiffer Publishing Ltd., 1996).

YOUNG, JAMES E., 'Between History and Memory: The Uncanny Voices of Historian and Survivor', *History and Memory*, 9/1 (1997), 47–58.

—— *Writing and Rewriting the Holocaust* (Bloomington and Indianapolis: Indiana University Press, 1988).

ZERUBAVEL, YAEL, *Recovered Roots: Collective Memory and the Making of Israeli National Tradition* (Chicago and London: University of Chicago Press, 1995).

ZUCKERMAN, YITZHAK, *A Surplus of Memory: Chronicle of the Warsaw Ghetto Uprising*, trans. and ed. Barbara Harshav (Berkeley and Los Angeles: University of California Press, 1993).

ZYLBERBERG, MICHAEL, *A Warsaw Diary, 1939–1945* (London: Vallentine-Mitchell, 1969).

ŻYWULSKA, KRYSTYNA, *I Came Back*, trans. Krystyna Cenkalska (London: Dobson, 1951).

INDEX